Praise for

How to Turn Boys into Men
Without a Man Around the House

"Essential reading for single moms raising boys. How I wish I had this helpful, reassuring guide sixteen years ago!"

> —Andrea Engber, founder of National Organization of Single Mothers and coauthor of *The Complete Single Mother*

"All parents wish their children came with operating instructions. For single mothers with sons, this book is the one must-have manual on everything from understanding the psychology of boys to using positive discipline techniques. The authors have clearly and thoughtfully outlined strategies that single moms can use to successfully mother their sons at every age—without losing their sanity or sense of humor along the way."

> —Holly Robinson, frequent contributor and columnist for *Parents* magazine

"A majority of American children will spend all or part of their childhoods with a single parent, usually a mother. Appreciating their oftentimes lonely and exhausting demands, Bromfield and Erwin speak directly to single mothers of boys, offering them developmental knowledge and practical advice that will help them understand and manage their sons. Any mother who reads this book will have the feeling that someone helpful is standing by her side."

> —Michael Thompson, Ph.D., author of *Raising Cain* and *Best Friends, Worst Enemies*

How to Turn Boys into Men Without a Man Around the House

A Single Mother's Guide

⸺⟨಄⟩⸺

RICHARD BROMFIELD, Ph.D.

CHERYL ERWIN, M.A.

PRIMA PUBLISHING

© 2001 by Random House, Inc.

Published by Prima Publishing, Roseville, California. Member of the Crown Publishing Group, a division of Random House, Inc.

PRIMA PUBLISHING and colophon are trademarks of Random House, Inc., registered with the United States Patent and Trademark Office.

Library of Congress Cataloging-in-Publication Data
Bromfield, Richard.
    How to turn boys into men without a man around the house : a single mother's guide / Richard Bromfield, Cheryl Erwin.
        p.   cm.
    Includes index.
    ISBN 0-7615-3630-2
    1. Boys. 2. Masculinity. 3. Single mothers. 4. Child rearing. 5. Parenting.
I. Erwin, Cheryl. II. Title.
HQ775.B68   2001
649'.132—dc21   200105134

01 02 03 04 05 HH 10 9 8 7 6 5 4 3 2 1
Printed in the United States of America

First Edition

Visit us online at www.primapublishing.com

To our mothers,
Marjorie and Thelma

The God to whom little boys say their prayers
has a face very much like their mother.

—James M. Barrie

CONTENTS

Introduction   xi

Note to Readers   xvii

1. A Fine Young Man: From Beginning to End   1

2. It's a Boy: The Wisdom and News on
   Boys' Development   13

3. He Needs Me, He Needs Me Not: On Attaching,
   Separating, and Independence   35

4. Keep Out of My Stuff: Respecting Boundaries,
   Privacy, and Separateness   61

5. Like Hand in Glove, Like Oil and Water:
   Mixing and Matching Temperaments   83

6. Making One Good Man: Instilling Values
   and Morality   103

7. Do Fence Me In: The Nuts and Bolts of Discipline   125

8. Evel Knievel, Wear Your Raincoat:
Fostering Self-Protectiveness and Resilience   147

9. Boys Will Be Boys Will Be . . . : Nurturing
Solid Gender- and Self-Identity   179

10. From Casanova to Prince Charming: Encouraging
Healthy Attitudes Toward Women and Sex   199

11. School Boys: Promoting Educational and
Career Success   221

12. Men 'Round the House: Optimizing the
Influence of Ex-Husbands, Boyfriends,
and Other Male Role Models   247

13. MotherVision: Knowing Yourself and
Your Blind Spots   271

14. Mothering Solo: Taking Care of You   289

15. Letting Go: Celebrating and Coping
with the Inevitable   307

Notes   319

Index   323

INTRODUCTION

It's a fact of life. The numbers are staggering and undeniable. More than one in three children are now born to an unmarried mother. Single-mother adoptions are on the rise. Half of all first marriages end in divorce; the percentage of second marriages that fail is even higher. At some time in their childhood a majority of U.S. children will live in a single-parent home, and the trend is quickening. Half of these children, of course, are boys—boys being raised primarily, if not wholly, by their mothers. Mothers like you.

Some experts tell us that the outlook for these boys is gloomy. They say that sons of single parents are more likely to have learning problems, to fail academically, and to drop out of school. We're told that these boys are at greater risk of abusing alcohol and drugs, getting into trouble with the law, being violent, needing mental health treatment, and, horrific as the thought is, committing suicide.

But isn't that what we expect of boys raised by single mothers? How can a woman possibly raise a boy to healthy manhood? Many people would instinctively agree with one divorced father who said, "Making a boy a man is a man's job! Fathers are what teach a son responsibility, honor, and courage."

Big words, aren't they? These big words might be more convincing if the man speaking them were not an alcoholic who had never kept a job, never saw his son, hadn't paid a penny of child support in years, and who, if he knew anything about doing the right thing, surely didn't show it. Of course, this one man and his shortcomings do not disprove the value of a father. His story teaches a different and unexpected lesson. Despite all the hurt and neglect he'd caused his wife and family, his son had actually turned into a boy any father could be proud of—for one reason only. That boy had a mother who somehow created a safe and steady home, gave him love and caring, and demonstrated, day in and day out, the very steadfastness, courage, and honor that her exhusband only crowed about—traits often judged to be the exclusive realm of men and fathers.

This is not to say that a good father isn't worth his weight in gold, for he is. We don't need researchers or clergy to tell us that any child, girl or boy, benefits from two happily married parents, or that a son benefits from a positive male influence. But the picture is far more complicated and involves more than just the presence or absence of a male role model. For example, we neglected to tell you that those tragic risks associated with single mothering are just as true for single fathering. Many of our greatest leaders and heroes, some of the manliest men, were raised by mothers, while many notorious villains came out of intact marriages and traditional father-headed families. Statistics describe only averages, and categorize groups of people. These numbers have their place, but they reveal little, if anything, about a specific home, such as the one you and your son share.

We, the authors—a child psychologist and a family therapist who herself has been the single mother of a son—recognize your realities: the financial burdens, the endless chores and demands that rest on you alone, the utter exhaustion, and the lonely self-doubt and despair, not to mention the societal prejudice and, perhaps, family criticism. And although the path—whether divorce or death, choice or abandonment—that led you to single motherhood is relevant, all that really matters is the path you and your son will travel from this day on. But how do you and your son get from nap-time under your watchful eyes to midnight curfews, from sweet dreams to talks of safe sex, from *Pat the Bunny* to freshman English?

Combining age-old wisdom with recent discoveries about boys' development, this book offers single mothers a map to better understand their sons and their parenting. Our approach is developmental, meaning that we look at single mothers and sons as they grow up together. For mothers whose sons are younger, our observations will guide your parenting through his childhood. For those of you who are further along with an older boy or a teenager, this book will help you understand the past and will serve as a foundation for the future. It is never too late to build a more effective, more loving, and more understanding relationship with your son, although, it's true, the earlier you begin, the easier the journey will be. What you do today will help to protect your son and promote his growth into the man you want him to become, making the risk of disaster less likely months or years down the road.

We'll explore the important developmental territory that you and your son will travel: attaching and separating, dependency and autonomy, boundaries and privacy. We'll describe methods of building character, resilience, and identity. Together, we'll problem-solve ways to foster healthy attitudes toward women and sex, promote educational and career success, and optimize the influence of ex-husbands, boyfriends, and mentors. We'll look at how mothers sometimes misperceive their sons, as well as how you can take better care of yourself, perhaps the most neglected demand of being a good mother. And finally, we'll face where it all leads—the eventual day you must let your grown son go off to be a man.

And yet as we offer strategies and suggestions, we want to confirm what you as the single mother of a son experience—the fears and the joys, the times you triumph, and the times you stumble. Rather than give you *the* right answers for parenting your son this very moment—such a "one size fits all" approach likely doesn't exist—we hope that our book helps you discover for yourself what to do in future situations. Our work with single mothers shows that they want and need not sugar-coated pabulum, but realism and honesty. They know better than anyone what they're up against.

Although self-congratulation will have its day, we did not write this book to blindly sing the praises of single mothers. Just as we doubt that only men can raise a son, so do we disbelieve that women are mythological deities who can always do it better. What makes single mothers heroes is not being women, but the bravery and resolve they show each day in raising their sons single-handedly.

Single mothers have little leisure time to read books for pleasure. They cannot be expected to study the latest research on parenting—a topic they already spend too much time on and may need a break from. And so we have tried to write a book that is engaging, enlightening, and useful. We hope you find it worthy of your time and of that most precious mission—raising your son.

NOTE TO READERS

Deciding how to address in a single book the needs of sons of all ages, from toddlers to young men, was a challenge. We considered chapters dedicated to specific age groups, but this felt artificial and made for a disjointed discussion.

Instead we have focused chapters on the major issues that affect mothers and their sons, integrating all of boyhood into each one. This, of course, makes perfect sense for single mothers of young sons who have much of their childhood still ahead of them. We realize this may momentarily deter mothers whose sons are well beyond the preschool period. Even for these mothers, however, we feel that understanding where their sons have come from developmentally will make for surer and more effective parenting in the days to come.

CHAPTER 1

A Fine Young Man

From Beginning to End

How can it be? He's all grown up. Just yesterday, or so it seems, she carried him everywhere. Hard to believe, looking at his young man's body. It's been years since the last time she lugged him upstairs to bed. His 53 squirming pounds nearly broke her back. The face she used to wash Gerber's spinach from, he now shaves himself. The eyes and smile that once lit up for her alone, now, it seems, brighten for everyone but her. The world that once revolved around their togetherness seems to have traveled to a distant galaxy, where he is now light-years from her presence.

Where did the time go? The hundreds of bath times, the thousands of bedtimes, the countless hugs, kisses, and giggles. He once needed her to do everything. And then, even when he didn't, he *wanted* her to do things for him. Sometimes she grumbled and complained aloud. More often, she silently relished the ways she was still an essential part of his life. What some considered thankless chauffeuring was, for her, a precious chance to hear about his school day and to meet the girls he liked. The boy-ravaged kitchen that she could have lectured and nagged about became instead a cherished opportunity to see her son with his friends, to get to know who they were, and, best of all, to know that he was safe at home. The demands for snack foods, clothing, or CDs created beloved moments when she could nurture the boy who, for all of his height and facial hair, was still her baby.

When you think of it, it's a pretty unreasonable thing to ask of anyone, especially a mother. It is thankless, unfair, and hurtful for a mother to give so much of herself, her flesh and blood, her energy, caring, and thought to another person, even if it is her son, so that one day he can just up and leave.

Today, though, as she watches her son walk across the stage to receive his diploma, treat his fiancée with respect and love, or simply live responsibly and kindly, she no longer questions the worth of what she's done. Her commitment and effort have paid off. Despite the battles and moments of utter despair, which often lasted much longer than days and weeks, she's succeeded in raising her son to be a man who will lead a good life. However trying, emotionally draining, and ultimately bittersweet, it's been a job well done.

We could have made this scene far more dramatic. Picture a young man setting sail to see the world, while his aged and haggard mother, depleted and abandoned, waves wearily from the dock. Yet the truth is, this quiet drama occurs each day, as sons leave the mothers who raised them. They begin leaving in small ways, moving farther and farther away from their mother's guiding hand. Eventually, filled with dreams and visions, sons move toward a fully independent life, while their mothers struggle to remind themselves that this is, after all, the purpose of parenting.

Savvy advertising agencies rely on this notion. The reason a McDonald's or Northwest Airlines commercial of a mother and son reunion brings tears to our eyes is that it tugs at the very real human feelings and vulnerability that lie just beneath the surface, ever ready to be awakened. Every mother knows this. The knowledge that everything she does is aimed toward her son's ultimate departure, his flying from the nest on his own, is in the back of her mind from the day of his first cry until he packs his bags and walks out the door. Even as she diapers her son, ties his soccer shoes, helps him study French, and finally adjusts the collar of his wedding tuxedo, she knows this.

> Eventually, filled with dreams and visions, sons move toward a fully independent life, while their mothers struggle to remind themselves that this is, after all, the purpose of parenting.

This truth can be even more piercing for single mothers. Carly, a 49-year-old nurse, adopted her son from Colombia eight years ago. Hardly a day passes that she doesn't notice something new about him. "Why," she asks herself, "can't I just be happy that he's learning and doing what he should? Why does every one of his steps forward feel like he's one step closer to the door?" Carly's torment is easy to understand. Carlos is her only child. She lost her father early in life and has never married; Carlos is the one and only man in her life. How could she not be torn?

Like many single mothers, Carly doubted her ability to raise a child and, more so, a son. She believed that a child is better off in a two-parent family. She felt solely responsible for the kind of man Carlos would turn out to be, a responsibility that weighed heavily on her shoulders. After all, she was doing most of his parenting by herself. This truth, besides straining the heart, carries big-time implications for mothering. A mother's vision of the man her son will become dictates much of what she does and how she does it and directly shapes the person he grows up to be. How she feels about his growing up and how she copes with those feelings influences her day-to-day parenting.

In the end, regardless of what Carly (and other single mothers like her) thinks, the process happens. And there is nothing, not one blessed thing, that she or any mother, single or married, can do to stop it. Oh, Carly can dress Carlos in baby clothes well past his first year (at some risk to his psychological health), just as she can baby him in other ways throughout his childhood. She can try to make his life with her wonderful and teach him that the outside world and adult life are bad and to be avoided. She can ignore his developing body and mind and look the other way, until one day she finds that he is gone, leaving only a pair of size 11 sneakers beside the front door. She can even unplug all the clocks and dig her nails into every moment, using every ounce of strength to keep today from becoming yesterday. But, of course, she will fail. For as surely as taxes and death, and with no regard to the number of parents in the home, time passes and sons grow up.

A Theory on Single Mothers and Sons

Scientists often conceptualize, as did Einstein with relativity, two accompanying theories to explain the world: one that describes more general phenomena and a second that focuses on more specific events or exceptions.[1] This model holds some relevance, it seems, to the task of single-mothering a son.

Though the following chapters will explore the special circumstances, demands, and methods of single-mothering a son, we cannot dismiss the obvious. For of all the truths about single-mothering a son, one stands supreme. She is, above all, the parent of a child.

Like a jazz pianist wannabe who must first learn the fundamentals of the keyboard, with its scales and classical technique, the single mother must understand all that a married mother understands. Both need to know something, if not a lot, about how a child develops, what constitutes effective discipline, how to make nutritious lunches, and how to get an active, energetic youngster into bed. Both mothers need to know enough about children and themselves to help their children negotiate developmental frontiers that are fraught with landmines, for their children must equally attach and separate, and master the same psychological tasks that sons of married women do. The children must forge their own places in the world, with their own identities.

Children of all mothers—be they happily wed, divorced, widowed, or adoptive—must learn to keep themselves safe and make good choices. Marital status confers no advantage in a mother's knowing when it's time to call the pediatrician or give her child a Tylenol. To be a good single parent, you must first be a good parent.

Modern society's knowledge of parenting has been further spurred by the valuable work of developmental researchers. First, we learned that girls had been ignored and that our culture unknowingly squelched the voices and selves of the daughters we loved and wanted only the best for. Enlightened by these powerful findings, like-minded researchers set

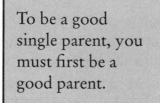

To be a good single parent, you must first be a good parent.

their social and psychological microscopes on the lives of boys and found a comparable deficit in what was believed about and done to boys. Researchers discovered the damage wreaked by society's stereotypes and assumptions about raising boys. Now mothers, whatever the structure and shape of their families, have both a new resource and a new responsibility. Single or partnered, they must recognize what boys are about, what they need from their mothers, and what risks they face.

The need for a specific theory doesn't end here, for single mothering is a much harder and more different task than parenting as part of a contented, well-functioning couple. In order to do the work of two people, single mothers must learn what has traditionally been done by fathers and men. Even if single mothers don't have the option of marriage or question the power of a father, it behooves them to understand his role and what he can offer a son. This knowledge can empower single mothers and help them to see more clearly what they can do and what they can't, what they want to do and what they don't, what their son needs and what, if anything, he lacks. Seeing and understanding more clearly can only make single mothers more effective and can only make their difficult job easier and more satisfying.

This is not to say that a unified and elegant theory exists for single-mothering a son. There is no one "right" way to parent. Many right ways are possible—as are many wrong ways. The trick of "good-enough parenting" is to maximize the right stuff and minimize the wrong, forgiving the inevitable and frequent times when what we do is useless or hurtful.

Parenting, even under the best of conditions, is a perplexing challenge. Though notions of perfect mothers and fathers who know best are lovely, such ideals may do more harm than good. The perfect parent exists only in our imagination—or perhaps, on television—and this fantasy may lead us to beat ourselves up for every misstep that we or our children take. The good news is that much of parenting is made of skills, and skills can be learned and improved upon. While parenting does seem to come more easily to some, few mothers or fathers find all or even most of it to be second-nature. A great many parents, perhaps most of us, work hard at it with less success than we'd like. Our efforts sometimes feel like car tires stuck in the mud, spinning us nowhere fast.

Single-mothering asks a lot of a woman. Be both mother and father. Do the work of two people. Run a home on half the income. Juggle, sacrifice, and spend the night plugging the dam with your thumb. Understand mothering, single-mothering, fathering, and boys. Strive to grasp the big picture, but—even while making space for your unavoidable mishaps—*do* sweat the details, for they make a difference. It can be enough to make a mother wish she never had . . . Wait, that's another discussion. Did we say sacrifice?

> Researchers have discovered the damage wreaked by society's stereotypes and assumptions about raising boys.

The single mother of a son, like any other mother or father, gets better as she goes along, if she keeps practicing and taking risks. This is the only way genuine learning occurs. Single mothers and their sons grow together, and each minute is one more laboratory *in vivo* in which to work on their mutual project. As one mother told her son, "You've never been an 11-year-old boy before. I've never been the mother of an 11-year-old boy before. This is a big experiment for both of us, and we're going to make mistakes. Lots of them." Embracing such an attitude can be a lifesaver during the many storms both single mother and son are sure to weather.

What Others Think

Who cares what others think? Some rare individuals don't. They know what they think and that's enough.

What Do You Think?

Should married couples stay together for the sake
of the children?   *Yes   No   Uncertain*
Is a two-parent household better for children?
Yes   No   Uncertain
Are children raised by a single mother at greater
risk for emotional, educational, and behavioral
problems than those raised by two parents?
Yes   No   Uncertain
Are single-parent households a problem in our
society?   *Yes   No   Uncertain*
Does the increase in single-parent households in-
dicate that people in unhappy or dangerous
marriages have more options today?
Yes   No   Uncertain
Are diverse family units more accepted today?
Yes   No   Uncertain
Is it important for children of single mothers to
have a male role model?
Yes   No   Uncertain
Is it just as challenging to be a married mom as a
single mom?   *Yes   No   Uncertain*

(Look on the next page to compare your views
with other single mothers.)

But most people, including single mothers, do care. Single mothers are part of families, workplaces, and communities, and they may be deeply concerned with other
people's prejudices and attitudes. As if it weren't sufficiently tough to raise a child alone, single mothers are

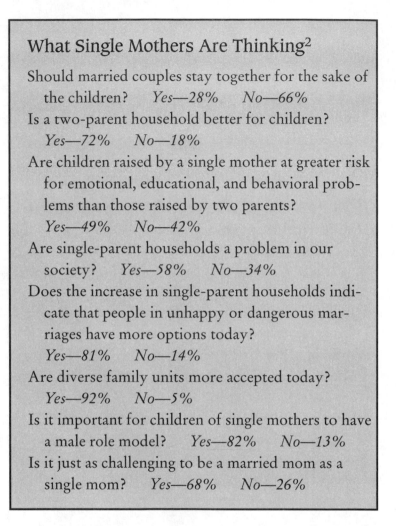

What Single Mothers Are Thinking[2]

Should married couples stay together for the sake of the children? *Yes—28% No—66%*

Is a two-parent household better for children? *Yes—72% No—18%*

Are children raised by a single mother at greater risk for emotional, educational, and behavioral problems than those raised by two parents? *Yes—49% No—42%*

Are single-parent households a problem in our society? *Yes—58% No—34%*

Does the increase in single-parent households indicate that people in unhappy or dangerous marriages have more options today? *Yes—81% No—14%*

Are diverse family units more accepted today? *Yes—92% No—5%*

Is it important for children of single mothers to have a male role model? *Yes—82% No—13%*

Is it just as challenging to be a married mom as a single mom? *Yes—68% No—26%*

sometimes told that they are selfish and foolhardy, neglecting and destroying not only their beloved children, but the community those children will, supposedly, grow up to ruin. Single-mothering a son—why, that is an even greater sacrilege. Everyone knows that boys need fathers—real men—to raise them. Don't they?

Let's face it. America has never been the friendliest of nations when it comes to children and families. For all of its singing about freedom, the nation boasts some ugly and discouraging realities, many of which are especially relevant for single-mother homes. Despite cutting-edge medical technology and widespread wealth for some people, the United States still suffers high infant mortality rates, high drop-out rates, and widespread poverty. This is shameful.

If you are a single mother by choice or are planning to become one, some people out there will undoubtedly try to shame you. But beware: It may be your own self-criticism that stings the most and your own biases and assumptions that you battle. A recent survey of single mothers suggests that they tend to agree with more mainstream views. Most single mothers think a child deserves and thrives with two parents, and they report accurately that children of single parents are at greater risk for a wide variety of problems. How much these views are a product of society or represent more genuine self-assessments is unclear and is well beyond the aim of this book. You might, however, consider your own beliefs about single mothers. Your attitude and self-confidence as you approach the task of raising your son alone will make a critical difference in your success.

Knowing the score is never a bad thing. Statistics convincingly suggest that single mothering is a monster of a job with major perils, though no more so than single fathering. (A recent study at Ohio State University found that single fathers are no better at discipline than are single mothers.) Whether you are the single mother of a son by choice or by circumstance, the task is formidable. But it is doable.

Any number of successful men, respected by their communities and sometimes by the entire world, have been raised by single mothers. Raising a boy on your own does not doom him to juvenile delinquency, unhealthy relationships, or a second-class life. Remember, your own attitude will be a powerful influence on the boy you love. Believe in the best for him. Devote yourself to learning all you can about his development, his strengths, and his liabilities. Do your best to parent him effectively, and hang onto your faith even when the road is long. It is possible to both recognize your own frailty and approach your journey with confidence. Your son will be stronger and wiser if you can.

> The perfect parent exists only in our imagination—or perhaps, on television—and this fantasy may lead us to beat ourselves up for every misstep that we or our children take. The good news is that much of parenting is made of skills, and skills can be learned and improved upon.

And for those of you who have felt the sting of others' criticism or judgment, know that the best revenge is to prove the world's and your own doubts unfounded. Raising your son to be a good man will be your best revenge, your sweetest dessert. It will also be your greatest pride, accomplishment, and satisfaction, all wrapped up in one. Yes, you can do it. This book will help you begin.

CHAPTER 2

It's a Boy

The Wisdom and News on Boys' Development

What are little boys made of? (a) Frogs and snails and puppy dog tails. (b) Enough curiosity to kill a clowder of cats. (c) More pep than the Energizer bunny—and far more courage. (d) ". . . a tiny molecular lever that reaches into a strand of DNA and pries a kink into it, setting in motion all the changes necessary to convert a sexless 35-day-old embryo into a boy."[1] (e) Spit and vinegar. (f) A rake and an ol' cake.[2] (g) Testosterone, and pretty much nothing else.

Were this a multiple-choice question, savvy readers might answer "(h) All of the above." But even they would be wrong. Little boys (and the bigger boys and men they become) are made of lots more than just these ingredients. And, as we all know, not all boys are the same. Some are neither curious nor courageous. Some prefer painting to paintball wars, reading in an easy chair to running wild outside. This chapter touches on what we've long understood about boys, as well as recent research findings, to help us apply these insights to boys we really care about—the actual sons in our lives.

Huck, Dennis, and the Beaver

Watch any little boy in a department store while his mother shops for a dress.

———◦◦◦———

"Stay right here for a minute," the mother instructs, while pointing to a cozy chair. Within seconds, having tumbled and rolled in the chair, the boy scans the women's section. Bored, he walks around, noting the colors and patterns, rubbing his hands over the rough wools and the cushy cashmeres, pulling the racks, even tapping the fixtures and assorted ornaments on the walls. Losing interest, he runs to the far corner, to an oversized, wheeled rack used to move clothing around the store. The boy hangs from the high bar and swings. He soon finds that if he swings hard enough, he can ram into the padded cushion of the winter coats hanging behind him. The pressure and softness against his back feel good. Better yet, when he swings forward, his outstretched foot can reach the dozens of heavy-duty hangers on a nearby hook. Every kick brings the satisfying sound of crashing hangers. The boy soon establishes a steady rhythm. Squish, crash. Squish, crash. While he swings, he sings along with the piped-in music. That he doesn't know the song doesn't matter, nor does it discourage him from using the words of a different song he does know.

"Reid!" His mother grabs his hand and sternly walks him back to the chair. "This will only take a few more minutes." Reid sits and asks his mother if she's still going to take him for treats. She reassures him that she will.

From the chair, Reid peers out to the main store. The movement and symmetry of dueling escalators catches his eye, until his view is obstructed by a man pushing a huge box on a dolly. He wonders what's inside the box, maybe Gameboys or his favorite candy. I'm hungry, he thinks. I'm dying of hunger. Now sitting on his head, he can see the cosmetics counter where grown women in long black aesthetician lab coats are drawing on the faces of other grown women. It'd be fun, he decides, to put a moustache and whiskers on his mother's face. Now that he notices, he can smell the fragrances of perfume. He hears the soft, dull ping, ping, ping of the elevator and wonders what that is.

A saleswoman snaps her fingers to catch his attention. She looks at the floor, and he can tell she means to sit up straight and get his feet off the chair. Not a bad boy, he does so with a smile.

Yes! His mother, he sees, is walking to the register. He can tell the end is near. *Vanilla swirl with sprinkles, skeet ball, here I come.*

As he wanders toward his mother, he notices a display of pastel blue, yellow, and pink bottles stacked in a pyramid. One seems out of place. He tries his best to fix it, but the bottles all fall.

"I told you I meant it." His mother grabs his arm firmly. "I want you to stand right next to me and not move." The boy squirms. "I mean it," she repeats with that no-more-nonsense look on her face.

Unnerved by the tension, her discomfort only accentuated by the obvious disapproval of the older saleswoman, his mother can't find her credit card. She needs both hands to dig through her pocketbook. By the time she finds the card and pays for the dress, he is gone. "Reid? Reid?" she calls softly, embarrassed to speak louder.

Undeterred by all the fuss, even by his mother's upset, Reid bursts out from inside a dress rack. "Mom!" he crows with a wide grin, certain his mother is as happy to see him as he is to see her.

Although we mock June Cleaver's designer house-dresses, string of pearls, and frightening perpetual good mood, we understand why she liked her young Theodore. Whatever his antics—playing hooky, filling pockets with worms and chewed gum, falling headlong into a billboard soup bowl—his boyish zest for life won out. Clearly, his mischief and goofy schemes were born out of innocent love, wonder, and fear. That he could make his mother smile was not just pure Hollywood. It is something that lots of boys can do, despite the thousand-decibel noise, mess, and trouble they sometimes make.

Ask most people to describe an "average boy" and you're likely to hear a description that is part Huck Finn and part Peter Pan. Many generations of folk wisdom, literature, and culture have made assumptions about what makes a boy a boy. Interestingly, some of these observations have been confirmed by those conducting research on boys today. What are these traits? (Mothers whose sons are not so "typically" boyish, please stay tuned, for we will soon meet your sons.) Let's explore some of the attributes shared by these fascinating creatures we call "boys."

High Energy

Boys, we usually believe, are spark plugs, energetic little engines that can run and run and run and still be looking for something to do. A morning soccer game and afternoon swim use up nothing that twenty wiggling minutes of cartoon-watching can't restore. Up with the sun, they are always looking for action until the sun goes down and they collapse into sleep. In fact, research tells us that as a group, boys are more physically active and impulsive than are girls the same age,[3] and many of their mishaps are attributable to the quest for activity that their fidgety fingers and jumpy legs are always on. Dangerous though it is, the toddler who sticks a paper clip into the outlet is not "up to no good." That four-year-old wants neither to electrocute himself nor to trip the main circuit breaker. He's just trying to occupy himself, employing an inborn drive to investigate the world around him (and yes, he needs constant supervision until he's learned the principles of electricity).

> Many generations of folk wisdom, literature, and culture have made assumptions about what makes a boy a boy. Interestingly, some of these observations have been confirmed by those conducting research on boys today.

Indeed, to many youngsters, the world is a wonderful laboratory, and they are the "mad scientists." Wouldn't it be great if we could somehow harness that high-octane energy and put it to good use? Some boys could have the yard mowed, a pie baked, and coffee brewing by the time their yawning parents come downstairs. Unfortunately, the minds and bodies of little boys are not ready for that sort of work. They are driven to explore, to play, and to learn what their bodies can and can't do.

Learning about themselves is the focus of young boys' early development (as it is for young girls). Like the crazy chimpanzees we marvel at on the Discovery channel, our baby animals need to romp and wrestle—a lot. That is why they can make a playground out of almost any place, whether it's a church vestry, the dentist's waiting room, or the dress department at Macy's. While their sisters are content sitting beneath a shade tree quietly playing with Barbies, the boys climb in the tree's branches, plotting ways to disrupt the peaceful scene below. They can't help it that their engines run fast and hot, any more than Ferraris and Corvettes can. That's how they're built.

High Curiosity

Are boys curious? Nail a wooden box shut, put it in your basement, and suggest to your son that he ignore it. His desire to obey you notwithstanding, he will focus on that box as if it were Long John Silver's buried treasure chest. He will use tools, his nails, even his teeth to get in there. Even as a splinter wedges into his cuticle and a nail slices his thumb, even when he realizes that his curiosity has gotten the better of him, that he's used a hammer to break the box, and that he's "dead meat," he can't stop himself.

Boys need to know—for that reason alone. They climb high to survey, dig deep to uncover, tiptoe clumsily and hide under beds to spy. What's a clock but a machine to take apart and understand? Want a boy to read something? Put it in an envelope, mark it *Top Secret,* then hide it.

———❦———

Elaine was driving home after a long afternoon of too many errands and too much traffic. Duncan, her three-year-old son, had been patient and cooperative in the shops, but spent the entire ride home asking question after question. "How come?" he would inquire about the trucks, the buildings, and the sky. And when Elaine answered, another "how come?" was sure to follow.

Finally, he wore out his mother's patience. "Duncan," she said, fatigue and irritation seeping into her voice, "that's enough!" Elaine glanced into the rear-view mirror and saw her son's gray eyes gazing back at her. "But mom," he said soberly, "I want to know these things."

———❦———

When and how, we have to wonder, did curiosity get its bad rap? *Webster's Collegiate Dictionary* defines "curiosity" as "a *blamable* (italics ours) desire to seek knowledge." Although endless questions can annoy even the most patient mother, is curiosity itself deserving of blame? In an earlier age, curiosity was downright dangerous: The *Oxford English Dictionary* tell us that curiosity—the human wish to know the meaning of life and God's ways—was judged to be dangerous, full of hubris and overreaching pride, tantamount to "spiritual drunkenness and adultery."[4] Whether descended from ancestral proscriptions or simply because it is so unrelenting, boys' curiosity can torment their mothers.

And yet, what would the world be without curiosity? Every mother should read de Kruif's fascinating *The Microbe Hunters* and his accounts of Louis Pasteur and others compelled to understand the unseen world of microbes. Our world would be a more difficult, dangerous place without the explorers whose curiosity drew them to strange and unknown places, whether on other continents, under the sea, on distant planets, or deep within the gelatinous recesses of our brains. Unlike Sherlock Holmes, boys don't need a pea-soup fog on the moors to sense intrigue. They can see mystery on the clearest day in their own backyards.[5]

High Volume

Here's a lame riddle: Why don't many boys mind the ear-shattering, head-splitting noise at the local video arcade? Because they can't hear it above their own yelling. (About as true as it is not funny.) Boys, we suspect, are responsible for the national movement to hold birthday parties at rented bowling alleys, gymnasiums, swimming pools, and self-proclaimed fun-towns. Who can blame their mothers? If 16 boys is 16 times the fun, it can be 64 times as noisy, 256 times as wild, and—well, you do the math.

It is almost always the boys who are the sound effects specialists. They can produce the roar of motorcycles, the wail of police sirens, the flutter of helicopter blades, simulated farts, and burps that become a private language. (Is there a boy out there who hasn't burped out "Ralph" and then giggled delightedly?) The louder the transgression and more unbefitting the setting, the better. A belch in school or the synagogue is worth a great deal more than one on the playground.

Boys' conversation sounds like a parliamentary debate on speed through an echo chamber. Each one talks louder than the last, as if screaming will get him heard. The sound of boys can be hard to take, especially for mothers who come home at the end of the day longing for tranquility and lacking their sons' inborn love of noise. Were the volume on our stereos and televisions stuck on high, we'd all listen and watch a lot less and find ourselves praying for just a little peace and quiet.

High Aggression

Give a boy a drum and he'll bang it all day. Give a boy a spoon and he'll bang that, too. For that matter, give a boy a cupcake, a glass coffee table, or your eyeglasses to hold and he'll happily bang all of them. Girls walk down the street holding hands, arm in arm. Boys walk down the same street, poking each other's ribs and whacking every tree and lamppost with their hockey sticks.

―⟨⟩―

Johnny and Dicky, 10-year-olds, are next-door neighbors. They are fighting on the ground, first one on top, then the other. Though mostly wrestling, they've both gotten in a couple of good punches. They are best friends and both are extremely pissed off. Johnny gets up and kicks the Monopoly pieces everywhere. "Take your damn game, cheater," he says. He vaults the chainlink fence between their two yards at just the spot where their constant leaping has broken it down. "Loser," Dicky calls back, getting up and kicking his own game, too, before storming into his house. Best friends, they fought over a dice roll that hit a rock. Best friends, they would be playing baseball together within the hour, though this would be far from their last skirmish.

———*ΩΩ*———

Many boys get mad and get aggressive. Many boys get frustrated and get aggressive. Come to think of it, when many boys get hurt and sad, when they get most anything, they are prone to get aggressive. If someone hits you, you hit him back. Someone says something you don't like? You hit him. Worried about your grandfather's health, but unable to bear or share it? Say something to annoy another kid, then when that kid gets mad and hits you, you hit him back—harder.

> Many boys get mad and get aggressive. Many boys get frustrated and get aggressive. Come to think of it, when many boys get hurt and sad, when they get most anything, they are prone to get aggressive.

For many boys, aggression tends to be a fact of life and must be noticed and accepted before we can help our sons do anything constructive about it. This is not, mind you, the same as saying boys equal violence. Boys often feel at a loss to handle conflict and injury verbally (for reasons we will explore later). This difficulty can present problems for them, their peers, their parents, and their teachers. But, as later chapters will show, we don't have to accept this fact as destiny. Meanwhile, be sure to wear your shin guards before telling the boys. And, needless to say, many of our sons, even those with ample testosterone, are not at all aggressive and are the ones to make peace, while young girls hone their hatchets (often verbal ones).

Low Impulse-Control

"I couldn't help myself." "It just happened." "It was Jeannie's fault." "I wasn't even there." "The devil made me do it."

Pretty cheap excuses, huh? You can almost hear an adult's replies: "All your friends somehow managed to stay out of it." "So the money just walked out of my purse and jumped into your pocket?" "Jeannie says she didn't do it and she doesn't lie." "Well, you were the only one seen throwing a snowball." "Blaming the devil, now, that's a good one."

Actually, developmental research suggests that the last excuse may indeed be a very good one—blaming the biological devil, that is. Without any question, boys are apt to leap before looking, to act and then think. Boys don't have nearly as much capacity as girls do to speak before doing and to think before saying. For boys, it's precisely the opposite. Boys tend to take longer and to need more trials to learn from experience, and they tend to be less deterred by punishment. Mark Twain might have been writing about boys when he said, "Good judgment comes from experience. Experience comes from bad judgment." That may be why, for example, the little boy we met earlier shopping with his mother kept up his behavior despite his mother's and even a salesperson's reprimands. Their displeasure somehow wasn't enough to quell his exuberance.

Modern technologies such as PET scans and MRIs have enabled scientists to discover biological evidence for some of these differences. Politically correct or not, boys' brains do differ from girls' brains in structure, func-tion, and chemistry. Although exceptions exist to every gen-eralization, boys' brains are less well equipped for impulse control, social skills and understanding, and language. (Obviously, most do eventu-ally develop these skills, but tend to do so later than girls.) It shouldn't surprise us that the human brain, which is soaked in and influenced by numerous chemicals and hor-mones throughout its development, is a highly sexualized organ and plays a major role in determining the nature of boys and girls.

> For many boys, aggression tends to be a fact of life and must be no-ticed and accepted before we can help our sons do anything con-structive about it.

Boys' impulsivity not only leads them to be more ag-gressive against others. It can also propel them toward destructive promiscuity, drug and alcohol use, and illegal activity, as well as less dramatic, but chronic, irresponsi-bility, defiance of authority, abusive relationships, and daredevil behavior, all of which, however indirectly or unconsciously, also express aggression against them-selves. Individual temperament, culture, and parenting style can profoundly affect the fate that any innate, gender-based tendency toward impulsivity seems to impose.

Delayed Verbal Skills

Consider the gifts that early and strong speech provides. Verbally endowed children have the ability to say what they want clearly and with less frustration. They can tell you what hurts or why they are crying. Language—one of the most complex skills any human being acquires—is the foundation for human communication and connection, so it is logical that children who develop verbal skills early in life have a head start in making sense of their world.

Language offers both a mother and her child a means of negotiating around struggles and an effective avenue for implementing discipline. The capacity to use words enables a child to learn self-control, to speak instead of merely acting on every impulse. Socially, language skills make everything easier and can enlist the admiration and encouragement of adults such as parents and teachers. All of these assets, in turn, promote self-esteem, success, and resilience.

Unfortunately for boys, these advantages are more likely to be enjoyed by girls. Girls learn to use the left hemisphere of the brain, the part that is primarily responsible for processing language, much earlier than do boys. And the parents of girls are more likely to converse with infant girls than with infant boys, reinforcing language skills early.[6] What are boys left with? Although there are exceptions—first-born children, including boys, are often quicker to acquire verbal skills than later-born children, for example—boys are indeed likely to be slower to gain the ability to express their needs, thoughts, and feelings in words rather than behavior.

In addition, the style boys usually employ to communicate differs from that of girls. In her book *You Just Don't Understand: Women and Men in Conversation*, Deborah Tannen states that when men and women communicate with each other, they might as well be talking across different cultures.[7] Girls, for instance, are more likely to ask, to invite, and to offer choices, while boys (and the men they become) are more likely to issue directives and commands. Not surprisingly, men and women (and boys and girls) sometimes misunderstand each other because their approach to language can be so different.

Politically correct or not, boys' brains do differ from girls' brains in structure, function, and chemistry. Although exceptions exist to every generalization, boys' brains are less well equipped for impulse control, social skills and understanding, and language.

Many boys confront almost every iota of their experience from a weaker position. Not having the words to speak one's mind and heart can be frustrating beyond belief. (An acknowledged link exists between children who suffer speech delays, for instance, and biting and other aggressive behavior.) Sure, boys can kick or throw a punch, but is that real power? Imagine yourself having to argue with William F. Buckley, Jr., in a foreign language that you've just begun to study. Actually, this analogy is inadequate, for losing a debate is not usually a catastrophe. Instead, imagine having to fight for your job with a new and critical boss, or defend yourself against a false accusation, or salvage a rapidly sinking romance, again, in a language you barely speak. Now you get our drift.

Highly Competitive

Boys love to win and hate to lose. But not as much as they just love to compete. Even after the last pitch is thrown, they race to the water fountain, fight for the front seat of the van, then battle it out in a cutthroat game of punch-buggy.[8] While this competitiveness lies near the heart of many boys' love of sports, it is also evident in the attitudes of nonathletic boys toward their own interests. Some boys love to do better than everyone else in school or band or compete academically on junior high school math and college bowl teams. The skaters spend their afternoons trying to out-grind each other, while the gangsters freestyle their rap head-to-head. All the boys strive to get off the best insults in the banter that typifies almost every group of boys. And it is sad but true that the boys doing alcohol and drugs also want to be the "best at being bad" and can be heard boasting about how "wasted" they got the night before.

Boys bring that competitive spirit to almost everything in their day. When they aren't directly vying for a place in line or for the last cookie, they are daring us with a bet, wanting to prove us wrong, or having to have the last word. Does this need to compete, we wonder, partially fuel boys' addiction to video and computer games? When no one else is around, they can play against other boys online or against the computer itself. So desperate are boys to compete that they are also known to spend countless hours competing against themselves, building extensive domino knockdowns, shooting free throws, or seeing how long they can juggle a soccer ball.

> Boys bring that competitive spirit to almost everything in their day.

Although we've read about schools that attempt to teach children to be noncompetitive, we suspect that the drive to compete is here to stay. In fact, entire sports leagues are designed to foster cooperation and teamwork among youngsters rather than competition. In these leagues, each player receives a trophy and no official score is kept. But ask any boy on either team, and he can immediately tell you who's really winning. Eliminating all competition seems akin to teaching boys to walk totally erect on their hands. With enough training, coercion, and incentive, they could do it for a few minutes or even an hour. But it would never become the natural mode for most boys.

Heartfelt Boys

Buzzing, energetic, boisterous creatures looking for a good game or a good fight, searching for self-control and the words they can't find. Though this sounds like some of the boys we know, the portrayal is sorely lacking. By

What Are Boys Made Of?

While there are exceptions to every rule, here are some ways that your son may differ from his female peers:

More physically active and energetic
More curious
More likely to be loud
More likely to be aggressive and to act on impulse
Slower to develop verbal and social skills
Fonder of competition
Better gross motor skills
Less-developed fine motor skills

its sin of omission, it suggests that only girls care about communicating, connecting, and doing the right thing. By focusing on the outside of boys, by credentialing their behavior alone, it disregards the soul of boys. This deficit in society's thinking—and the enlightening success of the girls' and women's movements—has spurred the recent boys' movement, which, for us, means research into and writing about boys as whole children. Though many of the "new" insights have been understood for decades, their recent presentation in a new and crystallized light is a necessary and healthy advance. What else, then, are boys made of?

To begin, much of what boys are made of is not readily visible. For reasons of constitution (how their brains and bodies are built), environment, and culture (to be elaborated in detail throughout the remainder of the book), boys tend to keep their inner selves well protected, not only from the world-at-large but from themselves. But why are boys so guarded? Why, like so many under-developed splinter-nations, do they spend most of their resources defending their psyches, leaving little energy to pursue the aspects of life that bring human relatedness?

The road runs astray early, say Daniel Kindlon and Michael Thompson, authors of the revealing *Raising Cain*.[9] From a young age, boys are directly and subtly "steered" away from their emotional lives. That boys speak less of feelings does not prove that they feel any less than girls or that they are without human emotion. In fact, some studies show that very young boys cry more frequently and more intensely than do girls and seem to feel things deeply indeed, especially such things as separating from a parent or not getting as much parental attention as they want.[10] Infant boys also find it harder to calm themselves once they are upset. Mothers of young sons often have to work harder to keep their babies happy than do mothers of girls.

What many boys do miss are the psychological and verbal skills to recognize what they feel and to manage those emotions. Unlike their female peers, they are less able to go to those they love when they are distressed in-ternally. And so they are deprived of the listening, ac-cepting, consoling, and guiding that all children need and that the mothers of boys are so often longing to provide. Because boys cannot easily ask for help from others, they sometimes struggle to develop the ability to monitor and cope with their emotions on their own, a skill that is essential for healthy adult relationships.

In this spiraling and unfortunate cycle, boys stumble through their childhood emotionally illiterate. Given how few resources they have to negotiate the high seas of adolescence, is it any wonder that so many drown or wash up on dangerous shores?

Too much hyperbole, maybe. But how can any of us deny what is happening in our society? Is it just a coincidence that with rare exceptions, the young people who have taken guns to their schools and shot their peers and teachers have been boys? And it's not just the crime or riots on the news. William Pollack, author of *Real Boys*, describes it as a "silent crisis" that's taking a high toll on a nation of boys and men.[11] Michael Gurian, a man as deserving as any of the title "father of the boys' movement," conceives of it as an epidemic that is wasting boys' moral health. Few disagree with the call to arms to do something to help our boys. Single mothers in particular search for the skills and the strength to understand, guide, and nurture their sons.

And so we look at our sons as they belch and kick cans down the street, and as they mutter a perfunctory and meaningless "fine" when we ask how school was today. They smile on the outside even when they hurt inside. It is all but impossible for a boy to tell his mother that a bully called him a faggot or spit in his face, or that he felt humiliated when he couldn't do a division problem on the blackboard. Too many boys stew in their shame alone, licking their wounds when no one is around

Understanding Your Son: How a Mother Can Help

This book is devoted to helping mothers sift through the world's assumptions about boys. For the moment, however, here are a few ideas to ponder as you seek to support and nurture your son:

Learn to know the real boy, not just the public one. Being a mother means becoming an acute observer of the person your son is becoming. What are his individual strengths? His weaknesses? What are his greatest joys and his deepest dislikes? When he's having a terrific day, what precisely made that happen? Discovering what brings out the best in your boy will help both of you as you grow together.

Learn to listen to your son's feelings and help him find words to express them. It may surprise you, but no one is born knowing exactly what a "feeling" is. You can help your son cope with his emotions by calmly and kindly labeling the ones you see. For instance, you can say, "Looks like you're feeling frustrated," or "That must have made you feel proud." By listening and identifying feelings, you send your son the message that you want to understand him—whether he's ready to talk just now or not—and that his feelings are always acceptable, even when his behavior might not be.

Read to your son. Because boys often are slower to develop verbal skills, reading together (and turning off the television and computer) can provide opportunities to explore the world of language and help boys prepare for school. Make reading aloud fun: Use different voices for different characters and pause occasionally to share ideas. Your librarian, teacher, or other parents can give you recommendations for books that boys will enjoy.

Play with your son. Yes, he'll laugh at your gun and animal noises. But playing the games your son loves will give you real opportunities to see him in action, as well as to model for him attitudes and skills such as sharing, problem solving, and empathy. You may be surprised at how strongly you bond during the times that you laugh and play together.

Make an effort to be calm and kind when dealing with your boy. Because boys may tend toward anger and aggression, it's usually wise to avoid yelling and anger when dealing with them. You can be firm and enforce necessary boundaries without resorting to excessive control, physical force, or anger.

Remember, so many of the boyish traits that challenge you today can mature into strengths and attributes that will help your son thrive as a man.

to see. Even as they hang out with the gang, with their supposed best friends, they often do not let on that anything bothers them. What they do let out instead is anger and aggression, their most reliable shields against the sadness, loneliness, and anger they feel.

Having to be tough and without need of support is a burden that none of us should carry. It is not a question of turning our boys into girls, as some have implied. Boys need to have all of their complex selves understood, protected, and nurtured. It is as true for poets and musicians as it is for the toughest "jock." It is this basic truth, perhaps more than any, around which our book is centered and on which our plan for prevention and remedy rests.

CHAPTER 3

He Needs Me, He Needs Me Not

On Attaching, Separating, and Independence

"When I'm grown, I won't need you anymore, will I?"

"What?" Hunter asked, not really hearing three-year-old Larry as she turned onto their mountain road in Stowe, Vermont. She and her son had spent the weekend in Montreal, and they'd had a blast, the most fun she could ever remember having. They'd chased swans with their pedal boat, frolicked in the hotel pool, and spent hours just walking, hand in hand, laughing at the street jugglers while eating cotton candy and tri-colored Popsicles. It was a trip that neither wanted to end.

Hunter had listened to Larry chatter all the way home. "It's dark." "The stars are bright." For almost four hours, he had talked nonstop. "My stomach's hungry." His guard was down, maybe in some kind of trance, she thought, because of the relaxing darkness and drone of the car. She was too close to see that it was the intimacy lingering from their wondrous day together. With little to distract him on the rural highway, only distant lights and his own reflection, thoughts and feelings had free rein. His usual self-censoring at rest, Larry gave minute-by-minute updates on the state of his mind and body, speaking anything that came into his head. Who could blame Hunter for having tuned out?

"When I grow up, I won't need you, will I?" Larry said, undiscouraged that he had to repeat himself.

Hunter felt a hard, sudden kick in her belly. That he'd spoken the words so innocently only made them feel that much more honest and real to her. She turned on her windshield wipers until, seeing that her vision was still blurred, she turned them off and instead wiped the tears from her eyes.

Larry's words were neither provocative nor a bid for her attention; he had spoken them as matter-of-factly as he'd described the itch on his big toe and his thinking that seven was a better number than four.

Hunter pulled her car into the driveway and shut off the engine. "Why did you say that?" she asked, turning to Larry in his car seat, as if he could have explained.

But Larry was sound asleep.

—◦◦◦—

For all mothers, moments like this one are inevitable, when they realize that if a mother does her job well enough, her beloved son will one day leave her. It seems almost unbearably poignant that a three-year-old boy can sense it, too. And yet, isn't that how it is with children? The things they say can be goofy and side-splitting one instant and then, seemingly out of nowhere, utterly revealing in their candor.

For what it's worth, Larry is now thirteen and more connected to his mother than ever in his life, even as he is preparing for manhood. His words, however, were not empty declarations. They carried significance for him, as well as for the world of boys he unknowingly spoke for. But to grasp the meaning of Larry's words, we must return to where it all begins for mothers and their sons.

Hold on Tight

What does a mother do with a beautiful bouncing baby boy? After a deep breath and wishing herself luck, she will take him home where, lost in their *twoness,* she will begin a torrid love affair. Holding him to her warm breast, she will feed him when he's hungry and rock him when he's cranky. By caring for his physical needs—by offering warmth, sleep, and stimulation—she will begin to deeply persuade that little baby that the world is a safe and reliable place, worth trusting and investing in. By responding to his attempts to make his needs known—smiling back, gazing into his eyes, shifting her body so he can feed more comfortably—she will, bit by bit, demonstrate that he has the power to act on his world, that what he feels does matter.

What this mother is instinctively doing is building a secure *attachment* to her child. One of the pioneers of human development, Erik Erikson, believed that parents' primary task during a child's first year of life is creating a sense of trust. Children learn to trust their parents and the world around them when their cries are responded to, when their physical needs are met, and when they are touched and handled with gentleness, love, and care. Children who do not experience this sort of connection with a loving adult—children, for example, who are abused or physically neglected—may lose a great deal of their ability to trust and connect with others, predisposing them for both emotional and behavioral problems later in life.

Each time a mother holds, comforts, and satisfies her son, she adds to his inner sense of her enduring presence and goodness. That good feeling will become part of him and will influence the way he approaches his world. In the way that Leo Lionni's mouse, Frederick,[1] summoned the summer's sunshine when the winter grew dark and cold, the child will turn to that wellspring of mother-love for lifelong self-love and soothing.

Feel the Magic

When all is as it should be, a mother attends not only to her son's physical needs but to his emotions, seemingly without trying. He smiles, she smiles back. He hurts, she hurts. He protests in anger, she registers his complaint. Slowly and steadily, a mother's mirroring of her son's emotions validates the child's sense of what he feels, the bedrock of his coming to know and accept his authentic self.

But it isn't all hard work that makes for secure attachment. A young son needs his mother to enjoy him. Seeing his mother's eyes light up when he walks into the room, her irrepressible delight in his antics, and her easy contentment when he sits beside her convinces him that he is loved and is lovable. She will celebrate, too, his milestones, the first words and steps, as well as his daily and less dramatic attempts to grow. For she knows he needs her unconditional acceptance and love, when he stumbles and falls, as well as when he soars.

As mother and son grow together in these subtle but substantial ways, she will do her best to prove stable and reliable, her steadiness serving as a foundation for the man that she is helping to build. She becomes the safe harbor where he can always find shelter from the rocks and storms of life.

Creating a Secure Bond with Your Young Son

You may believe that when a child is born, his brain is fully formed and all that remains is to teach him what he needs to know. The truth may surprise you: Technological advances have taught researchers that the brains of young children continue to grow for the first three years of their lives. How parents guide and relate to a child during these early years can have a significant impact. The age-old parenting behaviors that build a

(continues)

loving and trusting relationship between you and your son also encourage healthy brain development. Here are some things you can do to help the process along:

Respond to your baby's cues. Coming when your son cries or squeals and attending to his needs are ways you help your son understand that he can affect his world and ask for what he needs. As children grow older, they can learn to manipulate adults with their behavior, but in your son's early months you don't need to worry about spoiling him.

Touch, speak, and sing. Those old nursery rhymes not only give you time to play with your son, they help him learn the rhythms and patterns of language.

Provide opportunities to play, and play along. If we've learned anything from the animal kingdom, it's that babies—be they chimps, bears, or humans—need play to bond, grow, and learn. Play, as the educator Maria Montessori observed, is the work of childhood.[2]

Encourage curiosity and safe exploration. (Yes, you should child-proof your home.) Your child needs space to roam, to learn to use his muscles and his body, and to investigate the world around him. Confining your son to a playpen or an infant seat may make life easier for you, but it does inhibit his ability to explore, to stretch, and to grow.

Allow private time for your baby. Your son needs time to explore his own body and to learn to soothe his own emotions. It may take time to find the right balance between attention, stimulation, and quiet time for baby, but it will help both of you develop a healthy relationship.

Use discipline to teach; never shake or hit. Babies are physically and emotionally vulnerable. Never forget that their motivations are only to experience and learn more about the world. They do not "misbehave," reject, or frustrate you on purpose or because they don't love you; they are just doing what babies do.

Take care of yourself and your own emotional needs. Mothering can be extraordinarily frustrating and demanding for even the best of mothers. The happier and less stressed you are, the better and more satisfying your parenting will be.

Love and enjoy your son. You both deserve that much.

(For more information on brain development, see *Rethinking the Brain: New Insights into Early Development,* Rima Shore, New York: Families and Work Institute, 1997 and *Your Child's Growing Mind: A Practical Guide to Brain Development and Learning from Birth to Adolescence,* Jane M. Healy, Ph.D., New York: Doubleday, 1994.)

The Urge for Growing

But a sailor does get the urge to roam, doesn't he? As cozy as safety can be, we all need novelty and adventure. Confident in his mother and himself, a toddler boy will want to explore. Courageously, he'll let go of his mother's skirt and venture off toward a box on the coffee table. He'll get only halfway there before he scampers back like a scared squirrel. *Just checking* (to see that his mom hasn't left him). But she's there, reading her magazine, just as he'd left her. And so, renewed, he heads out once more, this time making it all the way. He opens the box, but suddenly drops the lid and runs back to mom, who greets him with a welcome worthy of Ulysses' return from his Odyssey.

> *"I want to do it myself"* is the creed of the day. This drive toward self-sufficiency is healthy and strong and is a part of normal development.

And so this back-and-forth goes, each trip taking the boy farther and farther from his mother. Today he explores the land within his mother's horizon—meaning the bits of his world from where he can see her. Tomorrow he'll turn the corner to blaze territory that's out of her sight. Our little Magellans and Balboas are playing with separating, trying it on for size and liking how it fits.

The same inborn forces that, like the Sirens, call toddler boys to faraway lands invoke them to go it alone. *"I want to do it myself"* is the creed of the day. This drive toward self-sufficiency is healthy and strong and is a part of normal development. Watch a baby boy struggle to get that spoon of applesauce into his mouth or a toddler trying to button his own shirt. Despite the extraordinary frustration, they persist. *"Come hell or high water,"* their actions seem to cry out, *"we're going to do this by ourselves. If the floor drowns in applesauce, if we never get dressed, if it takes us the rest of our lives, we're going to do it."* (Of course, not all boys are natural-born mavericks. Some will need their mother's gentle nudging to go out and see what life has to offer them.)

This ongoing exploration fosters the child's sense of competency and autonomy, which are cornerstones to esteem and resilience. No less than in the four-legged animal kingdom, exploration prepares the child for the future when he's no longer a helpless infant and when his mother may no longer be nearby to feed and protect him. Like it or not, an essential part of mothering is weaning, gradually transferring responsibility and skills from mother to son. It is sometimes a painful process, but a mother cannot coddle a son for eighteen years and then throw him into the jungle to survive alone. He won't make it.

A Big Boy Now

His growing self-confidence enables a boy to leave his mother. He now can go off to school, where he'll be able to listen to and feel cared for by teachers. He'll be able to devote his energies to school and play without the preoccupied fear that he will lose his mother or her love while he is gone. During this period, he will be more independent in many ways, even as he still needs his mother for much in his life. Many mothers believe their sons need less parenting as they grow and mature, but nothing could be further from the truth: They simply need their parenting in a different form, one that encourages and guides a boy's journey toward healthy adulthood.

Of course, while the teen years can be easier for some mothers, for many others adolescence can throw a wrench into the works. For some parents, it will feel more like gallons of tar pitch. In an abbreviated and symbolic form, teenage boys will revisit and renegotiate the development tasks of previous years. They will need to establish their sense of autonomy and initiative on a new, more mature level. They will set unreasonable tightropes for their mothers to walk high over the rush-hour traffic on Madison Avenue. They can sometimes make demands of their mothers that seem all but impossible to meet: Hold me, but don't smother me. Guide me, but don't tell me what to do. Love me, but keep your affection to yourself (and for heaven's sake, don't display it in front of my friends!). Keep me safe (from the world and myself), but don't limit what I do. Help me, but let me make my own mistakes. Expect greatness for me, but don't pressure me. On and on the list of impossibilities goes. At times, all that a mother can do is to watch from shore while her son jumps from ice floe to ice floe, just barely keeping out of the frigid water. For his dear life she will try to grab and hold onto the elusive lifeline he ambivalently throws her, even as she side-steps the many traps and landmines his adolescence inevitably leaves for her.

Wrong Turns, Dead Ends, and a Way Out

Our portrayal may make the mother and son connection seem natural and foolproof. Eventually, however, even the most loving mother and son will encounter challenges. Any parenting relationship will have moments of confusion and hurt (as well as great joy), but the relationship between mother and son is intricate and demanding. Finding the right balance between guidance and independence, encouragement and wisdom, holding on and letting go, can prove astonishingly difficult.

Difficulty Attaching

Unfortunately, sometimes creating a secure attachment doesn't happen as smoothly as it should. If the average single mother's son is anything like his peers, he will be more colicky, cry more, and be harder to console than the girls in the neighborhood. (This can be more likely for some adopted babies.) In the classroom of mother and babies, where an easy baby can help teach a mother what to do, these more demanding baby boys use methods that aren't the most educational. In short, their behavior sometimes frustrates, rather than encourages, their mothers' natural instincts. Mothers who don't mesh well with their sons can feel a constant sense of failure and criticism. They may feel rejected and ineffective. If this is their first child or first son, they may unfairly judge themselves unfit as mothers (at least, as a mother of boys), causing unnecessary stress and fueling a painful cycle that can drain an entire childhood.

It may help to remember that boys do mature more slowly than girls. Developmentally, they are slower to recognize their mothers' faces. They smile later and less frequently. *"It's him,"* these mothers must remind themselves, not to judge but to understand that they face a developmental challenge.

> Mothers who don't mesh well with their sons can feel a constant sense of failure and criticism. They may feel rejected and ineffective.

The same is true for adoptive parents whose sons don't readily surrender to their warm arms because of temperament or trauma during their early weeks or months. A mother must be willing to acquire the concepts and skills to provide her son with what he needs, despite his pushing her away. As any mother or father can testify, trying to quiet a screaming infant can be tough; doing it while beating yourself up for being a bad parent is more than twice as difficult.

Think of your son as an experiment. Perhaps you've seen the same old ways fail and fail. Perhaps trying what you've been told to do, or have read somewhere, or what your neighbor did with her son has failed, too. Eventually, effective mothers learn to discover and trust their own wisdom. Get creative. For example, when trying to soothe your irritable toddler, hold him on your side, up high or down low. Try rocking or sitting perfectly still. Notice if he likes pacing fast, walking slowly, or rhythmically waltzing around the kitchen. No matter what your eighth-grade music teacher said about your singing, try a lullaby, maybe even your favorite rap song. Your tone-deaf folk melody may be just the thing that distracts him from his bodily discomfort and rejoins him to you.

Observe and notice. If that little twist you did stopped his crying, try it again. Play with it. Things like the speed and tempo of your movements do make a difference.

Sometimes doing less is better than doing more. While your daughter may have loved disco dancing, your son may enjoy watching your pinky finger slowly bend and unbend, over and over again. Discovering ways to soothe and manage your baby boy are worth much more than their weight in gold. Each of the countless little tricks you design will give you more rest and peace of mind, and they will promote your son's evolving inner sense of well-being and self-regulation.

Sometimes it helps to take a long-range view of parenting and to remember that changes are best made gradually. Even as you act in the moment, think months or years into the future and let that broader perspective and your long-term goals for your son motivate you. If he won't nap, but he and you need sleep, make that your one project of the month. Read, consult, and get advice. Give your experiments 100 percent of your effort and be patient. Real change usually requires persistence, more than one half-hearted behind-the-back toss. Ask yourself, Is he really incapable of napping, or does he refuse to sleep because the room's not fully dark, the music you play downstairs is too loud, or you are inconsistent in establishing a routine? Or could he have discovered, in the instinctive way children do, that if he just whines a bit longer, you'll come back, sigh, and read him another story?

> It may help to remember that boys do mature more slowly than girls. Developmentally, they are slower to recognize their mothers' faces. They smile later and less frequently.

Try to be there more, and, perhaps, act less. Secure attachment occurs because of the mother's calming presence, and it takes uncluttered time, free of the distractions of everyday life (no small task for busy single mothers). Establish time when you have no other obligations or preoccupations. Shut off the telephone ringer and don't pick it up. Hunker yourself in a big comfy chair and do nothing but listen to your son tell his tales, or allow him to read or play with his Legos while leaning against your legs. If you are a constant doer, try and harness this compulsion. Your son, as high-paced as yourself, may need someone to teach him to relax, to wind down, and to sit comfortably with himself.

By implication, of course, we are talking about a mother's ability to recognize and validate her boy's feelings. Many mothers, ill at ease with their own unresolved conflicts and hurts, have little patience and few resources to hear their sons' upsets and worries. A little boy's "I'm afraid of dying" or "What happens if a burglar gets in?" can terrify a mother who fears the same things herself.

And yet our sons desperately need us to hear their inner thoughts. They need to watch us bear them without falling to pieces. When a mother can listen calmly and accept her son's fears and worries, her acceptance itself can detoxify an overwhelming thought. And we all know how comforting the simple sharing of one's troubles can be. The act of listening—truly hearing your son's heart—may be all he needs.

Unfortunately, many mothers struggle to accommodate their sons' emotional needs. Conservative statistics suggest that a third or more of mothers may be depressed or anxious. This number is even higher for single mothers, who must deal with more stress, despite having fewer resources to rely on. Depression is a serious illness; it can cause a mother to struggle with her own inner hurts and preoccupations to the exclusion of all else and often makes her emotionally unavailable to the son she loves. Anxious mothers may convey fears that dwarf their children's own, making their sons unnecessarily timid and scared. Depressed mothers may lack the energy even to physically care for a young child and may be unable to experience joy and enthusiasm for their sons. Children of these mothers are at greater risk of developing depression and anxieties of their own, and their ability to learn and develop may be affected.

It is important to note that depression and anxiety are not choices, nor are they signs of weakness. As many as one out of every ten mothers suffers from significant postpartum depression. Many are embarrassed and ashamed, blame themselves, and never receive adequate help. Single mothers who feel that their depression or anxiety is compromising their mothering should seek help. A wide range of treatments has proved to be beneficial. If you are reluctant to seek help yourself, do it for your child's sake. When depression or anxiety is reduced by treatment, studies have shown, parenting becomes more enlivened, responsive, and satisfying, and children almost immediately resume their normal developmental course.

A Word About Depression and Anxiety

It isn't a subject most people enjoy talking about, but single mothers tend to suffer more depression and anxiety than do mothers with partners. Beyond making life feel dreary and difficult, depression and anxiety have a very real effect on children. Research shows that the children of depressed mothers develop verbal and social skills more slowly and have a greater tendency toward depression themselves.

Depression is more than just feeling tired or sad. Depression drains the feeling out of life, leaving little ability to feel joy, pleasure, or satisfaction. Depression brings with it fatigue and can disturb both appetite and sleep. Depressed people can isolate themselves from others and become unresponsive to those around them, even to the children they love.

Separating Too Early

Imagine attachment as something that takes hold early in infancy but that deepens and broadens over childhood, even as a child moves away from his mother. When it develops as it should, a boy will separate inch by inch on his own terms and at his own pace, acquiring responsibility and independence in small increments that he can handle and integrate. But that is a growing rarity in today's world.

Anxiety can result in intense feelings of fear and discomfort. Sufferers sometimes believe they are having a heart attack and experience sweating, a pounding heart, sweaty palms, or a choking sensation. They may fear the scrutiny of other people and believe that everyone is watching and judging them harshly. Anxiety, too, can affect sleep and appetite, and, if social anxiety, it can isolate single mothers from the comfort and support of others. Her fears and worries can inhibit her mothering and make her a less effective mother, sometimes fostering anxiety in her own child.

If you suspect that you suffer from depression or anxiety, do not suffer unnecessarily. Seek help. Varied treatments, involving both talk and medication, can help. Talk to your health-care professional or a licensed therapist who can explore these options with you.

—◦◦◦—

Ryan was a nine-year-old who lived with his 37-year-old mother, Stacey. She'd adopted Ryan on her own from Korea. The first few years were any adoptive mother's dream. Ryan was an affectionate, bright, and caring boy. He was a pleasure to mother and for most anyone else to be with. He was secure in his attachment and took great pride in his growing ability to do things for himself. Despite her considerable self-doubt, a doubt fueled by the ceaseless criticism of her father, Stacey had mothered him admirably. Everyone could see it. Everyone but Stacey's father, a man who set himself up as the family authority on boys and men (even though he'd never had a son of his own).

"You'll make him a sissy boy," her father warned, when Stacey proudly described the lovely breakfast Ryan had made her for Mother's Day. "It's unnatural for a boy to cook and wait on his mother."

That Ryan was an athletic and assertive boy was inadmissible evidence. Eventually, Ryan's grandfather wore his mother down. "He cries too much" meant he cried at all. "He fears too much" meant he could admit and talk about his fears. And "he acts like a girl" meant he liked playing the flute. Most of all, Stacey's father said that the boy was too attached to her. "What's going to happen to him if anything ever happens to you?" the father asked, citing how he'd lost his mother at an early age and how it had devastated him.

As wrong as her father's accusations and concerns were, they touched Stacey's own insecurity. A modest woman used to being domineered by her father, she felt that luck had carried her through the first few years, but now she worried that she would really do some heavy-duty damage.

And so, afraid she'd ruin her wonderful son, Stacey cut the apron strings. Under her father's approving eyes, she instituted a new regime. She no longer tolerated tears, telling Ryan that boys don't cry. She no longer indulged long-winded tales of his experiences and feelings. "Let's get going. We have a lot to do," she'd say instead, encouraging him to take action and be determined (the way to train boys to be men, her father explained). And when Ryan was wounded by some word or deed, she urged him to get over it. The plan worked like a charm. At first, it was hard to act in ways she felt were cruel to her son. Her own heart broke each time she told him to keep his heartache to himself. But it soon got easier. Ryan eventually stopped crying, stopped complaining, and stopped telling her about his days at school. Sure, he no longer spoke about his dreams either, but then, that was the price of raising a man, and it came with good news. He no longer whined about hurt feelings and he could now watch a movie like *ET* without a sniffle.

It had been a near miracle. She'd transformed a sensitive toddler into a thick-skinned fourth-grader, well on his way to being a tough and macho man. Sure, she didn't like the swearing and his angry outbursts, and sometimes he scared her, threatening her that she couldn't tell him what to do.

Occasionally, she wondered if she'd made the right choice, particularly when he demanded that she make his lunch and buy him a treat. In spite of his bossy stance, he actually did less for himself than other nine-year-olds. And he didn't look too happy either. But, as her father had drilled her, raising a boy to become a man is not supposed to be fun or pleasant. It is a loving mother's duty. In those moments when she felt weakened, ready to bring back the old days, she'd remember her father and think of how proud he'd be, if he were alive, to see how Ryan had turned out. She'd done it.

—◦◦◦—

Some mothers, like Stacey, distance themselves from their sons because of family pressure and self-doubt. Others do it because our culture says it should be that way. Whatever the reason, the premature separating of boys from their mothers has become a problem of, some say, epidemic proportion.

What is the big deal, anyway? As Ryan's grandfather had learned through the school of hard knocks, we all have to leave home and mom eventually. Why prolong the inevitable? And why make marshmallows out of boys, weakening their ability to handle life without their mommies? What that bitter man knew inside in his soul, but could not bear to see, was that his own premature separation, the early loss of his mother, had shut away a tender part of himself and his own humanity. A big piece of him had died with his mother. Tragically, the lesson that could have salvaged both his life and his grandson's was lost to them both.

The way Stacey pushed Ryan away was unusually abrupt. She started off with love, respect, and joy, then made a deliberate choice to reverse it all. More often, the choice is less conscious and happens gradually from birth by a process that Dan Kindlon and Michael Thompson call "emotional miseducation." Parents, they say, essentially teach boys not to feel, not to be vulnerable, and not to rely on the relationships that can comfort and sustain them. Lacking the social, language, and affective skills of girls, boys are hit with a double whammy. We inhibit and close down what feelings and relationships they can tolerate. When hurt—by insults, failure, or rejection—they find themselves unable to express their pain in words or to seek consolation from loved ones or friends. Like cornered animals, they are left to defend themselves with posturing or playing dead, which in boys equals cruelty and aggression, or silent and despairing withdrawal.

When Ryan's misbehavior forced the family into therapy, things changed. Because of the early and strong attachment she'd nurtured, Stacey was able to recover the Ryan of old. He was happy to return to the land of the attached and feeling (though he had lost time to make up for). Sadly, most mothers and sons who are in this predicament have not had that beginning of health and connection. When those sons start showing up in truancy reports, in the courts, and on the corners late at night, it can be too late. Some children do end up where no amount of love or caring, where not even a super-hero, can bring them back.

Keeping the Connection Alive

As boys grow, their needs, feelings, and relation-ships with their mothers may change. Here are some suggestions for strengthening a healthy bond with your growing son:

Be available. Being a single mother is a full-time job. But remember that listening, talking, and understanding require time. Just because your son is older doesn't mean he doesn't need your atten-tion. Scheduling special time into your week, time to be with your son or to share simple activities, can provide moments to stay connected. You can

(continues)

read together, work in the garden, ride bikes, or play a game. What matters is that you find and reserve time for you and your son.

Make an effort to understand his interests. Just because he loves video games doesn't mean you have to learn to play. But then again, there's no reason not to. Your own instincts will give you clues about how much involvement your son wants from you. If he loves sports, attending his events and learning the rules will help you connect with him. Showing curiosity without judgment will open the door to sharing values and ideas. Note and nurture the activities, whatever they are, that you genuinely enjoy doing together. (For one family, it might be downhill skiing; for another, baking cookies or browsing bookstores.)

Listen with empathy. Really listening will help you stay connected, despite the changes time can bring.

Be flexible and try not to take it personally. Your relationship with your son may seem a lot like a rubber band: He pulls away, stretching your love to its limits, then returns to be close to you again. Insisting on intimacy and affection may make him pull further away. Remember that his journeys away from you aren't personally rejecting of you but are a part of his natural growth and development. It is one of life's paradoxes. By allowing your son to move away, in safe and appropriate ways, you actually enable him to stay close.

Dependency

Recall little Larry, telling his mother how someday he won't need her? Even at that young age he was struggling with his dependency. He knew how much he needed his mother, perhaps even more than she knew. It scared him. How precarious it must be to feel that your life depends wholly on another person. To Larry, his mother was the food he ate and the oxygen he breathed. He was torn between wanting to forever be his mother's baby and wanting to be completely self-sufficient.

However much a boy adores his mother, the degree to which he relies on her can make him feel vulnerable. A boy's childhood is partly organized around this struggle. In a healthy relationship he will come close, then retreat, come close, then retreat, over and over. He will alternately be baby and man, trying to find a comfortable place where he can grow up.

—◦◦◦—

Neal was a complex young man, just as he should have been at his age. Cocaptain of the seventh-grade soccer team, he was a solid student as well. He volunteered for the food pantry drive and the clean-up of the town fields. To the adults in his school and community, he appeared to be maturing well and on the right path.

And his single, divorced mom agreed, except when he was home and behaving more like his seven-year-old brother. "It's astonishing," she explained, "it's like living with Dr. Jekyll and Mr. Hyde. One hour he's a civilized young man and the next, he's having a Jello fight, crying that I love his brother more, asking me to tie his shoes, or trying to crawl into my bed at night. And all this, mind you, after I bump into one of his teachers who tells me what a pleasure he is to have in class."

—◦◦◦—

Fortunately, for both her son's and her own sanity, Neal's mother sought the ear of good friends, married and unmarried, who also had teens. She liked the comparably bad news she heard. All these women had their own horror stories to tell. She heard from one mother, for example, that her son Nigel, whom everyone called "Mr. Nature"—the one boy everyone expected to be a veterinarian or savior of wildlife— had taken to not feeding the family dog. "Let it starve to death, who cares?" Nigel was quoted as saying. A second woman described how her son, every other mother's favorite houseguest, was eating his baby nephew's applesauce and spinach for his own snacks at home. *We're all nuts*, Neal's mother quickly learned, which meant, *We're all normal*—a realization that brought enormous comfort.

> However much a boy adores his mother, the degree to which he relies on her can make him feel vulnerable. A boy's childhood is partly organized around this struggle.

Neal's mother wisely refrained from making a big stink about her son's vacillating moods and behavior. She took them in stride and soon came to trust that they were not a sign of disturbance and faulty parenting, but were a necessary part of growing up. Relieved of that burden and worry, she even came to enjoy Neal's weirdness in the way she could when hearing of other mothers' and sons' mishaps. A mother's goal, be she single or married, is not to build a young John Wayne, a tough guy who needs no one, but to help create a man who will be what Kindlon and Thompson have called "interdependent," able to live comfortably and satisfyingly in close relationships that leave space for independence, dependence, and all the space in-between. The mother who understands this, who leaves room for her child's to and fro, will help him to both need and not need her in ways that are flexible, adaptive, and connected—for their lifetimes.

CHAPTER 4

Keep Out of
My Stuff

Respecting Boundaries,
Privacy, and Separateness

Most of us readily acknowledge the importance of boundaries in our everyday life. We want shades over the windows and doors on our bedrooms. We hire surveyors and build fences to mark our property. We screen our telephone calls and request calling options that block telemarketers. We put passwords on our office computer and resent our bosses bothering us at home. We don't want our own visiting parents probing us about our finances and rifling through our papers. Though each person's needs are different, all of us need privacy in certain areas of our lives.

The boundaries we create in relationships, between our selves, our partners, or our children, are no less important than the more public kinds of limits that we attend to. Boundaries contribute to our personal comfort, our emotional health, and our ability to own our feelings, thoughts, and actions. But the questions that issues of boundaries imply can be subtler, vaguer, and more personally threatening. *What are my thoughts, and what are yours? Where do I end and you begin? Who am I without you? How can I live without you? How close is too close?* The question of boundaries, and the way each of us implements them in our relationships, can be a challenge for many married parents. For single mothers of sons, these issues become even more critical, for obvious reasons: She's the only parent, she's female, and her son is male. Being a single mother of a son brings a hefty dimension of both peril and possibility to the task.

In this chapter we will look at the developmental relevance of boundaries and find ways to help our sons become persons unto themselves, capable adults who can comfortably tolerate and commute between dependence and independence, togetherness and separateness, intimacy and solitude—all necessities of healthy adult functioning.

Just the Two of Us

In the modern math of mother and baby, one plus one equals one. As far as a baby is concerned (and when things go well), the universe consists of himself and his mother.

His needs are her needs. His hunger is hers. His colic is hers. She is he and he is she. In fact, research indicates that infants do not have a sense of "self" in the way that older children and adults do; they seem to view themselves as an integral part of their parents. But unlike corporate America, which aspires to merger as an endpoint, mother and child fuse early, then move toward separation.

Through early childhood, by experience and brain growth, the baby comes to learn that his mother is a separate person from himself. He learns that she no longer "reads" his mind as to when he needs feeding, but that he must tell her and ask for what he wants. Whereas he once thought she disappeared when a peek-a-boo face cloth covered his eyes, he now sees her come and go independently of where he is and comes to see both himself and her as existing even when they are apart and out of each other's sight. Experiencing the discrepancies in what he feels and she feels, and discovering that they have different reactions to each other and to the things that happen in their lives, further helps him to develop a firmer sense of himself as a person distinct from his mother.

The bulk of this growing up occurs within the child's psyche. For example, early on, the child who is well taken care of develops an image of his mother as good. But when she crosses him—if she runs out of milk, lays him down when he wants to be held, or otherwise frustrates him—he can't stand it, and for that instant, needing to protect that good image, he must see her badness as that of another woman, not his mother. To feel such rage toward the mother he loves and depends on might seem overwhelming and frightening to a young and needy baby. Over time, however, that same child, experiencing more goodness than badness, will integrate his perceptions into one: a mother who, being good *and* bad, is "good enough." This major developmental step toward a capacity for ambivalence allows the boy to simultaneously hold opposing thoughts and feelings. It also allows him to see other people, like his mother, as being just as complex as he is and as full of their own contradictions.

Related to this development is the child's capacity for what psychiatry calls reality testing, the ability to discern outer reality from one's inner world and, consequently, to discern reality from fantasy.

———

Kevin was three when his mother took him to see *Snow White and the Seven Dwarfs*. It was his first trip to a theater. Kate, his mother, had carefully told Kevin that some of what happened in the movie might be scary.

Excited about this new experience, Kevin paid no attention to his mother's warning—until, that is, the scene where the evil queen drinks the potion and becomes the wicked witch. At that moment, Kevin made a noise like a tea kettle boiling over and leaped onto his mother's lap. He refused to budge for the rest of the movie.

As they walked to the car, Kate tried to understand her little boy's reaction. "Honey, I told you it might be scary," she said, "but it's just a movie. It wasn't real."

Kevin looked at her with outrage. "It was too real, Mom," he said. "I saw it!"

———

Young children magically believe that what they think and feel is real and powerful. Each thought, each perception, has the potential to become fact. That is why harboring a hurtful thought toward someone they love can frighten them and provoke anxiety. To a young child, wishing his sister's death is tantamount to killing her. It is also the reason why so many young children, despite the reassurance of their parents, believe that some misbehavior or flaw of their own was responsible for a divorce or other trauma.

Over time, with his maturing self-control and ability to express himself with words, a boy will realize that what he thinks and feels is within him and may be quite different from what exists in the outside world. He'll see that what he thinks and feels does not telepathically come true, nor can his thoughts be read by others like X rays. He will come to distinguish what's in his head and heart from that which comes from the outside. He'll know his hunger from his mother's, his anger from his teacher's, and his love from his girlfriend's.

> Young children magically believe that what they think and feel is real and powerful. Each thought, each perception, has the potential to become fact. That is why harboring a hurtful thought toward someone they love can frighten them and provoke anxiety.

The boundaries that demarcate our selves, while sometimes overlaying our physical skin, are mostly in our heads. They can be thick and rigid, or permeable and flexible. Some people struggle to establish any boundaries at all. Whatever their nature, boundaries have everything to do with how well a person can function and relate to others, how much he can enjoy life and succeed, and how much he struggles and suffers.

These are big issues. What, specifically, can single mothers do as parents to be sure their sons have healthy boundaries and a healthy sense of self?

Cut the Cord

Janette loved her son Jason even more at the age of three than on the day of his birth. She loved him so much that she never put him down. After all, she'd waited four years to adopt him. Her friends and family ribbed her as to why she bothered to buy him shoes, since his feet never touched the ground.

And Janette knew her Jason—her "baby," as she called him—as well as she knew herself. Even better, she'd say. He seldom had to ask for anything. Like magic, his mother gave him food, fun, and attention. She cut his food into pieces and dressed him as if he were still a helpless infant.

"I know, I know. One day he's going to have to do things for himself. But he's going to be a baby for such a short time. Why should I give it up before I have to?"

———

Soon enough Janette learned why: Her son was becoming intolerable. By the time he was four, she couldn't put him down without loud and protracted tantrums. At those inevitable times when she couldn't fulfill his needs perfectly—something that happened with alarming frequency—he'd brutally demand her attention. He had actually hit and bitten her. She suddenly also understood what teachers had told her for many months, that Jason was falling behind. He wasn't handling the tasks of a typical preschooler. She could see it for herself when she noticed how much more able and contented her friends' boys seemed to be.

Janette backed off. She began to encourage Jason to do more for himself and to teach him the skills to succeed. He didn't like this change at first, but when he realized that he really wasn't losing his mother, he began to feel good about tying his own shoes and brushing his own teeth. His self-confidence improved, and he became willing to try new things. Though it saddened her to see him growing up, Janette now discovered a different blessing. She began to take pride and joy in her son's growth and saw that there was life for the two of them beyond babyhood.

It has been said that the simplest way to destroy a person's self-esteem is to do everything for him. Hidden in Janette's efforts to do everything for her son was a subtler message: Jason began to believe he was not able to do anything for himself and that he needed his mother's special service. As Janette and Jason discovered together, he was quite capable of learning, growing, and, eventually, taking care of himself. Mothers must love their sons enough to encourage the growth of healthy separation and competence, rather than fostering dependence by loving them "too much."

The Family Bed

Of all the topics that occupy parenting and child psychology, none is more controversial and disagreed upon than where children should sleep. Some families have slept their children's entire childhood in one big cozy bed, and their sons have turned out strong and healthy, just as have many sons who, since birth, have slept only in their own beds in their own rooms. Of course, other families have tried everything in-between, also with great success.

We approach this sensitive question from a perspective of probable outcome. Some families, we recognize, are so good at what they do, and some children are so temperamentally resilient, that where and with whom a child sleeps is inconsequential to the admirable outcome they get. But for other children, the results are more disturbing. The issues for an adult female and a growing male are undoubtedly more complex than those faced by traditional nuclear families. What, we must ask, *can* it mean for a son to sleep with his mother, especially in the single-mother home?

Many people—and indeed, whole cultures—believe that sleeping with a parent can foster a child's inner sense of security and attachment. The sons of single mothers certainly have those same needs and will sometimes benefit from the comfort of physical closeness—when they are ill, for instance, or have had a terrifying nightmare. But children don't need to sleep with parents in order to feel securely loved. Furthermore, sleeping with parents can pose risks to a child.

A child's inner sense that he has to sleep in his parents' bed can enforce his fear that he can't be alone. In fact, some behavioral psychologists believe that learning to fall asleep in one's own bed is one of the earliest steps toward a healthy sense of self. When a child does not learn to sleep by himself and to master his fears of aloneness, he can grow even more fearful and dependent. Instead of producing contentment, sleeping in his parents' bed might make that child more apprehensive in the long run and might undermine his ability to sleep by himself. Eventually, too, most parents want their privacy (and their bed) back. And the longer they wait to move a child to his own room, the more difficult that transition will be for everyone.

As the child grows to school age, the issue of sexuality begins to loom larger. With the closeness, lowered defenses, and sleepwear of nighttime, sleeping with one's parents can over-stimulate a child. It is undoubtedly a sensitive issue, but some single mothers so want the closeness of physical company that they turn a blind eye to their son's developing sexuality, continuing to share a bed

> A child's inner sense that he has to sleep in his parents' bed can enforce his fear that he can't be alone. In fact, some behavioral psychologists believe that learning to fall asleep in one's own bed is one of the earliest step toward a healthy sense of self.

with him long past the time when it has ceased being appropriate. Because there is no father to both physically and symbolically keep the boy in his place, that boy can become vulnerable to anxiety- and guilt-inducing

Sleeping Alone: Establishing Healthy Habits

Although nothing is wrong with a Sunday morning cuddle with your little boy or comforting him with a snuggle after a bad dream, it is wise for mother and son to establish healthy and separate bedtime habits. Here are some suggestions:

The earlier you begin, the better. It is usually easier for your son to learn to sleep alone when you organize your home that way from the beginning. If keeping him in your room makes nursing easier, let him sleep in his own crib rather than in your bed. Then you can move his crib to his own room when nighttime feedings are no longer necessary. Remember, you aren't being cruel. You are teaching him confidence and contentment.

Establish a bedtime routine. For the first several years of their lives, children learn best by routine and consistency. Try to start bedtime at the same hour each night, and organize the tasks in the same order. You can even have your son help you make a bedtime chart listing the steps in his routine. For instance, you might brush teeth, wash

fantasies of having his mother, not just sexually but exclusively (as he imagines a husband might).

For these reasons we suggest the easy route, training a child to sleep in his own bed. If your son already sleeps with you, it may be wise to consider moving him out.

face, put on pajamas, read two stories, say a prayer, then turn out the light.

Once the routine is established, stick with it. If your son comes to find you or wants to crawl into your bed, tell him simply "bedtime" and kindly but firmly carry him back to his own bed. Then leave. He'll know when you mean it (just as he'll know, and whine, if you don't).

Set the stage, but leave the sleeping up to your son. Falling asleep is your son's job. You simply cannot make him do it. But you can make the task easier for him. Trial and error will help you learn whether he likes his room dark or with a nightlight, silent or with soft music, cool or warm. Once you have made him comfortable, leave the room and leave the sleeping to him. Lying down with him or staying until he falls asleep may encourage him to need this attention from you and can open the door to manipulation that will cause problems later on.

(For more information on issues related to sleep, see *Solve Your Child's Sleep Problems* by Richard Ferber, New York: Simon and Schuster, 1986.)

Honor Solitude

Being alone has gotten a bad rap. Learning not only to sleep on one's own but to be comfortable by oneself is a valuable psychological skill. We often tend to think of

being alone as lonely, rather than as precious time to enjoy one's own company, be free from social demands,
and be open to one's own thoughts and fancies. Our
modern society and parenting have tended to untrain
children from what is a natural step, growing able to be
with oneself.

At birth, most infants demonstrate an innate ability to
self-soothe—that is, to quiet and calm their own bodies
and emotions. Infants send cues to parents that they need
time to self-soothe by breaking eye contact. When a parent insists on playing, touching, and stimulating a baby,
that baby may eventually lose the ability to calm himself
and may struggle later on to tolerate solitude and unfilled
time. How does a single mother help her son develop the
capacity to be confident and comfortable alone?

Foremost, when she sees him contentedly being by
himself, she leaves him be. It is such a human and motherly thing to call your child to see this, hear that, try this,
do this with me, and so on. Often a mother is the one
who draws her son out of his happy and solitary play-
time. She feels a need, perhaps, to join in, or, feeling guilt-
ridden about working, she thinks she needs to provide
"quality time" every waking moment. Or she may be
lonely herself or may never have learned to enjoy her
own company. *Come play with me, come be with me,* she
may ever invite. A mother needs to occupy herself and
learn to enjoy her son's ability to build block castles on
his own. Mothers can rest assured that their sons will let
them know when their attention is needed.

Some sons are not so drawn to solitude. They want
their mother's attention all of the time. When their

mother invites them to read a book, paint a picture, or work on a model on their own, at that table, in their rooms, they will have none of it. They must have mother involved every minute. When she is busy, they lose interest in what they are doing or obnoxiously grab at her.

These children will need gradual shaping, a planned weaning from mother's constant presence. If this sounds like your son, leave the room for a minute here and there, making little of your departing and returning. When your son asks for your help with something, give just enough—a nudge, a hint—withdrawing to leave him with his own initiative and industry. Don't let his cries of pain fool you. No loved boy will die of loneliness. He will learn how to be alone without feeling abandoned and unloved, a healthy skill for life and relationships.[1]

Out of My Head

To love our sons is to want to know them. What, we wonder, are they thinking, feeling? Many mothers want to know their sons' dreams, wishes, and fears, just as they want to know what happens when their sons are in school or visiting their fathers. However natural a mother's wish to know might be, some mothers are too quick to offer a penny for their son's thoughts.

———

Six-year-old A.J. had been in therapy for nine months. He'd done wonderfully. His depression was gone. Both his single mother and his teacher noticed how animated and joyous he'd become. Once as stiff as cardboard, he'd now shown himself to be a graceful athlete. And yet in all those hours and in spite of all these gains, he still had barely spoken directly about one thing that he felt or thought. He revealed the reason for his discretion in his very last hour of therapy.

"I ain't telling you," he said with a big smile, when asked what he'd miss most about coming to therapy.

"But don't feel bad. I don't tell anyone. They're all too nosy," he explained.

———⌘———

That his mother was the nosy one was no mystery. A loving and warm woman, she just couldn't stand not being privy to A.J.'s thoughts and feelings. And the more she needed to know, the harder she worked at getting into his head, the higher and thicker the walls he built to keep her out. When we met months later, she described how well A.J. was faring and, with a giggle, said that he'd recently begun talking to her about everything.

"It may sound crazy, but when I stopped bugging him to talk, that's when he started talking to me. He even tells me what he has for lunch now, whether it was good, if he put ketchup on it." Her voice hesitated. "I think all I really wanted to know was that he didn't hate me, that he loved me." That was the last thing she had to worry about.

No matter how many communication techniques a mother learns, there is no guarantee that her son will always be willing to talk to her, anymore than she will always share her intimate thoughts with her own parents.

Boys love to know that their mothers care and will listen, but they want to retain the right to choose when, what, and how much to reveal.

As A.J.'s mother discovered, the less a mother *insists*, the less her son might *resist*. Wise mothers listen more than they ask. They are patient and allow space and time for sharing to happen. They must also accept that as their boys grow and mature, those sons will increasingly want to keep certain matters private.

Out of My Body

One's body should be one's own. Our bodies are sacred. Not only as the shrines that body-builders adore, but more deeply as the place we—our minds, psyches, and souls—live and grow. Children need to feel in charge of their own bodies. They need to feel that their bodies are strong, healthy, and good. And even as they do what they can to stay healthy and fit, they need to accept and love their bodies as they are.

> Children need to feel in charge of their own bodies. They need to feel that their bodies are strong, healthy, and good.

Single mothers can help their children grow into their bodies in many ways. Caring and touching their sons lovingly in the early years will lay a foundation for good feeling and a sense that having a boy's body is a good thing. Giving them space to rule their own bodies will facilitate their sense of belonging in their own skin.

Making a federal case out of eating or toilet-training may invoke struggles that, over time, can lead to a child's developing an excessive and rigid need for control in both his general lifestyle and, more specifically, through his body. A mother's fanatic pursuit of cleanliness, too much worry about sickness, or herself playing doctor (e.g., routinely examining her child or making mountains out of normal body sensations and variations) can erode her son's faith in the integrity of his own body to function ably, leading to hypochondriasis and a pervasive sense of being defective and not quite well.

Physical affection, while always needed, will need to be monitored and adjusted as your son grows. A son can never be too well loved, meaning cared for in a way that meets all of his developmental needs. However, a son can be too well loved in a physical sense. He can receive too many kisses and hugs and may be confused by physical touch that is compulsively given or inappropriate in its intensity, location, or passion. A preteen giving his mom a backrub is probably not the best idea. Nor is it wise for a mother to frequently caress her adolescent's neck or walk arm-in-arm with him, like girlfriend and boyfriend.

We admit we feel somewhat mean and heartless talking so coolly and objectively about regulating the physical affection mothers show their sons. And yet parents have no choice. Painful as it is, our sons grow up. Our relationships change. Our task is not to stop loving our sons, but to find new and healthy ways of showing that affection, even as they grow beards and find girlfriends of their own.

Lethal Whispers

Benjamin is a 38-year-old loan officer. Though a handsome and intelligent man, he has yet to find a wife. He has had several long-term relationships and they've all failed. When his last girlfriend, Mary, left him, she told him he needed help.

As Benjamin explained it, he just couldn't trust Mary. No words and no actions could ever prove her love enough to settle him down. He forever doubted her fidelity and suspected that when he wasn't around, she degraded him to others. In reality she loved and respected him as much as he ever could have hoped. Benjamin recognized that the problem was his because he hadn't been able to trust any of the eight women he'd been serious with.

Though Benjamin's difficulties had many sources, his own relationship with his mother had been especially troublesome. Divorced when Benjamin was in early elementary school, his mother made him her confidante. Some of what she told him humored and flattered him. After all, to have been his mother's best friend was quite a tribute.

But as time went on, she'd show him her bank book and confess her worry about their finances. She'd tell him about her loneliness and the nightmares in which she pondered suicide. And she'd tell him, too, about her romances. Though her caricatures of the men she dated and worked with made Benjamin laugh, they also made it clear that his mother saw men as pathetic, weak, and worthy of humiliation.

Everything he heard his mother say about men stuck in his head. Eventually, he was sure Mary thought and said the same things about him behind his back. Every last word.

—◦◦◦—

It is common for single mothers and sons to share an intense relationship. These sons often show a highly developed, almost uncanny ability to read their mother's emotions. Exquisitely attuned *Mommy-o-meters,* these boys can feel their mother's sadness even before their mothers do.

Likewise, these boys may bear the weight of their mothers' depressions and anxieties. They may believe it is their responsibility to keep their mothers alive and engaged. Without being aware of it, such sons devote their lives to making their mothers happy, distracting their mothers from hurt and disappointment. To that purpose, these sons are prone to editing their own feelings and needs so as not to hurt, disappoint, or anger their mothers.

Alice Miller, in her classic *The Drama of the Gifted Child,* painfully described how such a child essentially can become an object that his mother unconsciously uses to fill herself and to offset feelings of emptiness or deadness. Ignoring his own needs, wanting to make his mother notice and attend to him, a son develops a false self that, while for the moment filling some need of his mother's, will eventually leave him empty and separated from himself. Bleak as this sounds, it happens.

Who's the Parent, Anyway?

Many single mothers have told their sons, with a mixture of pride and need, "You're the man of the house now." It rarely occurs to a loving mother that she may be setting her son up for a task that he is ill-equipped to

handle. And when he does succeed in that role, in behaving as if he were the man of the house, it can create a
whole new set of problems.

It's wrong when a boy imperiously tells his mother
where they are going that night or what they will eat. It's
wrong when a teen not only chooses his mother's new car
for her, but determines that she will purchase the $4,000
luxury package. It's wrong when a boy sets his own out-
landish curfews and his mother has to ask *his* permission
to use the car. It's wrong when a fifth-grader has an equal
vote in his mother's retire-
ment investments or consults
to her divorce settlement. It's
wrong when a son acts like
some kind of little emperor,
while his mother tiptoes
around His Highness.

Finding the right ground
can be tricky. The son of a
single mother is the male of
the house, and he knows this.
What would looking the
other way accomplish? And
some of the ways he may fill
that role are good for a boy.
Give him chores and appropriate responsibilities, a good
number of them. If he's a

Physical affection,
while always
needed, will need
to be monitored
and adjusted as
your son grows.
A son can never
be too well loved,
meaning cared for
in a way that
meets all of his
developmental
needs. However,
a son can be too
well loved in a
physical sense.

strong boy, let him mow the lawn, take out the trash,
and clean the basement. Thank him for his cooperation
and help. These tasks are good for any boy. Ask his

Private Eyes

Many single mothers, like many of their married counterparts, enjoy comfortable relationships with their sons. At an early age these sons may be given complete access to their mothers' bedrooms and the bathroom. The mothers dress and bathe in front of the sons, as do their sons in front of them.

Though this issue is not exclusive to the single-parent home, as her son grows older the single mother must take particular care to preserve her privacy for her son's sake. That she and he are of the opposite sex makes boundaries here of special significance. As a general rule, she probably won't go wrong insisting on privacy when either she or he are going to the bathroom or showering. Likewise, even though she may need a second hand or opinion, she may do best not asking her son to hook up her dress,

advice when it is genuinely called for, and involve him in finding solutions to the problems you face together. Treat him as grown up as he really is.

But a boy should remain a boy. Do not forsake your own adult role and responsibility. Seducing a son to be a partner or forcing him into pseudo-adulthood is unfair and will backfire. If you really need help deciding which bank to use, is your sixth-grader, however smart, the one to ask? You're going to be driving the car, so why not buy one that you like? If he's so fond of turquoise, let him paint his mountain bike. You want a red car. And for that matter, why should Timmy have a say in rub sun block on her back, consult on whether the black or tan stockings look best, or tell her whether that new dress makes her look sexy for a date.

Although she doesn't want to make her child uptight about sexuality and the human body, she might want to keep in mind the intensity of the single mother and son relationship. If a boy sees his mother walk around the house partially dressed, or she nonchalantly allows her bathrobe to fall open when on the phone, he may experience sensations that are seductively inviting, as well as overwhelming and shame-inducing. Most boys are most comfortable when their mothers practice modesty around them. While they may fantasize about hot chicks for themselves, and so-called Oedipal wishes aside, few boys truly want to see their moms sunbathing topless.

the landscaping when he won't raise a finger to help do the yard work? Let your son earn the privilege of having more input into the decisions you make. A boy cannot truly become the man around the house until he grows up properly as the boy around the house.

It's tricky, yes, but it is possible to find the right balance. A mother–son relationship is healthiest, and paradoxically may be most truly loving, when the boundaries between them are clear and respectful, and when these boundaries allow both parent and child to learn to know and cherish themselves as well as each other. Your open eyes and good sense will show you what is reasonable.

CHAPTER 5

Like Hand in Glove, Like Oil and Water

Mixing and Matching Temperaments

Just imagine if mothers used personal ads to advertise for the baby of their dreams:

> *Olly olly oxen free. Stop hiding and come find this remarkable single mom. The Easter Bunny meets Meg Ryan. More zest than a French mustard and a 100-megawatt smile. Blueberry picking, homemade donuts, and tuning my mountain bike are mere appetizers to my day. Prefer video games to conversation, tag to moonlight dinners. Love fishing and tree-climbing, Michael Jordan and Tiger. Wanna race? Looking for like-minded baby boy for childhood of*

*fun and games, to share life's mysteries, and maybe
wrestle a little bit, too. Clara, Personals, Box 561.*

Now this sounds like a mother who is psyched for a boy, doesn't it? We hope she can put up with the diapers, the naps, and the many months before he can run on his wobbly legs. For his first few years, his version of "party hearty" might clash with her own. But let's not get hung up on the details and lose sight of the bigger picture. What a mind-blowing concept: a mother seeking exactly the baby she would like—more so, looking forward to the son she dreams that her baby will one day become.

Consider that all-American boy, even if he doesn't really exist (and putting aside for the moment the unique variations of every child's personality, his gifts and weaknesses). As we learned in chapter 2, the typical boy is active, invigorated, loud, socially clumsy, and competitive. Now consider a different woman, one who can't stand to be around people of that ilk. She changed jobs once because her boss was "like that," and she's had catastrophic blind dates with men who are "like that." What happens if by some fluke she gets the boy that Clara wanted? Storks sometimes screw up—we know that.

———

Strong enough to handle a painful and combative divorce, in other ways 33-year-old Helene was a delicate creature. Her allergies aside, she had little need for the outdoors, finding it cold and wet, bug-infested and dirty. To her, great vacations meant museums, bookstores, and trendy restaurants. Her 10-year-old daughter, a budding artist and violinist, agreed, and mother and daughter were like best friends. But her eight-year-old son Nicholas had a different perspective on life and what made it worth living.

For years Nicholas had tried to physically engage his mother, but he always seemed to hurt her. As a toddler his sharp and flying elbows gave her bruises, and his hugs felt more like headlocks. "Your mother's a gentle thing," she'd tell him while she backed away and held her arms up to defend herself. Nicholas would laugh at what he thought was playfulness and come at her even harder, until she got mad and punished him.

"We're just peas from different pods," was how Helene saw it. "I'm a cerebral person and he's all energy, all body. I want to talk with him about his thoughts and feelings. He wants to scale me like I'm a jungle gym."

In spite of her wit and complaining, Helene felt awful and ashamed that she wasn't giving her son what she believed he wanted and deserved.

—⟨⟨⟩⟩—

Helene's daintiness need not have compromised her relationship with her son. Nor did Clara's quest for a boy after her own heart guarantee anything more than her sometimes being able to enjoy with a son the high adventure that she sought for herself. But it does underscore what for years was almost too obvious to notice. The same forces and dynamics that lead one person to like or dislike, to get along or not get along with another person apply to two people even when they happen to be parent and child, mother and son.

Some significant inborn differences exist between males and females, boys and their moms. In addition, both boys and girls have a wide range of temperaments, those personality qualities that make us who we are. A person can be introverted or extroverted, active or quiet, timid or fearless. The differences between them can intrigue and engage a mother with her son, or become almost insurmountable obstacles to a real, heartfelt connection. How can a mother approach the differences she perceives between herself and her son? And where are those differences most likely to appear?

Our Chromosomes or Crummy Homes?

Child psychology has made its share of mistakes. Arguably, one of its whoppers was the once-held view that "refrigerator mothers" caused their children's autism. Living with cold, unresponsive mothers, so went the theory, led their rejected children to withdraw emotionally into autistic shells. Autism was seen as a purposeful, if unconscious, defensive maneuver that emotionally protected a helpless child against a toxic mother. "It's all in the environment" was the message of the day.

Since that time, we have learned that quite the contrary is true. Autism, for instance, is a neurological syndrome that involves deficits in language and social processing. Mothers do not cause autism any more than they cause dyslexia or diabetes. The coldness once believed by medical experts to cause autism was actually the sad but understandable reaction of mothers whose children habitually rejected their smiles, hugs, and warmth. We can only imagine the frustration and guilt those falsely accused mothers felt.

Such missteps cautioned us and heaved the pendulum to the opposite extreme. Biology as destiny became the cry. Suddenly, almost by the hour, medical research was finding the evidence of biology in a panoply of human functioning, whether it be depression, anxiety, obsessive-compulsive disorder, learning disabilities, distractibility, or many subtler aspects of personality. Advances in brain science, neurochemistry, and genetic research catalyzed this explosion and fueled a necessary backlash. Standing atop their rapidly accumulating mountain of data, these scientists declared bad biology, not bad parenting, as the cause of so many childhood disorders and problems. Mothers, they proclaimed, were the victims, not the perpetrators, of difficult children.

> The same forces and dynamics that lead one person to like or dislike, to get along or not get along with another person apply to two people even when they happen to be parent and child, mother and son.

And so it goes, from one extreme to another. Fortunately, the pendulum is settling into a more balanced rhythm. The findings of developmental researchers have confirmed what any mother of two or more children has already experienced. Babies are not all alike. Endowed or saddled with different genetics, they are born with different brains and bodies and different temperaments. Some babies are notoriously hard to console, while others coo and smile their way through infancy. Some are doers, while others are observers. Some love rough-and-tumble play; some hate it.

And the baby watchers did not stop there. If babies have their temperaments, mustn't the adult women they grow into have these still, even when they become mothers? That interacting of temperaments proved key: How a mother and child "fit" together (or don't) explains much of what happens in their relationship. Temperamentally compatible children and mothers work more easily together than those whose temperaments don't match. Some mothers and sons fit like a hand in glove; others mix about as well as oil and water.

Nature and nurture both matter. Nature provides a basic template of who a child is and what his potential and vulnerabilities are. At the same time, it offers a window of opportunity for environment to make its impact, forces that can be substantial and that can last many, many years. Genetic research seems to tell us, for example, that certain genes predispose a young man for both aggressiveness and risk-taking. How he is raised—the values he learns, the boundaries around him, the respect and trust he feels for the adults in his life—shape whether those traits contribute to his prowess on the football field or a life on the wrong side of the law. Depending on how we treat him, a shy child can become either a socially anxious or a confident man. A wild child can end up an irresponsible lout or a good man full of life. It's what parents do with that window that counts.

Making the Most of Temperament

Let's return to Clara, ten years from now. She indeed got the prototypical boy she advertised for, but they aren't doing as well together as she'd planned. Each more strong-willed and competitive than the other, they battle more than they get along. Clara's frenetic schedule, busy enough for two mothers, clashes with that of her son, who has signed up for enough sports to satisfy two average boys. Neither listens to the other, compromises, or can say, "I'm sorry." He hates school and does poorly. He needs help with his homework, but he and Clara only get into power struggles when she tries to assist him.

> Genetic research seems to tell us, for example, that certain genes predispose a young man for both aggressiveness and risk-taking. How he is raised—the values he learns, the boundaries around him, the respect and trust he feels for the adults in his life—shape whether those traits contribute to his prowess on the football field or a life on the wrong side of the law.

"Be careful what you ask for, because you might get it" is not our point. We wish to stress that there are no sure things when it comes to parenting. Few parents are so well matched to their child that whatever they do works and they have no pitfalls to avoid. Few parents are so poorly matched to their child that they cannot adjust what they do to give their child what he needs. In other words, you cannot always choose what you receive in life, but you certainly can learn the skills to deal with it effectively.

Clara, we confess, was born of fiction. But Alice and Eddie are a real mother and a son.

Forty-two-year-old Alice divorced three years ago when her only child, Eddie, was one year old. A highly valued office manager for a large real estate agency, Alice strove to run her home in as orderly a fashion as she did her office. But it seldom worked. Eddie, so it seemed to her, lived only to frustrate her every wish. When she needed his cooperation, especially in the morning when she rushed to get to work, he was least willing to give it. "You've never seen a child fight his clothes or his car seat the way Eddie does," she lamented. "I can't ask him to do anything. The smallest request leads to a world war."

Taking Eddie to school was a nightmare. He would hang onto his mother's legs and scream for her not to leave. When the teachers told her he did fine once she left, she felt both hurt and angry. "I don't know why he makes such a stink," she asked. "He often doesn't like being with me anyway."

Bedtimes were bad, too. They lasted upward of three hours, involving stories upon stories and lengthy negotiations. For all of Alice's threats, the night often ended with Eddie falling asleep much too late in his defeated mother's bed, teeth unbrushed.

Whatever the time of day, Eddie needed life to go his way. If he didn't get his cereal in his blue bowl, he would throw the cereal and wrong-colored bowl across the kitchen. If Alice shut off the computer before he was ready, he would smash the keyboard. He protested much of what Alice did and threw frequent tantrums.

Unlike his mother, who managed her life with the efficiency of a Swiss watch, Eddie dragged his feet. Transitioning from one place to another, from one activity to another, unsettled him and stymied his mother. "Why can't he just go with the program?" she wondered. "It's hard enough being a single mother without my child tripping my every step."

Common or not, Alice's and Eddie's dilemma was significant. Despite their love for each other, they were headed for years of strife. Sadly, for all his indignation, Eddie believed he'd failed his mother, and she believed that she'd failed him. Fortunately, even large problems can sometimes have simple solutions. Alice was wise enough to ask for help and learned to facilitate their home life rather quickly. Let's look at the ways she successfully confronted a mismatch of temperaments.

Acknowledge Frustration

Frustration and conflict are inevitable in even the most harmonious of mother–son relationships. But complaints, criticism, and anger (especially about temperament characteristics that may be beyond his control) can hurt a boy and, ironically, invite more resistance. Constant criticism can make his mother feel like a bitter nag, not usually a role she wants or enjoys. Still, it's important that a mother admit to herself and face squarely the parts of her relationship with her son that bother her.

The most active ingredient in the stew Alice and Eddie were brewing was her frustration that she couldn't run her home the way she ran a realty office. Eddie didn't take orders well; his mother's priorities didn't appear anywhere on his personal agenda. Neither could truly understand the perceptions and feelings of the other. Little boys are, by nature, labor-intensive and demanding of maternal energy, and the mess Alice's family life had become was complicated further by her divorce and by having to raise Eddie by herself.

Awareness is always the first step toward change. When Alice acknowledged her frustration over her constant battles with Eddie and how their temperaments clashed, she was able to take the first steps toward ending the war.

Educate Yourself About Development and Temperament

Not everything that children do is "misbehavior," and rarely is it as malicious or personal as it feels to a beleaguered mother. One step toward defusing temperament differences with your son is to learn how your son's development—his physical, emotional, and cognitive abilities and growth—affects his behavior.

> One step toward defusing temperament differences with your son is to learn how your son's development—his physical, emotional, and cognitive abilities and growth—affects his behavior.

For instance, preschoolers are hard at work learning about the world around them and discovering their own autonomy and independence—one reason why they so like to say no to their mothers. Adolescents, too, are moving toward individuation and adulthood. While teenage behavior can be unattractive, mothers will cope with it more effectively when they understand the context in which it occurs. Many personality conflicts can be resolved calmly and without hurt feelings when mothers learn not to take it personally (admittedly, easier said than done) and to focus on finding solutions.

Study the Behavior

Misbehavior happens for a reason, although often neither the parent nor the child is aware of what that reason is. Although you might have to take action, it is worth pausing to ask yourself some questions, to seek the message in your child's behavior and words: Where does this behavior come from? What is it asking for? Is it as bad as it seems at the moment?

Alice asked such questions and got some interesting answers. She found that Eddie's protests at school and bedtime spoke of his upset at not having more of her time and attention at home. She found that many of his demands, like that for his blue cereal bowl, made sense to him and were not malicious. Because he was unable to control important matters in his life, like his mother's comings and goings, micro-managing the little things felt good and gave him a symbolic sense of power to offset the helplessness he felt.

Eddie also told her, when she asked, that he sometimes slowed down because she went so fast. He feared that if he didn't drag his feet on the ground, she would just go faster and faster. By searching for the good in what can seem the bad, Alice took a major step toward understanding her son and managing his behavior more effectively.

Look in the Mirror

If it takes two temperaments to tango, a mother's and a son's, then a mother must take time to discover her own contribution to the dance. Is she calm and reflective or inattentive and flighty? Is she irritable and moody, buoyant and optimistic, or comfortable only when she calls the shots? Alice determined that she'd always liked things to be black and white. That is why she enjoyed managing an office and planned on becoming an accountant. Numbers add up neatly and when they don't, you can figure out why and straighten them out. She saw herself as a control freak. What she wanted most from Eddie was his compliance. It wasn't that she didn't love him. She was an impatient person who was lost as to how to shape a child's behavior. "He deserves a flexible mother," she decided. "One who can enjoy struggling with him."

Few parents enjoy struggling with their child, and Eddie didn't need or want a new mother. Alice was right, however, that Eddie did need a mother who could adapt to his needs and temperament with flexibility. Identifying her own rigidity and need for control enabled Alice to respect and accommodate the same qualities in her son.

Empathize

Even more than being loved or admired, being understood is arguably the most powerful of human experiences. But it's not easy to empathize with your child's feelings when they're negative and appear to be aimed directly at you. Mothers revel in hugs and kisses, but feel confused and hurt by unpleasant behavior and words—and the two can sometimes happen within a single hour.

Alice bravely worked to better hear Eddie's frustration over the burden that her temperament could put on his. When Eddie understood that his mother wanted to listen, he told her, sobbing, that sometimes he thought she didn't like having him for a son. Alice found a way to compassionately convey to Eddie that she grasped his hurt and understood how she'd made him feel. Despite his young age, these moments of empathy and openness opened channels of communication and allowed four-year-old Eddie to choose more cooperative behavior much of the time.

Don't Blame

Temperament is no one's fault, any more than are blue eyes or red hair. Neither mothers nor sons deserve blame for being who they are, but both are responsible for their choices and behavior. Self-blame and guilt accomplish little that is constructive and, ironically, may even bring out the worst in us. Too much self-criticism overwhelms a person. Calling herself "the most awful parent in the world" made Alice unhappy, but it also may have let her off the hook in subtle ways, unwittingly distracting her from her less-catastrophic but real

Building a Bridge: Conveying Empathy to Your Son

No two people, no matter how much they may love one another, see the world in precisely the same way. Strive to do the following and you will strengthen the bond of love and respect between you and your son:

Accept your son for who he is—right now. Most mothers, when asked, can provide a list of traits and behaviors they wish their sons could change. The simple fact is, though, that we do not choose our temperaments, nor does any of us have the ability to determine the behavior or feelings of someone else. You will be much better able to solve problems with your boy when you can accept his liabilities, as well as his strengths, and help him learn to manage both.

Listen. Your son speaks to you with his behavior and his body, as well as with his words. A communication tool known as "active listening" teaches parents to listen to their child's feelings, then to reflect that feeling back without judgment. For instance, when your son slams the door and stomps off to his room, you could tell him, "Get back here and close the door quietly!" or "What happened now?" Or you could say calmly, "Looks like you're feeling pretty angry." Children long to be understood. A nonjudgmental reflection of feelings can invite your son to tell you more about what has happened, and you can work together later to resolve the issue of the slammed door.

Show genuine curiosity. Your son's world is a fascinating and complex place, and one way to understand his behavior and feelings is, quite simply, to ask. Be sure you truly want to know the answer. Children usually can tell when parents have an agenda in mind. Inviting your son to explain his own perceptions can give you information you might otherwise miss. For example:

"What do you like about [name of least desirable friend]?" instead of "I think he's a bad influence on you."

"Tell me more about your favorite rap music," instead of "I hate that stuff."

"How do you think we should solve this problem?" instead of "Do it because I said so!"

(It's important to note that listening and showing curiosity do not mean you agree with your son's opinions or behavior. You are creating a respectful atmosphere in which you can work together to resolve differences.)

Treat your son with respect. Empathy and love thrive in an atmosphere of mutual respect. Many times parents insist that their children show respect, while failing to respect their children. Note that respecting your son does not mean giving him adult privileges or responsibilities. It does mean choosing not to shame or embarrass him in the name of discipline and recognizing his right to his own thoughts and feelings, even when they're different from your own. Mutual dignity and respect build a foundation on which your relationship with your son can thrive.

shortcomings. Remembering that parents, too, are human and imperfect allowed Alice to pursue a healthier and less-damning self-inquiry that she could bear and that proved beneficial.

Focus on Solutions

In addition to seeing and empathizing with Eddie's feelings, Alice needed to examine their situation as logically as she might a problem at the office. When and how, she tried to notice, did clashes occur? What factors and conditions exacerbated them? What resolved them most quickly? Sensing that her relationship with Eddie was too emotionally loaded and too close to see clearly, Alice applied the case study method used by business and law schools. She imagined how she would have advised a mother like herself who had a son like Eddie. Playing family therapist consultant, Alice interviewed her hypothetical mother. "What traps," Alice asked herself, "lay before this mother and her son and how might they avoid them? How can that mother break the issue of temperament down to bite-sized pieces that can be dealt with? And how can she prioritize them to make them bearable and doable?"

> Self-blame and guilt accomplish little that is constructive and, ironically, may even bring out the worst in us. Too much self-criticism overwhelms a person.

Now Alice's temperament became her ally. Exploiting her strong problem-solving skills, Alice readily came up with several excellent solutions to her own problems. Spontaneity is wonderful, but many parents find that they are more effective when they act thoughtfully than when they react emotionally. Careful thinking and planning pay off.

Build on Strengths

Alice had learned as an office manager that criticism never brought out the best in her employees. Borrowing from that experience, Alice made a deliberate effort to think in terms of Eddie's and her own strengths. He was, she noticed, not just stubborn, but strong-willed, like her. His abundance of energy was healthy; it was her exhaustion at the end of her hectic day that made him seem so oppressively hyperactive. Even his "bossiness" she came to see as an asset, in that it was Eddie's active attempt to deal with a developmental task and, if properly guided, might one day evolve into leadership.

But we are talking about more than semantics. Denial and euphemisms are seldom, if ever, catalysts to family harmony. But, as it did for Alice, trying to see her son's behavior in a context of capability and potential can help a mother see the positives that her frustrations have blinded her to. And all of us, including young children, respond in a much more positive way when we don't feel criticized or blamed. Getting reacquainted with the good things in our sons, in itself reparative, can almost magically cut down to size the problem we think we face and renew our acceptance of both our sons and ourselves.

Be Creative and Varied

Alice and Eddie ended their battles by listening, understanding their unique temperaments, and looking for mutually respectful solutions to the problems they faced. We suspect that as time passes, they will encounter new challenges and will need to work together to solve them over and over again.

It is the process that matters, rather than the specific solution. Children are ever-changing and one strategy—one remark, one tone, one technique—will not work for long or in all situations. Children will outgrow and outfox them. Each effective ploy you devise expands your repertoire and adds tools to your parenting toolbox. And if you have more than one child, you have probably already discovered that what works with one child doesn't always work with the second. To understand temperament implies seeing all at once the ways that two children (and you, their mother) can be so alike and so different. Parenting is perhaps the toughest and least reflected-upon human endeavor. Use every resource available—other parents, professionals, books, articles, classes, anything.

And do not hesitate to be creative. Alice tried several strategies before discovering the ones that worked. She came to view her feelings of being stuck as a signal for change, allowing her to find new ways of looking at and handling her son.

A son comes into this world with unique limitations and possibilities that his mother and his home can profoundly influence. The child psychiatrist Stanley Greenspan has described this give-and-take as a dance between mother and child, one that can be as graceful as Fred and Ginger's.[1] But even as Greenspan wrote this lovely metaphor, he knew that, at times, all parents can dance with two left feet. Sometimes our parenting needs fine-tuning; other times it needs a major overhaul.

The chapters ahead show us that mothers usually do not need a whole new language, but an adjusting of the factors that make up good-enough parenting for any child: giving love, acceptance, empathy, attention, structure, and discipline. By opening her eyes to the patterns that get lost in everyday life, a mother—whether her son's temperament runs against or alongside her own—can widen and smooth the roads that run between them.

CHAPTER 6

Making One Good Man

Instilling Values and Morality

There is one thing on which parents, teachers, spiritual leaders, pediatricians, child psychologists, and even grandparents agree: Children need love *and discipline.* For many parents, however, delivering the disciplinary goods can be difficult. Single mothers in particular may wrestle with the concept of discipline, particularly as their sons grow taller, bigger, and stronger than they are. It is crucial that mothers discover effective ways to guide their sons' behavior from their earliest years, to instill character and values, and to avoid the power struggles (and, sometimes, physical struggles) that can become so destructive to both mother and son.

Parents fail to provide effective discipline for a number of reasons. Sometimes they truly believe that what they are doing is best for their children (despite growing evidence to the contrary). Sometimes they are determined not to do what their own parents did. Sometimes they want their children to be "happy" and believe that boundaries and discipline are just too tough on a child's tender self-esteem. And sometimes parents are just too weary to deal with discipline—a feeling most single mothers have experienced from time to time.

Regardless of the reason, failure to establish effective discipline rarely leads to a positive outcome. All too often, parents surrender to whining, demanding, discontented, and misbehaving children. We all know the immediate cost of that leniency—the crying, the fighting, the noise. But an even greater price is the burden our lax parenting places on our children and their development.

> Good character and psychological health don't just happen. Nor is love enough. Without proper discipline, children go forward on shaky ground.

Good character and psychological health don't just happen. Nor is love enough. Without proper discipline, children go forward on shaky ground. When children self-rule, when they live by the royal *me,* they grow into tortured adults, along the way torturing everyone else with their ill-boding *I*s: *I*nconsideration, *I*rritability, *I*rresponsibility, *I*mpulsivity, *I*mmaturity, *I*llusions of *I*nvincibility, *I*nsatiability, and *I*mmorality.

Deprived of consistent and dependable limits, structure, and expectations and ignorant of where they end and others begin, children fail to learn tolerance for the many experiences in life that are less than exciting, are less immediately rewarding, and that involve stress, failure, and hard work. As a result they may grow into underachievers who cannot sustain interest and effort in their learning, work, or connections with people.

At worst, children who are not disciplined can be prone to delinquency, depression, impulsivity, drug and alcohol abuse, sexual mishaps, and troubled relationships. And not so obviously, inadequate limits can lead even quieter and more compliant children to experience unnecessary anxiety, withdrawal, and problems with anger.

Although the prognosis can sound enormously gloomy, restoring order to the home is not as daunting a task as it may seem. In this chapter we explore the meanings and dynamics of morality and discipline, while in the next we detail the actual methods of discipline.

Morality and Discipline

Discipline is necessary for moral growth to proceed. However, morality is more than your son's good behavior and obedience to your rules.

Morality means having a strong inner sense of right from wrong. It encompasses the ability to live ethically in a complex, stressful, corrupt, and tempting world—especially when no one is watching to tell your son what to do, when he is being told to do something he shouldn't, or even when the conventional "right" is wrong.

Integrity, it has been said, is doing what is right even when no one is looking. Your son's good moral judgment is based on his having a strong character and a great deal of trust in his own values. Children who are raised with discipline alone, but who are not taught and encouraged to act and judge for themselves, may well behave but may fail to morally thrive.

Children must be taught to exercise good judgment and responsibility by being given opportunities to practice—and it is inevitable that they will make mistakes. Without this practice, however, children can rely only on values and limits that come from outside themselves (what is called an external locus of control), a situation that may place them at the whim of their peers or leave them rudderless when no authority is present.

Wisdom, character, and good judgment grow from an internal locus of control—the ability to weigh options, consider consequences, and act with wisdom and responsibility. This skill is not inborn; it must be taught. Moral growth occurs only by being exercised regularly—inch by inch, judgment by judgment—in homes where moral parents offer their children ample age-appropriate opportunities to prove and earn their greater trust.

What Is Discipline?

Discipline is all of the ways that help your son to behave well and learn to live a moral life. In fact, the word *disci-*

pline comes from the same Latin root as the word *disciple* and has a very simple meaning: "to teach." Discipline includes setting limits, providing structure, discouraging misbehavior, inspiring good behavior, educating as to what is expected, and encouraging effort in the right direction.

What Does Discipline Accomplish?

Although it's good for children to say "thank you," politeness is just one small aspect of what discipline aims to achieve. Proper discipline contributes to a boy's ability to know right from wrong; manage his anger; use good judgment; exercise self-control; tolerate frustration, as well as shortcomings in himself and others; assert reasonable needs and worthy causes; respect others; love others; and work with pride and care. In sum, sound discipline, along with love, is the best guarantee a parent can give a child for his psychological well-being, a sound foundation for a son's experiencing comfort, joy, and satisfaction throughout his lifetime.

> *Signs That Your Discipline Is Amiss*
> Your son doesn't listen to you.
> He mistreats you.
> You frequently make excuses for his behavior.
> You rescue him from consequences outside
>   the home.
> You do his chores or homework for him.
> You yell a lot.
> You feel like a nag.

You say mean things to him.

You find yourself having to make bargains and
promise rewards for every ounce of cooperation
and good behavior.

You repeatedly threaten, warn, and count to three,
but seldom follow through, with no change in
your son's behavior.

You tend to let things slide and slide until, overwhelmed, you explode with frustration and anger.

You feel as though you are being manipulated, but
can't figure out how to change things.

You find yourself explaining to him, on and on,
everything you ask of him.

You seldom, if ever, just say no.

You are unable to discipline in public.

You often rationalize why you cannot follow
through on a consequence.

You walk on eggshells so as not to upset or displease
him.

Much of the time parenting feels like driving an out-
of-control race car.

You have moments, lasting days, weeks, or longer,
when you do not like your children (or yourself).

A Cry for Parenting

Your son needs boundaries and structure to grow
straight. Like a tomato plant that bends toward the sun
and water, a boy who forever bothers his mother is
searching for the limits he needs to grow well. His in-

creasing misbehavior is meant, to a great degree, to test you, his mother, to find out what outrageous action or word will finally evoke your reaction and get him the discipline even he knows he requires.

In fact, being calmly and consistently disciplined is one way that children initially learn trust. When discipline is both kind and firm, children can relax, knowing that the parent is on duty and that their world is a safe place. Although he would never acknowledge it, deep down your son wants such help. You may be astonished by the cooperative and contented child you discover when you can successfully follow through with discipline.

Proper Discipline

Good discipline is doled out:

Fairly, not heaped on one child over another, and not dispensed whimsically, depending on your mood or on how your day is going

Responsibly, taking ample credit or blame for its success or failure, acknowledging your part in creating the problem in the first place

Consistently, with sufficient regularity

Judiciously, with thought and care as to its whys, hows, wheres, whens, and whats

Compassionately, with concern and empathy for how it makes your child feel

For good reason, meaning, in your son's best interest

With love, driven by your loving wish that your son grow into a self-confident, contented, and decent human being

Custom-Made Discipline

Sound discipline takes account of your son's development, meeting him where he is. It uses words he understands. It uses consequences that sting but don't assassinate. It uses time periods he can appreciate. It assumes the need for certain struggles as part-and-parcel of a son's separating and growing into a mature person. And it follows from a sensible realization of what is reasonable behavior to expect from a boy of that age, level of maturity, and in the context of that situation.

This means that within the same family, children may differ in how much and what kind of discipline they need. An occasionally raised eyebrow may work for one boy, whereas your stronger-willed son may require much more frequent and robust discipline. Likewise, a child may need more discipline at particular times or in particular areas. To strive for equal parenting of all children is likely to fail because it will not give each child the discipline he developmentally needs.

There are many ways of assessing how successful your approach to discipline is. One, not surprisingly, is the degree of cooperation you receive from your son. Another is the confidence you feel in following through. Many mothers choose disciplinary methods (ones they've read in a book, heard from a neighbor, or seen on a talk show) that they actually feel uncomfortable using. You will be more effective in providing discipline for your son when you are able to act with confidence. If your heart tells you "this isn't working," you probably should listen.

Perhaps the best way to discover the long-term results of your discipline is to check out what your son is learning and deciding about himself, you, and the world around him. This often is not at all what parents think it is. As your son grows older and more articulate, you can (and should) talk with him about what he is thinking, feeling, and deciding. It's the best evidence that the lessons and values you are trying to communicate to him are getting through.

How Strict Should You Be?

Many modern mothers fear that harsh homes produce angry, beaten-down, and revengeful children. And, in fact, they can. However, and contrary to what we might expect, studies show that children from stern (not abusive) homes fare better in many ways than those from overly permissive ones. Children from lenient homes often do not learn how to cope with the limits and frustrations of life and can be prone to even greater problems with anger and anxiety than those who receive loving, firm discipline.

The best discipline avoids either extreme. It is neither too lax and permissive (which can create self-absorbed, manipulative children) nor overly controlling and severe (which can lead to defiance or sneakiness).

We should aim for a balance, to be parents who—while kind, fair, and supportive—can, when necessary, exert our values and enforce our own and society's rules.

The Many Functions of Limit-Setting

It is self-evident that setting clear limits helps to keep us, our sons, and those around them safe. But that is not all limits do for our growing sons. By not allowing them free rein, by curbing what they do, parents help their children learn to tolerate the frustration of not getting what they want when they want it, strengthening their ability to delay gratification (a patience that many adults sorely lack). Our limits on their physical aggression force them to use words instead of hitting or kicking, thereby increasing their self-control.

> Contrary to what we might expect, studies show that children from stern (not abusive) homes fare better in many ways than those from overly permissive ones.

Setting limits also demonstrates that you, as a parent, do not fear your son's reactions to your discipline and that they will not manipulate you. "Be angry, disapprove, even dislike me for now," your steadfast action tells him. "Your momentary unhappiness will not keep me from doing what I must as a good parent."

Further, by allowing and acknowledging a boy's feelings—a mother gives him a much-needed chance to vent, in small and manageable ways, his bigger feelings of helplessness and frustration. Few sons can articulate their conflict over growing up and their occasional wish to stay mommy's little boy. Many more boys, however, can comfortably blast their mothers for picking them up late or packing the wrong school snacks. Unpleasant though these moments may be, listening to and acknowledging your son's feelings will help you to avoid the larger disagreements that can eventually drive you farther apart.

Mothers' Rights

A son is a most cherished thing in a single mother's life. Shouldn't her son's needs and rights rule the house 24 hours a day, seven days a week? Heck, no. Children deserve the best parenting we can give. But it's important that you not forget your parent's rights, too.

As a good parent you deserve:

Authority and respect
Some recognition and appreciation for what you do
Private times and places that exclude your children
Time to spend not only with your children, but on other loved ones and yourself
To trust your own judgment concerning discipline and other child-related matters
To pursue interests beyond your children
To consider what you want, too, when making family and personal decisions

Forgiveness for the inevitable moments of moodiness, impatience, and other human conditions often taken to be the exclusive province of children

Failure to treat yourself with respect does more than deprive you; it can harm your son, who must learn to treat others (including the women who will eventually enter his life) with dignity and respect.

What Is Smart?

Is a brainy nuclear scientist who creates weapons of mass destruction smart? How about a manufacturing wizard, whose profitable Fortune 500 company flushes its hazardous waste downstream? And what of political leaders who shamelessly double-talk, blame others for their failures and—perhaps the thorniest chink in their credibility—deny doing anything solely in their own self-interest? Are these bright, confident, and highly achieving men *really* smart?

What we think of as "smart" implicitly involves values. Our conscience leads us to think more highly of men, or boys, who don't devise ways to kill their fellow man, who exercise care not to befoul the world they live in, and who refuse to steal from those who trust them to protect their welfare. We are not against success or capitalism, for the unsuccessful can be just as "not smart" when it comes to how they conduct their lives. It is not so much what a person does as how he does it, with how much conscience and compassion. That, to us, seems to be the rightful definition of what constitutes "smart."

A great deal has been said and written in recent years about character. School programs seek to build it; books and experts expound on what it is. We believe that each parent must thoughtfully consider the attributes and qualities she desires for her son, the character she believes will help him become a capable, confident, compassionate man. Each act of discipline every day of a boy's life should move him in the direction of those qualities. It is no easy task, but it is critically important that all parents consider and take responsibility for the character their children are or aren't developing.

Concern for the World

We don't need statistics or reminders to know that our world and society are in deep trouble. Our sons will live their lives in the world we are creating. How can we not, for their own good, raise them to care about the world they live in? How do we make them boys, and eventually men, who care about their environment and world?

We give caring. By reliably mothering your babies— feeding, soothing, and admiring them—you foster their sense that the world is a good and safe place. Responding to their cues and gestures shows them that they can act on their world and influence the important people in it. This early sense of trust and power is the foundation for a vital and responsible life.

We show caring. Helplessly in love with you, your children strive to be just like you. What kind of model do you present? Do you respect and care for the world, or do you neglect, befoul, or exploit it? And what does your abuse of the environment, your children's home, say to them about your love for them?

We confirm their caring. When your young children show caring for other people or things, even if in play, encourage and celebrate it with your enthusiasm, pride, and explicit praise. Belittling or ignoring a boy's concerns or deeds will eventually take the joy and zest out of his interest in the environment. Your admiration can only help to sustain it.

We enforce caring. Children need limits, even in their dealings with nature. And when they transgress, they need firm consequences. They must learn that soiling nature is as much an offense as is marring the living room wall. They must learn that the world *is their home,* too. Children who are glibly excused from their actions are liable to become entitled adults who see themselves as being above the laws of nature and human consideration.

We teach caring. Children love to learn about nature—whether from a book, on a television show, or on a walk with mom. Every fallen leaf, every cooing dove is an opportunity to educate. As you teach, strive to stay at the child's level; for example, hearing that there may one day be no clean water to drink or air to breathe can frighten and discourage a child more than it inspires.

Instilling our children—the consumers, parents, CEOs, and policy-makers of tomorrow—with an environmental conscience is one of our greatest challenges. By helping them accept that they are part of the world,

Growing a Social Conscience in Your Son

Encouraging character and concern in your son for the world around him is not difficult. You can build these activities and ideas into your home and your life together. Everyone will benefit.

Talk about ideas. When you watch the evening news or listen to the radio, when you read the newspaper, or when you watch a movie or television program that deals with the environment, poverty, bigotry, or the other issues our society faces, take time to explore these issues with your son. Instead of lecturing, ask what he thinks. Sharing your values with your son and learning about his will help you encourage character and compassion.

Create a caring home. If the environment is important to you, take time to recycle, choose products carefully, and invite your son's help. Practice honesty, mutual respect, and generosity toward others. Speak about these values often and let them guide your daily interactions with those around you.

Put your ideas into action. Your son can learn that he has the ability to change the world around him, despite his youth. You can choose to make caring for others a part of your family life. For example: Take outgrown clothing and toys to a shelter, adopt a family for the holidays, join in a fundraising walk for a cause you both care about, or simply spend an hour a week picking up trash in your favorite park. Imagine what the world might become if each family acted on what it believed.

mysteriously connected to every bird and tree, to every other living and nonliving thing, we can provide them with a richer legacy. And by doing so, we may become just a little bit "greener" ourselves.

Loving Our Sons Too Much

As Cheryl Erwin and Jane Nelsen wrote in their book *Parents Who Love Too Much*, contemporary parents often express their love for their children in ways that are counterproductive, sometimes even destructive. In a tragic irony, these parents focus on giving their children what they want rather than what they need.[1]

—✿—

Jeff was a handsome, athletic, and bright second-grader who was having a hard time of life. He didn't like his teacher and felt that she picked on him. He put little effort into his school work and was rejected by classmates, who disliked his bossy, know-it-all attitude.

At home he was even worse. His mother, Franny, had been divorced for five years and had no control over him. The only way she could get him to do what she wanted was to bribe him with treats and toys. Trips to the candy and toy store were a regular part of her daily schedule, even though she barely had time to do what she needed to and didn't have money to spare.

Franny began indulging Jeff right after the divorce. Abandoned on a day's notice by her husband, her esteem was crushed when he ran off with a much younger woman. Thoughtful parenting according to Dr. Spock was a luxury that was way beyond her. All she could do at that time was to survive. That she was able to feed Jeff, keep him safe, and get him to school was a miracle in itself.

And so, as a toddler, when Jeff would refuse to get dressed or get out of the car to go to day care, Franny resorted to material rewards. "Put on your shoes," she'd promise, "and I'll buy you another Lego set this afternoon." It "worked," but soon grew into a problem of its own, one that quickly grew too large for Franny and her son.

———◦/◦/◦———

When she finally became unable to handle Jeff's louder and longer tantrums and realized she couldn't afford the more expensive toys that he demanded, Franny sought professional help. With some parent guidance, she came to understand that her indulgence harmed rather than helped her son. It weakened his character and was rapidly producing a miserable and insatiable adult with no inner sense of motivation and no consideration for the needs of others, including his hardworking mother.

Unfortunately, Franny's insights changed much more quickly than did Jeff's behavior. Although she stopped bribing her son, Jeff would have none of it. His demands grew more demanding and his protests grew more volcanic. *You have to buy me that! If you don't take me to the toy store, I'll never listen to anything you say!*

Despite growing discouraged, Franny kept at it. Steadily, if with much tumult, Jeff began to respond. Once he really believed that his mother meant it, he began to surrender, showing more kindness, consideration, and patience than his mother had ever thought possible.

His improved attitude and happier disposition, the proof of the pudding, motivated Franny to sustain her new way of mothering for the years to come.

Guilt and the Single Mom

We realize that in many cases we are preaching to the converted. Before reading this book many of you well understood that your sons need limits and structure. Even as you say okay or look the other way, you wince, sensing that you've given in and done your son a disservice. What keeps mothers from doing what they know they should? Why do single mothers sometimes fail to set limits or follow through, allowing their sons' emotions and desires to dictate life in the family?

There isn't just one reason, but our experience tells us that guilt is often the culprit. Many divorced mothers, especially those who asked for the split, worry that they've hurt their sons and deprived them of a live-in father. Many who are single mothers by choice feel guilt about their decision to parent alone.

Single mothers also feel guilt because they must juggle work, household chores, education, and some sort of personal life, often at the expense of time with their sons. They may feel guilty when, for example, their son is ill and they must choose between taking time off from work, paying for child care, or leaving him home alone, all difficult and painful choices. For the vast majority of single mothers work is not an option. Reports in the media that child care or mothers' working can possibly harm children only add to the guilt over a situation that is hard, if not impossible, to change.

Because single mothers already feel that their choices may be hurting their sons, they are prone to over-indulge and under-discipline. They may give in and give more to a son because they judge he's "suffered enough." "He has no father" (at home or perhaps anywhere), the guilt tells them. "I don't get to spend enough time with him. The least I can do is let him have that toy, this twenty dollars, some small joy."

Guilt is an understandable emotion, as is your wish to make your son happy. Guilt is useless and destructive, however, unless you are able to learn something from it. Rather than spoiling and pampering your son, put your guilt to better use. Let it compel you to give your son the discipline and character-building he needs so much more than any extra treat or videogame. He eventually will only love and respect you more for doing so.

The Danger of Hypocrisy

Children, especially teenagers, seem to have an uncanny ability to detect those moments when a parent's words and actions don't match. One of the toughest parts of raising children is accepting the reality that what you do is a far more powerful influence than what you say. We all know that vigorous toddlers strive to be just like their grownup parents—in clothing, speech, and action. It is inevitable that children, as once happened to us, will grow disillusioned with the most upstanding parent, for no mother or father is as all-wise, giving, or protective as young children initially believe.

There is no need, however, to make this natural disillusionment worse. What will a child think when he sees his father cheat in a game of basketball or hears his mother lie to her boss? And what is he to think when he is praised more for an A he obtained with his mother's excessive help than for a B he earned entirely on his own? What does he learn when his mother discourages him from confessing the truth about a late assignment, suggesting that he say, not that they went bowling, but that he was ill?

> What we think of as "smart" implicitly involves values. Our conscience leads us to think more highly of men, or boys, who don't devise ways to kill their fellow man, who exercise care not to befoul the world they live in, and who refuse to steal from those who trust them to protect their welfare.

The answer, though neither absolute nor the same for every child, is typically a discouraging one. A boy may easily lose faith in the trustworthiness of those he once counted on and to whom he looked for guidance and inspiration. If his ideals are dragged through the mud long enough, he may embrace the delinquent behavior he observes around him. If you value high grades, scholastic achievement, or monetary gain above all else, your children will know it and likely will live according to that creed.

Parents cannot have it both ways, living the low road and preaching the high. It's easy to blame society, the media, and successful men in the news for corrupting our children. But life isn't that simple. Morality begins at home; and rigidly enforced rules at home—no lying, no cheating, no whatever—will not suffice. Parents who want to teach their children to be good people must take a close look at their own morality and values.

Holding Court

Our sons need to be given a childhood filled with opportunities to exercise their judgment and to struggle with their own ethical decisions under the watchful, guiding, and fair eyes of parents—judges who are neither too lenient nor too stern. Rather than merely condemning or punishing, we must help our children understand the reasons, usually good ones, behind their lying. Avoid the black and white. Instead of treating a sneaked cookie as grand larceny, consider with your child what motives might have propelled him and what he could have done differently.

Conversely, do not be afraid of doling out justice. Children who are glibly excused from taking responsibility for their own actions time after time develop selective consciences that conveniently rationalize their misbehavior. Because they have successfully avoided the consequences of their wrong choices, they may grow into entitled adults who hold themselves above the laws of the land and, more important, the laws of nature and of human consideration and mutuality.

When you are parenting alone, raising a boy who has a conscience and respect for himself and the world can feel overwhelming. This task, however—arguably, the most challenging and necessary of our tasks as parents—is possible.

CHAPTER 7

Do Fence
Me In

The Nuts and Bolts of Discipline

Every mother wants her son to grow up to be a good
and ethical man. We understand that discipline is
necessary for that to happen. But how does a mother
provide effective discipline for a growing boy, particularly when she's a single mother?

It can help a great deal to recognize that discipline
and punishment are two different things. Punishment—
grounding, nagging, spanking, taking away privileges—
is often an emotional reaction to a child's misbehavior.
Discipline, on the other hand, is a thoughtful act intended to teach. Discipline can and should be both kind

125

and firm and can, with enough planning, happen without yelling or anger.

Few people do their best, tackle new challenges, or face their own weaknesses and mistakes when they feel discouraged, shamed, or humiliated. Yet that is almost always the attitude we assume discipline should produce. Don't children, especially our strong-willed young men, have to suffer in order to learn? Doesn't discipline have to pinch for the message to get through?

Well, sometimes, but sometimes not. Anything that teaches your son respect, cooperation, motivation, and strong character qualifies as discipline, even if it's only talking a problem over together. Because you may not always be bigger than your son, it is unwise to rely on physical force to control his behavior. Better to cultivate the quiet strength that comes when your son respects you and knows that you mean what you say and will follow through. To that end, we will explore parenting strategies to consider making a part of your discipline plan. All are designed to teach good judgment, responsibility, and personal accountability, as well as obedience.

Why Do Children Misbehave?

Children's behavior has a purpose. The problem is that we (and usually, they) don't know exactly what that purpose is. Many professionals who work with children believe that one primary motivator for behavior is the need to belong and to feel significant. When a child doesn't feel that sense of belonging and connection, he may try to evoke that feeling. Parents usually call these misguided efforts to belong and to feel significant "misbehavior."

Punishment and rewards are intended to change behavior, but they do not take into account why that behavior is happening. A boy might throw a temper tantrum because he's learned it gets his mother's attention, he feels a sense of power when he's defying others, he wants to hurt someone as badly as he's been hurt, or he feels discouraged and unable to live up to others' expectations. Although the behavior, a tantrum, can look the same, in each case the underlying reason differs.

You will be most effective as a parent when you can combine information about development, temperament, and discipline with your own inner wisdom and common sense about your son, and when your methods deal with both your son's behavior *and* the beliefs behind it. A child tends to repeat behaviors because these bring about something he wants. The riddle for parents is to decipher the code: to understand what purpose the behavior serves for a child and how to help the child achieve belonging, attention, and significance in a more positive way.

Natural and Logical Consequences

Natural consequences are consequences that naturally follow from a behavior or situation. Because they relate to the behavior in a direct and timely manner, natural consequences wield more power than more arbitrary punishments. A child often learns best when his parent steps out of the way and lets him experience the results of his own choices.

For instance, the natural consequence when your son refuses to eat a meal is that he will get hungry later on (unless you rescue him with a midnight peanut-butter-and-jelly sandwich). If he stays up too late, he will be tired the next day. And if he refuses to wear mittens when he goes out to throw snowballs, his hands will become very cold.

> A child tends to repeat behaviors because these bring about something he wants. The riddle for parents is to decipher the code: to understand what purpose the behavior serves.

The beauty of natural consequences is that they require little assistance from parents. In fact, sometimes they're most effective when you offer empathy ("Goodness, your fingers are blue!") and invite your son to participate in solving the problem ("What do you think you could do to warm your hands up?").

Sometimes, however, there is no natural consequence for an action, or the natural consequence is unacceptable. The natural consequence of his playing in the middle of the street, for example, is not one we want him learning from. The natural consequence of your son's getting a bad report card is simply that he is now the owner of a bad report card, something that may or may not move him to work harder. Obviously, in these instances parental involvement is called for. We call these parental interventions "logical consequences."

Remember that the success of any parenting method depends in large part on your confidence, your attitude, and your willingness to follow through. As whole generations of grandmothers have told us, "Say what you mean and mean what you say." Don't set up consequences you know you won't be able to execute. ("If you don't feed that puppy, he's going back to the pound!"). Be sure that consequences are reasonable and directly related to the misbehavior, and, as much as possible, take time to establish and discuss them with your son in advance.

———

Sheila's nine-year-old son, Henry, enjoyed athletics. To their family, fall, winter, and spring meant soccer, basketball, and baseball. Sheila enjoyed driving Henry and his friends to practice and watching the games. What she didn't like was all the laundry, especially the socks.

Henry went through several pairs of socks a day. And he had a habit of pulling them off from the top down, so they wound up in the laundry basket in muddy, sweaty wads. When Sheila did the laundry, she had to turn these crusty socks right-side-out, a miserable job.

No amount of lecturing and nagging made a difference. Sheila showed Henry how to take his socks off. It didn't matter. He wasn't interested. The laundry basket stayed full of damp, smelly, wadded socks.

Finally, up to her elbows in dirty laundry, Sheila had an epiphany: Henry wasn't going to change until she did. So, one day when in a calm mood, Sheila sat down with her son. She told him that she didn't like doing his socks, and that his unwillingness to help out frustrated her. From now on, she advised, she'd wash his socks in balls, just the way he'd put them in the laundry basket, and return them to him that way. It worked for a few days until Henry, not surprisingly, lost interest.

Knowing she had to follow through, Sheila laundered the crusty wads, putting washed-and-dried wads back in Henry's drawer. Most important, she did not nag, lecture, or scold. She simply did what she had said she would.

Henry soon grew tired of wrestling with his clean socks. In a matter of days Sheila found neatly turned socks in her son's hamper. Sheila had set up a reasonable, logical consequence and followed through with respect and dignity.

———✦———

Consequences are not always easy to recognize in the heat of the parenting moment. Because children tend to repeat troublesome behaviors, single mothers can and probably should plan out apt consequences for misbehavior they know is sure to come back.

As children mature, the issues change. Consequences and follow-through will be different for your adolescent son than they were for your toddler. You will need to sit down together and reach an agreement about expectations regarding curfew, driving, money, jobs, and other young-adult issues. It can be helpful to put agreements with teens into writing. Then no one can say later, "That's not what you said!" As always, when you have agreed upon a consequence, be ready to follow through without threats, lectures, or *I told you so's*.

When examining the misbehavior, ask yourself, *Is my son getting something from this behavior? What is he really learning, and deciding to do in the future?* When your fourth-grader didn't do his homework as he promised, should he be allowed to stay up late to watch that Giants game? If you allow it, what will he be learning about homework, his responsibilities—and you, as disciplinarian?

Teaching Skills and Communicating Your Expectations

Many otherwise competent and loving parents have a baffling tendency to assume that their children should somehow learn the rules and expectations of social behavior by osmosis. Unfortunately, it doesn't usually happen that way. The rules for behavior—for example, in restaurants, shopping malls, and other public places—must be taught. And it helps to do some preparation with your boy *before* you go out into the world.

For instance, let's say you take your son to see the blockbuster movie of the summer. The super-popcorn and bottomless-soda, however great a deal, does not automatically come with every movie ticket. If, without asking, your son grabs the five-dollar bill from your hand and heads for the refreshment counter, you have several choices. You can give him a stern lecture and threaten him with mayhem. You can take his arm and leave the theater. You can remove the money from his hand and let him

> The rules for behavior—for example, in restaurants, shopping malls, and other public places—must be taught. And it helps to do some preparation with your boy *before* you go out into the world.

watch the movie without snacks. Better yet, you could have done some teaching before you left the house.

What therapists call role playing, children call "let's pretend." Let your son be the parent, and you be the child. Ask him how you should behave at the movie (or the pizza parlor, or the toy store). Should you run around? Beg for treats? Grab money? Shriek or whine during the movie? Practice a bit, and be sure you explain calmly and clearly your expectations before you go. You can make an agreement about what sort of treats you will purchase and when. You can also (especially with an older child) set up in advance the potential consequences should your son not be able to follow the rules. Be sure you can follow through kindly and firmly. It may require your leaving the theater once or twice without seeing a movie, for example, to convince your son that you mean your end of the bargain.

Remember, discipline means teaching. It usually takes one or two lessons in teaching correct behavior (and following through when things don't go as planned) for your son to understand what is expected and to behave.

What About Choices?

Most mothers have heard the phrase "Give your child choices." And indeed, for a child addicted to power struggles, offering limited and reasonable choices is an excellent way to constrain his power while still allowing him to exercise choice and responsibility. Children can learn by having limited choices, such as which of two cereals to have for breakfast, which outfit to wear, and

Some No's of Discipline

Here are some common stumbling blocks in practicing effective discipline:

- Beware of empty threats, warnings, and counting to three. They frustrate you, weaken your authority, and may make your son more defiant. If you say it, be willing to follow through. If you can't follow through, don't say it.
- Don't shame, humiliate, or ridicule as a way to discipline. It is unnecessary and can teach your child to do the same to others. Nor does it lead to better behavior.
- Try not to discipline out of frustration, self-hatred, or resentment.
- Perfect consistency is impossible. However, habitual breaking of your own rules—because it is summer, a late night, or Tuesday—will erode your disciplinary legitimacy.
- Keep your discipline in line with the crime.
- Hitting and other physical punishments are never helpful. They're not necessary and can do harm if they get out of control. Physical punishment may also encourage aggression in boys who need no urging in that direction.

whether to brush their teeth or have you do it for them. The catch? You have to be sure the choices teach the right lesson and work for both of you.

Choices can be a useful way to teach children that they do have power over their own lives and can influence what happens to them, but the choices must be appropriate and reasonable. It isn't wise or helpful to ask a five-year-old if he'd like to go to day care today, when both of you know you have to go to work and he has to go to day care. Children shouldn't be consulted about decisions that are an adult's responsibility, such as finances, adult relationships, or whether or not you should move to another neighborhood. They can be given choices about simple things that enhance their sense of responsibility for their own behavior.

Keep in mind that too many choices can complicate the issue and can turn children into master manipulators. By relying too much on choices, some mothers have trained their children to be savvy deal-makers. "You can read your school book for fifteen minutes or go to bed right now, which is it?" she asks. "Five minutes," he counters, wanting to work out a choice more to his liking before he even considers a decision. As always, you must be willing to follow through with kindness and firmness, dignity, and mutual respect.

Routines

Many mothers dread bedtime or morning because at these times of day, they will engage in yet another battle with their children. Harried, fatigued mothers often find that getting out of the house in the morning or getting the kids to bed at night are when they are most likely to struggle.

Although there is no single solution to parenting challenges, having a reliable and consistent structure for these difficult times can be immensely helpful. Children, especially young children, learn best when parents are consistent and life is predictable. Having reliable routines can be an effective form of discipline.

If you find you are fighting World War III every bedtime, try organizing a simple routine. Let your son help you make a chart—not one to earn stickers or rewards, but more of a map that lays out the steps of your nightly routine. Begin at the same time each evening, and follow the steps in order. When your son gets distracted or balks, ask him, "What's next on your chart?" The routine becomes the boss, and both of you will know just what happens next.

Similar routines can be worked out for dinnertime and mornings. Making school lunches can become part of your evening routine, along with gathering books and homework papers. Consistency and clear expectations can take much of the guesswork and hassle out of these stressful times.

Positive Time Out

Time out may be the most overused, misunderstood method of discipline. Many frazzled moms count to three and then, when their child hasn't leaped to obey, drag him to the "time out spot" to think about what he did. Some mothers set a timer, one minute for each year of the child's age. And they may wind up spending most of their energy trying to get that child to stay in time out.

Actually, time outs can be a useful method. But they are best used as an opportunity to cool off, rather than as punishment. None of us does our best work when angry, out of control, or in tears. Time out can provide a child with the time to catch his breath, get a grip, and relax enough to do the real problem solving most conflicts require. In fact, mothers often benefit from a time out as much or more than their sons do.

Consider designating a cool-off spot for your son. It can be in his room, a quiet corner of the den, or some other place where he feels comfortable. Allow him to furnish his spot with things that help him relax—some books, a puzzle, a Koosh ball, or pillows. When tempers flare or he's angry and disrespectful, invite him to take a moment in his special spot to cool off. Tell him when he's feeling better, you will work together to solve the problem. Or tell him that *you* are getting too angry and need to cool off, too.

Some parents object, claiming that this use of time-outs rewards children for misbehavior. This isn't true. It helps children learn the vital skill of "self-soothing," the ability to be aware of and manage strong emotions. Boys often reflexively resort to anger, yelling, or even physical aggression when upset. A cooling-off time out can help them learn to deal with anger in a positive way, a skill that will benefit them for the rest of their lives.

Remember, you're not letting your son off the hook. When the outburst has subsided, you can then work together to follow through on a consequence, talk over a disagreement, or resolve a misunderstanding. We guarantee that the process will be much smoother when you and your son are calm and respectful.

The Magic of Encouragement

What, you may wonder, does encouragement have to do with discipline? Well, if misbehavior is frequently about a need for belonging and significance, finding positive ways to help your son find that belonging and connection should improve his behavior. Not surprisingly, this often happens.

Encouragement means noticing effort in the right direction ("Wow, you brought that D in history up to a C+!"), rather than rewarding only complete success. It means noticing what your boy does right, as well as the things he does wrong. It means being aware each and every day of his strengths and wonderful qualities and remembering to appreciate them, rather than focusing only on his flaws and difficulties. And it means remembering to celebrate success and to say "thank you," without adding, "now, if you'd only get that C+ up to a . . ."

But, once more, everything in moderation. One recent study found that aggressive behavior, even violence, may be triggered when children who have come to need and expect the constant approval of others encounter people who do not like them or situations when they do not receive praise and approval.[1] Praising our children all the time or showering them with compliments and superlatives for every slight move in the right direction can backfire. Encouragement means "to gladden the heart," and it comes from the heart. As simple an act as a loving squeeze of the shoulder may speak volumes to your son and may relieve him of the necessity to act out in some way to gain your attention.

Privileges and Appreciation

Many parents use privileges to shape a child's behavior. They dispense privileges when things are going well and take them away when children mess up. But this approach often undermines their parenting, because daily life becomes a constant negotiation over what is deserved, and it sometimes teaches children to behave properly only when some goodie is at hand.

Our sons need to learn the value of gratitude and appreciation—qualities easily missed in this era of affluence and indulgence. Discipline is about teaching and shaping character. It involves highlighting, for our sons and ourselves, the privileges we enjoy in the everyday routine of life, a lesson that has been grossly lost in today's society. Modern parents, particularly single mothers, can be as shortsighted as their sons when it comes to seeing the privileges that are everywhere. Isn't it a privilege to sit at the dinner table and eat a good meal? Isn't it a privilege to be driven to basketball practice? Isn't it a privilege to be taken to the bookstore, even if the book is for school?

Ironically, too many privileges and rewards destroy a boy's ability to appreciate them. Loving and effective discipline is meant not only to improve behavior, but to teach the skills and attitudes that will ensure personal satisfaction and happiness in life and relationships.

Creating a Disciplinary Environment

Some mothers find it hard to discipline their sons under certain conditions, such as in the presence of their own parents, in front of friends, in public, or even in their apartment, because they don't want neighbors hearing the scene that's sure to come.

You can confront these realities in three ways. First, do whatever you reasonably can to make your home a space in which you can comfortably discipline. Second, learn how to discipline in an environment that cannot be changed. It can be helpful to take your son to a quiet place—your car, the parking lot, or away from others—so that you and he can work

> One recent study found that aggressive behavior, even violence, may be triggered when children who have come to need and expect the constant approval of others encounter people who do not like them or situations when they do not receive praise and approval.

things out with some privacy. Remember, kind, firm discipline gives you nothing to be embarrassed about. Third, you may have to confront your lifestyle if, indeed, it leaves no room for disciplining.

Serious Business

It wasn't the first time that nine-year-old Sam had been in trouble. He disobeyed and lied to his parents routinely and was a slippery citizen at school. But his carefully planned theft of a friend's wallet and money was more than his divorced mother would tolerate.

Determined to stop Sam's wayward behavior, his mother agreed that a severe response was called for. She made Sam return the wallet with a direct apology—not that big a deal for the remorseless child—then added that he would have to do thirty hours of work around their house, one hour per day, to pay back the thirty dollars he'd stolen and spent.

But she never followed through. She felt bad that he had to work in the summer heat and understood his complaint that other kids made ten dollars an hour. Finally, she sabotaged the entire arrangement by refusing to stand over Sam day after day just to make sure he did his time. "I'm not going to be punished for his crime," she said. "Let his father do it."

—◦◦◦—

Well, Sam's father didn't do it either, and as you can guess, all didn't turn out for the best. Each time misbehavior is not dealt with, and the consequences are not enforced, a child drifts farther and farther away from adult influence. His already meager conscience shrinks further, leaving a boy like Sam even more vulnerable to the bad influence of his own and others' temptations.

Boys without conscience are no joke. When parents allow this to happen knowingly, they are the ones committing a crime.

Making Amends

Though consequences have their place, children also need the opportunity to have their *I'm sorry*'s and attempts to make it up acknowledged and appreciated.

—⚘⚘⚘—

Before the sun rose, five-year-old Gary thought he could make breakfast for himself. But the gallon of milk was more than he could handle. When he woke his mother, and she saw the puddle of milk on the kitchen floor, she screamed, "Whatever were you thinking?"

A very upset Gary ran to get the mop and furiously began to push waves of milk under the stove and dishwasher. His mother grabbed the mop from his hands. "Just go, get out! You've already done enough. You're just making it worse."

But on his way out, Gary noticed a river of milk creeping into the hallway. He took off his pajama top and tried to sponge the milk up, until his mother, seeing what he was doing, yelled at him again, accusing him of further bad judgment and sending him to his room for the morning.

When lunch came, and his mother let him out of his room, Gary never got the chance to apologize and explain that he was only trying to let his mother sleep late. He knew how tired she was. But he couldn't tell her.

———

Our point is not to suggest that Gary's mother over-reacted to the milk spill. True enough, some mothers would have taken it in stride, but a majority would have been aghast waking up to such a horrible mess. We instead stress Gary's need and obvious willingness to repair the damage he felt he'd done. He'd dirtied the kitchen and wanted the chance to clean it up. If he'd had the skills and strength to clean the milk, he would have done so and let his mother sleep (not to be sneaky, but to take responsibility for what he'd done).

> Boys without conscience are no joke. When parents allow this to happen knowingly, they are the ones committing a crime.

Whatever their misdeed, children want and need the opportunity to make it better again. When they don't get to follow through on this reparative work, the hurt they can feel and see (and may have been told) they've inflicted stays with them, leading to a more sustained sense of being a bad boy, a bad person. Experienced repeatedly and over time, these boys can stop caring, believing they can never undo and make up for the horrors they've committed, especially to the parent they love.

What could Gary's mother have done? She could have used the moment to guide Gary in his helping, showing him how to use a mop, for example. If she felt she needed to mop up the milk right away, she could have later taught her son how to wash a floor with vinegar or how to wipe off the bottom of the chairs and wastebasket with a wet sponge. She could have let him carry the trash bag of milk-soaked paper towels outside, put his own milk-covered clothing in the washing machine, or even taken him to the store with her to choose a container of milk he can easily hold. Any of these would have worked to alleviate Gary's guilt and enable him to make things right with his mom.

Beware that some children are not so good at picking the places or ways to make their amends. Teach and guide them toward better ways of helping out, while noting their good and heartfelt intentions, perhaps giving them the chance to help you out in a different way. Gary, in this case, could have helped cook dinner under his mother's watchful and instructive eye. While a child's apologies, his words of contrition, are important and should be respected, it is his earnest attempts to undo and make up for what he's done that deserve the most encouragement and acceptance.

When Nothing Works

Despite our best efforts, at times nothing seems to work; the harder we try, the worse things seem to get. What can a mother do at these times?

Call a truce: No one can devise a battle plan under siege.

Beware of acting out your frustration: One more day of childish misbehavior will fade into history, but your mean-spirited words or angry slaps may not.

Think in the long term: It's easy to lose sight of your larger parenting values in the heat of the fray.

Look inward: Sometimes giving yourself, not your child, a time out can allow you to see what you have contributed to the situation. An apology, when appropriate, can defuse a volatile situation and invite your son to do the same.

After the storm: Study the chain of events that led to the blowup. Crises do not rise out of thin air. This understanding can help you to squelch or, better yet, prevent the next skirmish.

(For more detailed information on discipline as a single mother, see *Positive Discipline for Single Parents, Revised 2nd Edition,* Jane Nelsen and Cheryl Erwin, Roseville, CA: Prima, 1999.)

The reasons discipline sometimes goes astray—meaning you do it too much, too little, or ineffectively—are as varied as the faces of children. You may be tired, depressed, unsure about how to do it, afraid of angering or hurting your son, or fearful that he won't love you. You may be rebelling against your own parents' discipline of you, believing that discipline will kill your child's lively spirit. You may unconsciously take pleasure in your child's misbehavior and defiance of authority. You may be preoccupied with other matters (like earning a living and keeping a roof over his head), worried that making him unhappy will lower his esteem, distracted by other relationships, or too guilt-ridden to do what you must.

Unfortunately, you and your son cannot afford to wait for insights into reasons that often run deep and are outside your awareness. Your son needs discipline today.

Start now. Choose one problem area where you believe you can make a difference and one method that feels right for you. As your approach to that one problem becomes more confident, you'll find yourself more able to effect change with your son's other behaviors. You will gain confidence in your discipline, and your children will require less of it. You may also find that as your disciplining strengthens and your child's behavior improves, you'll begin to see what kept you from doing it sooner. In short, you will halt and reverse that vicious downward cycle of misparenting and misbehavior, spiraling it upward to good things.

Be forewarned, however, that the forces undermining your discipline are unrelenting. Like gremlins forever throwing wrenches and pouring molasses in the works, these forces will tenaciously try to weaken and sabotage your best parenting efforts. Your guilt will goad you to give in and give up. *Don't*. Instead, grab your guilt by the horns, channeling it into avoiding a different regret: not giving your son the discipline he needs, not preparing him well for life. It's up to you now. Although advice can help, only you can mother your son. You know what needs to be done. And keep in mind, too, that however much your disciplining causes your son some tears and turbulence today, he will thank you tomorrow. In the words of that sports giant, just do it.

CHAPTER 8

Evel Knievel, Wear Your Raincoat

Fostering Self-Protectiveness and Resilience

What mother hasn't wished she could be a guardian angel who could forever flutter unseen above her son's head, watching out for cars that speed around corners, tripping up the bullies who would block his path? To many parents, the world looks like one big avalanche about to cascade on their children. Stray bullets, angry knives, street drugs, spiked party drinks, drunk drivers, AIDS, and other sexually transmitted diseases lurk around every corner.

Sex is everywhere—on the television, in the movies, on the Internet, and on the pages of sports and news magazines. And then there are those catastrophic illnesses and accidents that are just too awful to think about. These horrors are just a sampling of the bad things that can jump out of the dark to get our children.

When sons are just little ones clinging to your legs, watching over them is a breeze. You know where they are and what they are up to. You oversee what they eat and do. But as they grow and go off to day care and school, first on foot and then by bicycle and car, you are hogtied. Sure, you can give them cell phones and ask that they check in with you. But what are they doing all those other hours and minutes when they aren't calling to tell you, in impatient monosyllables, that they are fine? Your best bet, and only hope, is to raise sons who will watch out for themselves as vigilantly as would you, their mother, if you could be there.

Feed Healthy Self-Love

Love for oneself may be the most misunderstood concept in psychology. It evokes images of shallow men and women, like so many peacocks, preening their stylish hair in the mirror. People who love themselves, you might think, are people who have little love left over for others. After all, feeling good requires that people consider themselves better than the rest of us, doesn't it? Those who love themselves, you might suppose, fret more over their own hangnails than their neighbor's liver cancer. *Me, me, me!* is their motto—or so you may think. But such assumptions are inaccurate, confusing people who love themselves in a healthy way with people who are merely selfish and egocentric.

Likewise, the notion of loving oneself can strike us as trite, a perfect example of psychobabble. Even as we write this, we can hear *Saturday Night Live*'s Stuart Smalley feebly affirming himself. "I'm good enough. I'm smart enough," he says with a simper. But again we are mistaken. Trying to talk yourself into feeling good about yourself, trying to "get happy," does not translate into love for yourself. Genuine self-love depends neither on being superior nor on being good-looking. Genuine self-love doesn't have to be drummed up; it is just there, like the ocean and the air.

When a boy truly loves himself, he accepts himself for who he is. He has compassion for his shortcomings and can take pride in his best attempts to do better next time. He doesn't need to think that his eyes, his physique, or his brains are the most terrific, better than anyone else's. His goodness doesn't depend on the lowliness of those around him. Self-love doesn't rely on being so wonderful that a boy cannot help but love himself. The boy who knows authentic self-love is okay with his modest height, his frizzy hair, or his clumsy hands. He is okay with them for one reason alone: because they are his own. He realistically understands that all people have limitations and that few, if any, of us, are all or even most of what we hope to be.

> When a boy truly loves himself, he accepts himself for who he is. He has compassion for his shortcomings and can take pride in his best attempts to do better next time.

The worth of self-love, by the way, lies not simply in the joy of it, though that is good, too. Its greater value is in inviting the child to invest in himself. A child who loves himself is not only more likely to love others—and to be a better friend and citizen—but he also will treat himself more respectfully. Loving himself, he will not do things that put him in the way of danger (or will do these things significantly less often). He will care for himself as he might a precious autographed baseball card or a rare gem. When someone offers him a drag or a drink, he'll fear putting anything into his body that might hurt it.

Having said this, we understand that many of us never know self-love, and that a majority never know it perfectly. Like all goals, however, we and the boys we love can strive for the ideal and perhaps reach something pretty good. How does a single mother teach her son to love himself?

The simple answer, belying its true complexity, is by mothering him with love and care. Responsive and reliable mothering will cause a boy to feel in his emotional belly that he is lovable, worthy of love. As Dorothy Law Nolte prescribed in her poem *Learn What They Live,* we must give our children tolerance, encouragement, praise, fairness, security, acceptance, and approval and spare them from our criticism, hostility, ridicule, and shame. If we followed no other wisdom, we and our sons would do well.

Think Competency

Our sons' grandparents knew that people don't grow strong by being babied and indulged. They knew that their own resilience came from a tough existence—having little, working hard, and surviving tragedy, all without hand-holding. Their lives had taught them that economic hardship, if it didn't kill him, could make a man able to withstand almost anything. Our elders believed that pampering a boy and protecting him from the real world was the surest way to ruin him and make him unfit for life. Though we didn't want to listen—and some of us had good reason not to—our own mothers and fathers were right. The self-esteem parenting movement was a mess.

There is a good reason for this. Self-esteem does not grow from praise and kind words. Nor can it be "given" to children. All human beings must cultivate their own self-esteem, and it does not come merely from being happy. It comes from facing the challenges of life and learning that you can survive, even thrive. Self-esteem and self-confidence are not constant. They ebb and flow, depending on the situation. But once a boy has developed true self-esteem, he can always find his way back from disappointment and frustration.

Child therapists learn early in their careers that parents who strive too hard to make their children happy often fail miserably. Rewarding every inch of cooperation, celebrating every good catch, hanging every homework assignment on the fridge, delighting in every cute word ... Where does it end, and for how long does it mean anything to the child? Yes, there are children who long for their parents to watch just one soccer game, but is it really important that a child's mother watches every game?

Our well-intended efforts to protect our children from the frustration, loss, hurt, and failure we knew as children—and which yet haunt us—have boomeranged. We've created a generation of children who cannot withstand the bruises of daily life, let alone the tougher hardships guaranteed to wallop them sooner or later.

The solutions? One is to teach our sons real competency. Experiencing competency—learning that you can cope with both physical and emotional challenges—is the root of true self-esteem. Possessing real skills gives a child confidence and resources to make his way in life. When your son is young, create opportunities to teach and foster life skills. Invite your son to help you replace a screen door. When you bake a cake, let him help. If he makes a mess, teach him to clean it up. When you clean a closet, employ his arms to help empty it; use his mind to help reorganize it. Once you get in the groove of it, you'll find that little teaching moments are here, there, and everywhere.

Young children in particular are delighted to help adults. When they are toddlers, their favorite phrase is "me do it!" When you vacuum, they want to help. When you work on the car or hoe the garden, they love to be right beside you. Take advantage of this natural inclination to teach both skills and cooperation. It does not last forever. Mothers who tell eager little boys, "No, you're too little," often find themselves years later wondering why their 10-year-old boys refuse to help out.

Take Time to Teach

Never assume that your son knows just how to do things. Be sure you take time to teach the skills involved in doing jobs around the house and yard.

———⟨⟩⟨⟩⟨⟩———

Mitch was four, a bundle of energy, and his mother's most eager helper. And so, his mother, Zoe, was not at all surprised when, on a Saturday morning, he took out the vacuum cleaner before she could. Appreciating his industry, she smiled at her son as she went by on the way to put in a load of laundry.

Vacuuming, however, proved more challenging than either Mitch or his mom anticipated. Hearing a crash, Zoe ran upstairs to find her son, sobbing, standing over her favorite and now broken lamp.

"Oh, Mitch," Zoe snapped, yanking the vacuum from his hands. "Sometimes I wish you just wouldn't help me." Mitch ran from the room.

It took several days before Mitch again tried to help his mother around the house, and weeks before he'd even go in the room where the vacuum cleaner was.

———⟨⟩⟨⟩⟨⟩———

How might this story have ended if Zoe had taken a few minutes to show Mitch how to use the vacuum and steer it around tables? Realizing that she hadn't given Mitch the skills to do the job comfortably, Zoe acknowledged this and her son recovered his eagerness to help. When this sort of incident happens frequently and goes unexamined, however, it can permanently thwart a child's willingness to learn and contribute.

Here are four easy steps to teaching a younger, less experienced person how to do something new and different:

- *You do it, he watches.* Invite your son to keep you company as you vacuum, mow the lawn, or scramble some eggs. Offer simple instructions about what you are doing and why.

- *You do it, he helps.* Allow your son to work alongside you. Delegate some simple parts of the task. Offer encouragement and coaching, not criticism.
- *He does it, you help.* You are gradually transferring responsibility for the task to your son, with your support and guidance.
- *He does it, you watch.* Be sure your standards and expectations are realistic, and celebrate your son's effort, not just perfection. Experiencing even small successes will encourage your son to participate and to learn.

Be patient. No child learns it all immediately. Help just enough to let your son do what he can. Try not to show your frustration at his dropping some screws or dripping glue on the floor. Let your pride show in his effort more than in the product, if you can. And let the work and experience be the major reward. Too often, well-meaning parents high-five the feeblest endeavors, making a child feel like an undeserving phony and diluting the ability to enjoy true admiration when it has really been earned.

It helps to plan ahead. Consider your child's development and set the stage to foster his success. For example, if, when painting a fence, you fear eight-year-old Leo will dribble paint on the patio, take the time to cover the bricks. It's not fair to expect him to paint with the care and expertise of an adult.

As your son ages, his abilities will deepen and expand. His pleasure in doing things competently will stay with him. When we work with even the most delinquent of youths, we are struck by their wish to show what they can do well. We've yet to meet a teenager who doesn't jump to help us when he feels valued and has the skills to do a job.

Thicken the Psychic Skin

Tony looked every bit as angry as his mother, his brothers, and his teachers all said he was. His chip on the shoulder was palpable from a distance. He constantly fought with peers who, he claimed, ridiculed him. Teachers didn't like him and picked on him, he was sure, and so he gave their grief back to them. One who could dish it out far better than he could take it, Tony had a colossal sense of justice, or rather, of the injustice he always judged came his way. He felt mistreated at home, too, and reacted to every hint of insult—and he heard insults everywhere—with cannonballs of venomous retaliation. Only a sixth-grader, Tony and his life were already a wreck.

—◦◦◦—

Tony was not the only child like this in his school and city. Some of these children suffer true narcissistic disorders, a more difficult problem. But many more have a problem that is milder and what's called being "narcissistically vulnerable."

You may recall Narcissus from Greek mythology, a beautiful young man who, seeing his reflection in the water, fell in love with himself. Trying to find and be with that young man who was as wonderful as he, he fell into the pool and drowned. Today, "narcissism" refers to a preoccupation with oneself, a need to be considered superior, and an inability to withstand criticism or perceived disapproval. Narcissistic boys, and the men they become, can perceive disapproval even where it does not exist. They can become defensive, hostile, and unable to feel compassion for the needs or feelings of others. Fragile in the face of life, these children can read insult in the most kindly put piece of advice or feel rejection in the most neutral of comments. The smallest misstep can wholly deflate their sense of who they are.

Many boys deal with their constant sense of being attacked or unfairly dealt with (that is, narcissistic injuries) with a defensive posture that, while protective, causes more problems. Cut off from their hurts, and unable to ask for consolation, they are left alone with their rage, a rage they do not fully understand themselves and that is often directed at those who love them best. Many find solace in alcohol and drugs, sex and violence. In less dramatic cases they just stop caring and trying.

Some of these children arrive at this place of isolation and disappointment by way of perfectionism, an inner expectation that they should always perform well, achieve, or meet some ideal. When these children experience a setback or don't do as well as they hope (for example, on a test), they can experience intolerable self-hatred, arguably the most toxic substance known to man or woman. We often see boys, too, whose façade of failure and apathy is mostly to counter a buried but unrelenting belief that they must be perfect.

How does this come about? Tony's mother did all she could to help her son feel successful and fulfilled, in order to build his self-esteem and prepare him for the hard knocks of life. Like many of her fellow babyboomers, she'd followed this philosophy with the hope of sparing her child. She'd devoted her energies to pursuing the illusion of the perfect childhood, often at the cost of her own happiness and well-being, trying to engineer a world in which Tony would know nothing but good feeling. That, she believed, would fill her son up with a well of self-love and confidence. But, as we all understand now, such an approach achieves mostly its opposite.

How do we make our children less susceptible to perfectionism and narcissism? Well, it is important not to shelter them from life. A mother's duty is to protect her son from physical and emotional harm, but not from the everyday bumps and bruises of life. Sadness, disappointment, even failure are the training ground for the inner strength and willingness to face life that a young man needs. He needs daily exposure to the frustrations, trials, and falls that he will regularly encounter.

A child learns to cope through experience, not from a lecture or one-time fable. He needs to struggle getting that spoon into his baby mouth and he needs, too, to struggle with sleeping on his own. He needs to handle an occasional stern look from his mother, and he needs to manage an occasional poor grade. He can survive not making the All-Star team or being left out of a friend's birthday party—as long as his mother is there to help him believe in himself despite occasional setbacks.

It is a daily balancing act, but your job as a mother is not to distract your son from his upset or to trivialize it. It is to listen, to absorb and understand his pain without attempting to fix it or talk him out of it, to help him label and cope with it, and to believe that he can succeed. Analogous to the way the human body develops resistance to a disease, repeated exposure to the mishaps of life and surviving these will grant immunity to our sons' self-esteem.

> Analogous to the way the human body develops immunity to a disease, repeated exposure to the mishaps of life and surviving these will grant immunity to our sons' self-esteem.

It may seem obvious, but too much criticism can do damage here. A child who is made to feel as if he always screws up will come to believe that a screw-up is all that he is. He will expect and hear criticism even where it doesn't exist, reacting defensively to the most benign remark. Overflowing with self-criticism of his own, that child will himself become a harsh critic of the world, and so the baton passes on. Our sons benefit when we can learn to express our dissatisfactions or give our guidance in ways that don't attack the essence of who they are. In other words, while your son's choices and behavior may be wrong, he himself is not bad. And you might make an effort to learn from the feedback you receive from others. If people often say that you are picky or impossible to please, you might take their observations seriously and see if a change in your own attitude produces a change in your son's.

Sometimes, a son's vulnerability emanates not from your criticism of him, but from your criticism of yourself. Perfectionism seems to hand itself down the generations, even from parents who are determined to halt the pattern. A son who watches his mother have to do everything and have to do it right, can unknowingly adopt her attitude. He might try and do the "anything-but-mom" route and adopt a forced antiperfectionist stance, with utter refusal of responsibility, but in the end, he may need to see that he is indeed just like his mother. A mother who is driven to insist on ridiculously high standards for herself owes it to herself and her son to either moderate them or openly acknowledge this as her own issue and help her son to find his own place more toward the middle. Giving up perfectionism does not mean giving up high standards, motivation, and success.

Although children need to feel potent and worthwhile, they also need exercise in dealing with the frustrations, rejections, and the other assorted slings and arrows that life flings at them. And what better place to get that training than in a loving and supportive home, where the child's reactions to those hurts can be welcomed, accepted, and understood? Growing to tolerate and master the ways that life upsets us, however slow and painful, is the best path to our sons' resilience.

Foster a Work Ethic

Part of acquiring competence is appreciating the value of hard work. This value is rapidly dwindling in our children. Try and get a school-aged child in your neighborhood to mow your lawn or do some other job. Offer him $15 for an hour's work. Perhaps the boy is gung-ho the first time. But the second time he does a shoddy job, and he doesn't even show up the third week.

Many adults recall loving to help their parents around the house. That is a rarity today. Today's children seem to feel no need to work. It is usually parents who drag out the trash cans and carry in the groceries. Children often behave as if they have more money than they know what to do with. They are willing to work when and only when they need some hot cash for a CD burner or a skateboard.

Too many boys don't aspire to real jobs, the kind their parents have, for those jobs require too much work. They are boring. You have to sit at a desk all day. You can't dance and have sex there. What's worse, a boss tells you what to do. Dreams of being rich and famous—the cruel carrots and pipe dreams that our media hold up to our boys—plague our children and make careers as pimps, pushers, and pop stars seem appealing and possible. They all want to be players, to be "the Man." They long for instant fame, girls, jewelry, and cars, cars that likely sport the bumper sticker: "Hard work is for chumps and losers." Of course, many young men from many walks of life do know the value of money and hard work. A great deal of what happens depends on the lessons parents teach. But with the way of the world and the unrelenting onslaught of crass commercialism, parents find themselves facing a power to dwarf Goliath.

This disdain for work often betrays a hidden lack of confidence and competence. Many of these children are incapable, not of the work itself but of the character and resolve that work requires. Working their way up a ladder slowly and steadily is beyond them. Get them a summer job in a mailroom and they want to have the VP's office, salary, and parking space.

As one such boy put it when declining a generous invitation to work at a local gasoline station. "Who are they kidding? They'll have me sweeping the floor and doing oil changes all day." That the owners, skilled foreign car technicians, also cleaned up and did oil changes was irrelevant. Nor did the boy's total lack of knowledge about automobiles affect his expectations. He wanted to tune Mercedes and BMWs and wasn't going

> Too many boys don't aspire to real jobs, the kind their parents have, for those jobs require too much work. They are boring. You have to sit at a desk all day. You can't dance and have sex there. What's worse, a boss tells you what to do.

Family Work: What Can Your Boy Do?

Family work—the tasks that all families share—is an opportunity to teach your son life skills and the value of cooperation. Sometimes, though, parents sabotage this opportunity by asking children to perform duties they aren't ready for. Here, by age, is a list of tasks that your son can help you with. Remember to keep your expectations and standards realistic.

Preschool
Place napkins or silverware on the table
Rinse lettuce for a salad
Help with simple clean-up tasks
Dress himself, brush his own teeth, and perform
    other personal grooming tasks
Pick vegetables from a garden
Put cheese slices on hamburger buns
Use a kitchen mini-vacuum to clean up crumbs
    and dirt

Elementary school
Sort his own laundry
Pull weeds and help plant flowers

to settle for less. For those who wonder, he spent his summer instead "working on"—equals, playing with—a remote control car.

Working involves earnestness and diligence. A worker must be able to delay gratification; that is, he must work

Learn to prepare simple meals (grilled cheese, macaroni, microwave dishes, etc.)

Wash and dry dishes, or empty the dishwasher

Care for pets

Help with grocery shopping

Vacuum or dust the house; keep bathrooms clean

Middle school

Mow the lawn

Wash cars

Plan and prepare meals one night per week

Baby-sit (yes, boys love to do this, too, and will benefit from training, often available through your local school, library, or community college)

High school

Help with car maintenance (change oil, check tires, etc.)

Help with home repair tasks (again, proper training is important)

Remember, taking the time to teach the appropriate skills and asking for your son's help, rather than issuing commands, will most motivate your son to help out.

before he gets paid and must get paid before he has money to spend. A worker has to tolerate frustration and be able to work alongside others. A worker has to take orders and do what is asked of him, even if he deems it a waste of time or beneath him. A worker needs to be able to take

Reforming Lazy Bones and the Work-Allergic

What does a single mother do when her son wants no part of work and responsibility?

Convince yourself that work is necessary. A boy who won't work may grow into a man who can't work, and may be doomed to a hard life. He needs you to get him moving, and the sooner the better.

Seize the moment. There'll never be the right or best time to act. That you are changing the rules after all these years is neither contradictory nor unfair. In fact, examining your parenting and making corrections is a virtue to be proud of.

Plan. Decide how you will change things. What are reasonable expectations, considering his age, development, and other responsibilities? Strive to invite cooperation before resorting to rewards and consequences, although they may eventually be needed.

Announce your plan. Now that you've decided things will be different, you need to calmly and firmly spell it out for your son. "From now on," you might say, "I'm going to expect your help with work around the house. What things would you be willing to do each day? Each week?" You might offer a reasonable incentive for cooperation (perhaps time spent together doing some activity you both enjoy) or, less positively, you might invoke consequences for not helping. Be sure you can follow through on your agreements, and try to design consequences to teach and encourage, not to shame or set up additional power struggles.

Implement it, totally. If, after delivering a vigorous speech about the new regime, you grow half-hearted or soon forget it, your son will, too. Getting a nonworker to work can be tough, and will require consistency. Be willing to sit down with your boy and fine-tune your plan if snags arise. Involving him in making and executing the new family work system will enhance his cooperation.

Work with him. Some sons respond miraculously when they work alongside a parent. Rather than only assigning your son tasks to do on his own, create partnerships in which he can offer you a helping hand. These times, when you and your son are busy doing something together, can become opportunities for casual chats that lead to greater closeness and sharing. This approach also permits you to teach your son valuable life skills, and to watch that he is doing his work safely and well.

Watch him outside the home. If everyone on the "outside"—teachers, coaches, neighbors—praises your son as a worker, then the problem is between you and him. You may need to ask yourself why he is reluctant to show you the same consideration and effort he is so eager to show others. Don't forget to pat yourself on the back for raising a son

(continues)

who, for all of his laziness at home, is a responsible citizen out in the world. If, on the other hand, he won't work for anyone anywhere, your problem is much bigger and more serious.

Acknowledge his efforts. Note, just enough, even small changes. Simply thanking him today for bringing in his own dirty dish might lead him to bring in everyone's dishes next week. (After all, don't you feel more motivated to try harder when your efforts are appreciated?) But don't overdo it. Nonworkers tend to retreat when their efforts are celebrated too much or too joyously. Understated appreciation tends to go farther.

pride in a job well done (even if that job is making tuna sandwiches or bagging groceries). And a good worker must be able to do an honest day's work, which implies also being honest at work (i.e., he must not steal and must report hours accurately).

How do we teach our children how to work? How else? By asking them to work, via chores and responsibilities, from a fairly young age. Consider how even toddlers on a farm can collect eggs and feed the chickens. And as most parents know, toddlers generally want to please parents. Exploit that natural inclination. Find suitable jobs for your son as he grows. And note when he does them with good effort and care. Make the satisfaction of work something he feels deeply good about.

Whatever one says about Freud, he knew what he was writing about when he said that a healthy person must learn to love and work.

Teach Real Courage

Nothing scared Tad. His mother called him "the walking accident." Any day of the week, he was covered with bloodied scars, scratches, and homespun bandages. Whether skateboarding, roller blading, or BMX-biking, Tad pushed the envelope. He was the one the wild kids dared to do the riskiest skateboard tricks, to ollie off the school's eight-foot loading dock, and to tear ass over the creek's rock bridge. Several broken bones, two concussions, a detached retina, and who knows how many sprained ankles and fingers hadn't slowed him down. "I was born to ride," he'd proclaim, as he limped into the room.

—⟨⟨⟨⟩⟩⟩—

Sure, yesterday's boys swam in quarries and pursued feats of daring and strength. The risks are more serious now, thanks to the advent of technology and extreme sports. The greater availability of vehicles, for example, from skates to skis to dirt-bikes to automobiles, has given these young daredevils new and more powerful ways to defy gravity and to demonstrate their manliness and skills. How can we slow them down? Or should we?

Utter recklessness—not boyish and healthful adventure—is a worrisome sign. The leading cause of death in teenagers is accidents. Often, disregard for one's own well-being signals a lack of self-protectiveness, an emptiness that begs to be filled with excitement, a lack of more conventional competencies, or gloom about the future and a basic belief that "So what if I die?" The bravado of such boys often speaks to deep-seated fears they can't express, let alone heed. It takes a good amount of personal strength and confidence for a boy to admit fear and avoid something that is dangerous. To appear a coward is even more perilous and less acceptable than taking a risk, especially for the boy who, however big and tough on the outside, inside feels small and helpless. He is the boy who can master or cope with a fear only by doing it, no matter how stupid or risky.

As with so much else in a child's development, prevention is the key. When you are strong enough to foster resilience and self-esteem in your son, your child will grow to value self-care, to nurture and protect his own physical and emotional health. He will have enough confidence to say no or walk away from a dare without feeling any weaker for having done so. When he is not blinded by his own misunderstood emotions, he will clearly see that the other boys' egging him on serves to deflect their own anxieties and allay their own insecurities, and so he will not be trapped by their provocation.

Boys also learn by example. If they are trained to be wild men, dragged to do things that frighten them in the name of manliness, they will get used to it and maybe even come to like or crave the thrill. But that doesn't help the mother whose son was born a little Evil Knievel. What can she do? She can't do much about the genetic predisposition to thrill-seeking, but she can help her son to gain control of it. First, if your son is in real harm's way, you must act. Take away his mountain bike until he not only promises to stop, but really does stop riding off rock cliffs at the dump. Take away the car keys for a long time. (He's had three accidents in seven months of driving. Does he have to kill himself or someone else before we get it?) And if he adores a risky sport, brainstorm with him ways he can do it more safely: Insist that he take lessons, wear protective gear, and practice in a safe environment. If he is unwilling or considers such precautions geeky, without apology or further lectures forbid the activity until he's willing to comply.

Most mothers worry when their sons want to play football, snowboard chutes and cornices, or take that first overnight camping trip. As with so many things in life, these decisions require a balance between the opportunity your son has to acquire confidence, competence, and self-esteem and the need to keep him safe. Exercise your inner wisdom and common sense and invite his input. Then make the best decision you can.

Help your son develop other skills. As we will discuss later, a child who fails at school and has few successes elsewhere will seek ways he can excel and belong. He may understandably feel good about his prowess as a daredevil. If parents are proud of their golfing, their gardening, or their jogging, why wouldn't he love being the coolest skater on the block? If, however, that is his only claim to fame, he will forever be forced to take it to its

Facing Risk Head-On: Talking to Your Boy About Drugs and Sex

Many mothers feel uncomfortable discussing these issues with their sons. At what age should you begin? What if your son gets embarrassed or angry? And how do you bring up the subject without sounding like you're accusing him? Here are some suggestions that may help you approach these crucially important subjects:

Don't be afraid to bring up the issues of drugs and sexual activity. You can begin early, in gentle, age-appropriate ways, to introduce these subjects and to let your son know that you are willing to talk about them with him. As he grows, be sure you offer your own ideas and values about sex, relationships, smoking, drinking, and drug use. Stay calm and don't lecture, but do share your ideas and ask your son what he thinks and does. If you don't have these talks, your boy may get his information exclusively from peers and the culture around him, notoriously unreliable sources.

Be askable. Let your son know that he can ask you questions, and be prepared for him to do so. He may want to know about your own experiences. Taking a moment to think through what you want him to learn and decide will help you know what to share and how to share it. Strive for honesty. If you don't know how to best answer a question today, get back to him later, after you've had time to think.

Be informed. Do your best to know your son's friends and their families. Do expect your son to check in with you, and let him know where you stand about the recreational activities that may be popular in his group of friends (drugs and activities of choice often change from year to year). Many mothers wonder if they should spy on their sons, listening to their conversations, reading their e-mail, and looking through their desks and backpacks. It may be better to begin early having frank and open conversations about the risks your son will face as he grows.

Walk your talk. Sons will sense their mothers' hypocrisy. It simply will not work to give your son one set of rules while you do something different. If he sees you smoking tobacco or marijuana, drinking regularly, or having numerous sexual relationships, he may assume that this behavior is acceptable for him, too. Changing your lifestyle can feel unfair or too much of a sacrifice. But what other choice do you have, if your responsibility to your son is what matters most to you?

Stay connected. A respectful and loving relationship with parents is still a child's best protection against risk-taking behavior. Never stop working to know who your son is, not just where he is.

next level. What he sees on television—bikers, skaters, and even kayakers free-falling a hundred feet—will only inspire him more. As we discovered in chapter 2, boys have an inborn desire for aggressiveness and competition. Boys do what they must to be noticed and be special, to be somebody.

The leading writers on boys' development—Kindlon and Thompson (*Raising Cain*, New York: Ballantine, 2000), Michael Gurian (*The Wonder of Boys*, New York: Putnam, 1997), and William Pollack (*Real Boys*, New York: Owl Books, 1999)—agree that this is another indicator of what's wrong with the way our culture treats boys. Teaching boys not to cry, not to run to their mothers when hurt, not to admit fear, not to admit weakness, and not to give in may be good for making soldiers of them, but it doesn't create courageous men, men who can do what's right regardless of what others think and who can stand up for what they believe despite the odds. That is true courage, and mothers have a part to play in nurturing it in their sons.

> Teaching boys not to cry, not to run to their mothers when hurt, not to admit fear, not to admit weakness, and not to give in may be good for making soldiers of them, but it doesn't create courageous men, men who can do what's right regardless of what others think and who can stand up for what they believe despite the odds.

Promote Success in School

Study after study has shown without doubt that doing well in school protects children against all kinds of wayward behavior and dysfunction. This topic is so crucial that we focus on it exclusively in chapter 12.

Make Connections

In his book *Connect*, Harvard psychiatrist and author Edward Hallowell persuasively calls for all people to get more connected.[1] He rightly sees being connected as perhaps the single most potent factor protecting a person against depression, anxiety, physical illness, and existential despair. His prescription is as apt for young boys as it is for grown mothers. The fact that children who are lost and drowning, isolated from significant adults, use gangs as their life rafts tells us something about a boy's need for community and belonging.

A child in a single-mother home has only one parent present, one adult to provide belonging, a sense of worth, a listening ear, and guidance—and that adult is often overwhelmed with a host of demands on her time. In addition, emotional echoes from a divorce, abandonment, or death are issues that require time and patience to heal. It is no criticism of hard-working single mothers to say that their children may be at greater risk of feeling estranged and detached and at greater risk for joining the wrong groups in order to find a special place in the world. How can a mother keep her son involved?

Family Meetings

Family meetings are an encouraging and effective way to solve problems, share appreciation, and just check in with each other. But single mothers sometimes doubt their ability to make family meetings work, especially with an active boy. Having regular family meetings may mean you spend less time actually having to discipline your son. Give them a try and see what you think:

Set aside a regular time to meet, and make it a priority. Let your children know that you consider this time with them an important part of your week. Turn off the television and phone, clear the kitchen table, and sit down together.

Begin with compliments and appreciation. Look for the positive things each family member has done and encourage your children to do the same. Let this be a time when you can celebrate your strengths and accomplishments.

Keep an agenda board in a handy place. Post a dry erase board where everyone can reach it. Dur-

Dr. Hallowell suggests several ways, each of which can help a boy feel meaningfulness in his life, especially during the tumult and lostness of adolescence. A wise mother helps her son get and stay connected with:

Family: Maintain a strong family; attend family functions; be open and connected yourself to

ing the week, as issues and conflicts come up, write them down for consideration at the next family meeting, then be sure to discuss each one. Sometimes just the act of writing down our frustrations and having them noted is itself relieving and productive.

Brainstorm to solve problems and plan activities. Invite the opinions of each family member. During brainstorming, all ideas, no matter how unworkable they may seem, should be given a fair hearing. Once people have contributed their ideas, you can decide together which ones the family wants to pursue or implement.

Decisions should be made by consensus. Voting tends to create winners and losers. Work and discuss toward compromise and finding agreed-upon solutions. If you can't agree, you might need to table an issue until the next meeting. Use future family meetings to monitor previous issues and solutions.

End on a positive note. Conclude your meeting with a movie, a family activity, or a favorite dessert.

your extended family; allow your child to connect to relatives (including, when feasible, his birth father's family) even if you yourself are not.

Friends: Support his good friendships; make your home open to his friends; know and nurture his friends, too.

Art: Support your son's love of art and beauty; help him make it himself through painting, music, writing, and so forth; help him value this ability despite societal prejudices.

Nature: Promote and sustain your child's love of nature from an early age, and encourage his sense of being part of the breathing globe, one piece of a complex and rich existence.

Institutions: Being part of school, the YMCA, a boys' club, or athletic teams can create a sense of belonging.

Ideas: Being connected to one's beliefs and one's intellectual life can be quite sustaining and help a boy to make sense of a life that can feel emotionally jumbled and incoherent.

God: Faith in a higher being can provide much coherence and comfort to a child who believes. Numerous studies have shown that spirituality, a sense of connection to a power greater than oneself, regardless of denomination or type, is one of the key factors in building a healthy family.

Oneself: Coming to better understand, like, and accept oneself helps pave the way to psychological health. This connecting to oneself provides the surest footing in the journey called life.

There are no guarantees in life, and risk is, indeed, everywhere for our boys. Yet a thoughtful and committed mother can do much to nurture self-esteem, resilience, confidence, and good judgment in her son.

Although these strategies and ways of being require effort, time, self-reflection, and personal sacrifice, they hold the potential to preserve our sons more surely than any insurance money can buy.

Food for Thought

A recent survey of more than 12,000 teenagers in this country suggests that children who eat dinner with their families five nights a week are significantly less likely to be involved with alcohol, drugs, cigarettes, sex, and suicide than teens who eat alone. But sadly, another recent survey of parents indicates that a majority of parents and adolescents don't regularly share a family meal, a trend that is worsening.

Though parents living their fast-paced schedules don't need fancy explanations of why this is happening, they might wish to counter this trend in their own homes. Family meals, researchers agree, while tending to offer better nutrition, also offer children opportunities to be heard, be valued, feel belonging, and learn more about cooperation, in both the work that a meal involves and in the mutuality of discussion that takes place. Mark Goluston, a professor at UCLA, says that sharing family meals can build a foundation for learning team-playing, a skill necessary in today's corporate world.

(continues)

Some tips on cooking up healthful family meals:

- *Make family meals a high priority.*
- *Involve the children* in some aspect of the preparing, serving, or cleaning up after the meal (using that time to talk, too, rather than as a chance for you to go off and check e-mail or return a call).
- *Set a good example* at the meal, listening and refraining from unduly negative comments (using meal times as a place to complain or chastise your child will chase him away).
- *Learn to relax* at the table (you don't need to be at a 5-star restaurant to dine).
- *Be patient* (it may take some time for your family meals to grow as shared and satisfying as you might wish).
- *Have reasonable expectations* (a healthy family meal has plenty of space for debate, arguing, and disagreement; don't expect the peaceable kingdom).
- *Enjoy.*

(Adapted from a report by MSC.com correspondent, Beatrice Motamedi, in *All in the Family,* July 21, 2001).

CHAPTER 9

Boys Will Be Boys
Will Be . . .

Nurturing Solid Gender- and Self-Identity

Ah, don't we pine for the days of old, when it was all so much simpler. Back then, we all knew exactly what a boy looked like, didn't we? Rambunctious worm-digging, dirt-eating, dog-chasing, apple-stealing, school-hating, mom-loving creatures who could happily wear the same clothes for a month and who weren't afraid of anything except, maybe, their Saturday baths and old Sister Catherine's ruler.

Back then, telling boys from girls was never a question. Girls were the gentler ones with longer hair, carrying pink Barbie wardrobe-suitcases and skipping rope.

They were the ones wearing their mother's dresses and earrings. They liked being clean, helping mom around the house, studying for school, and pleasing the stern nuns of St. Peter's Elementary School (at least, more than the boys did).

In this new millennium the waters of gender have muddied. Women's studies, and their worthy child, girl studies, have revealed the lethal ways in which our society had unknowingly squelched its own beloved daughters. Studies in this area showed how girls were being raised to become acquiescing, accommodating, and enabling women who stand behind men and who value sophistication and sex appeal over contentment and confidence. We'd forced them to forsake their very selves, the saddest and costliest sacrifice a person can make.

That a culture could be so blind about its girls led others to wonder what had happened to boys. As mentioned elsewhere in this book, the current boys' movement has found just as many misconceptions and human tragedies as the girl's movement, including the ways in which we "emotionally miseducate" our boys, leaving them cruelly ill-equipped to handle life and its relationships.[1] The tougher side of boys, the side they show the world, reflects cultural socializing, as well as natural temperament. The bottom line is that much of what was believed about boys and girls just isn't true. Both genders are more complex than had ever been recognized. And despite their considerable differences, they share much more in the way of common humanity and psychological development than had been credited. Paradoxical as it sounds, we've learned that boys and girls are both more alike and more different than we'd realized.

Is it good news that research and universities are investigating and teaching gender? A trait that has such profound influence on our children deserves thoughtful and deliberate attention. And while we can yearn for the golden times of yesteryear, the evidence indicates that all was not quite as well as we'd thought. Many of our stay-at-home mothers felt more like they were chained-to-home. How many of our sons' grandmothers were bright women who would have enjoyed real careers, contributing to the world professionally, as well as by being good mothers? Sexual and physical abuse existed long before the news media made it a topic of common conversation. Many of our own mothers, as daughters, were victimized and then prohibited by the strait-laced conventions of the day from getting the help and support they needed when they were girls. And what of the men who didn't fit into the molds of what they "should" be, or who turned to alcohol, violence, and isolation as the only way to cope? How much did they suffer?

> The bottom line is that much of what was believed about boys and girls just isn't true. Both genders are more complex than had ever been recognized.

In this chapter, as in our parenting itself, our work is cut out for us. Old wisdom and recent findings, traditions and new ways, past prejudices and current openness, all carry big implications for our boys. Our heightened awareness of these issues has the potential to help us do better by our sons. For single mothers of sons, however, who do not share the trait of gender with their children, these issues can be even more complex and frustrating.

Genes, Jeans, and Jean

The genetics of gender are far beyond the scope of this book. We do know that heredity has a lot to do with how much of a "boy" a child is. If a fetus gets a Y chromosome from his father in addition to an X chromosome, he will genetically be a boy. It should come as no surprise that biology is a strong factor in gender. The sex hormones marinade the developing brain and make it—and the child possessing it—more like a boy or a girl. But boy behavior is genetically over-determined, meaning that not just one but many genes influence how masculine a boy becomes. Just what and how much that biological legacy determines can vary. Some boys are so inherently male that living in a house with 29 sisters and pink furniture couldn't deter their love for football and power tools. Other boys come into this world so biologically under-masculinized that bringing them up on a dude ranch would not deter their more feminine sensibilities. In short, some people probably do not have real choice about their gender or their sexuality, and the factors that determine one's degree of masculinity (or femininity) are imperfectly understood at this time. But for the majority of boys, the environment and parenting they encounter do make some difference.

Boys Have Normal Curves, Too

Many human attributes, such as height, are "normally distributed" and can be characterized by what mathematicians call a normal curve. A small number of people are seven feet tall, an equally small number are diminutive, but most people's height falls somewhere in the middle.

Boyishness—to group together a whole bunch of behaviors—is variable, too. Some boys are super-boyish, some are super *non*-boyish, and most are somewhere in between. Boyishness is a continuum of variability. Some boys are incredibly masculine; some are not. Some love sports; some don't. Many hate shopping for clothes; but some don't. Just because a boy is aggressive doesn't mean he likes sports. Just because a boy is highly competitive doesn't mean he's aggressive. (Some boys prefer to fight it out on the math team or debating club.) Rather than force our boys into limited, stifling, and misleading conceptions of what a boy should be, we must keep these subtleties in mind and refine our views to accommodate the kind of boys that our sons really are, the real people living below that male exterior.

Embracing Boyness

Realizing that there are frequent exceptions, which we'll soon explore, let's consider average sons and the influence of their single mothers' attitudes toward boys. Some of these mothers will appreciate having a male child. They will celebrate their son's masculinity and truly enjoy all the ways boys are different than girls. These mothers will accept a son as he is, relish his strengths, shape him where needed, work constructively on his weaknesses, and empathically nurture him, using the understanding of the "new" boy psychology. They will admire and enjoy their son's temperament and constitution, even as they confront places and situations where those traits get him into trouble.

A mother may scream about the mud he tracks over the clean carpet, but she will not assassinate her son's character for not being the "neat-freak" she is or blame his shortcomings on the fact that he is male. She may get on him for messing up the boxes she'd just organized, but she will not make him feel that his curiosity is a thing to be ashamed of. She may carefully help him learn to be more tactful with teachers, but she will not humiliate his ideas and best attempts to express himself. She might smooth over his social awkwardness, but she will not ridicule him into withdrawing. Though his mother will unavoidably battle with him (just as she would with a daughter), he will seldom, if ever, feel that she dislikes him for being a boy.

Some mothers and sons are not so fortunate. Because of who *they* are, some mothers do not mesh as well with their sons. Some mothers are extremely uncomfortable with aggression, their own and their children's. In the course of socializing their sons' aggression, these mothers can be overly harsh or rejecting. Some mothers do not at all appreciate their sons' robustness. Others cannot tolerate that their sons do not share everything with them. They see a son's reticence as a personal rejection.

The "How's school?" that brings an hour of revelation from their daughters may at best bring an unenthusiastic "Fine" that mothers may hear as "Leave me alone," rather than as the typically male phrase it is.

Unfortunately, it's also true that some mothers just like girls better, or at least feel more comfortble with them. Perhaps these women were physically or emotionally abused by a father or a male relative. Perhaps former partners abandoned them or treated them harshly or with ridicule. The fact remains that these women have sons to raise, little boys who depend on their mothers to shape their world, establish their sense of self, and encourage their journey into the world around them as healthy, whole men. What can mothers who are uncomfortable with males do to prevent their biases from doing harm?

Think behavior, not character. We must watch that we don't mistakenly equate behavior (which can be changed) with the essence of being a boy (which cannot). Beware of putting down the person your son is or making sweeping generalizations about how he and you just can't get along. Address the things he says or does in their proper context, without impugning his character or gender.

Confront behavior problems. We've met mothers whose dislike of their sons was understandable given their sons' behavior. But the problem was not their sons' being boys, as much as it was that these sons were insufficiently disciplined. Rather than condemn or feel a victim of their sons' aggression or wildness, perhaps mothers can work at being stronger parents who help their boys learn to manage themselves better, making themselves more likable.

Question your own motives. Try to identify what about his boyishness irritates you. Do you prefer girls because you are lonely and want a child whom you believe can listen to you like a mother herself or who will emotionally nurture you? Do you dislike boys because you envy your brother and resent the preferential treatment your parents gave him? Do you dislike your son's zest for life because it makes you feel more depressed and out of it than you already do? Harsh questions, we agree, but the circumstances call for them. Often, a parent's dislike for a child derives from experiences that have nothing to do with that child and that can be healed with time and effort.

Be honest with yourself. In our clinical work we've met loving mothers who feel horrible that they harbor any prejudice against their boys. They feel too guilt-ridden, however, to speak aloud such unmotherly thoughts. Unspoken and unexpressed, those feelings eventually make themselves known in their actions, body language, and attitude. Even as these mothers try to say the right things, try harder to like their sons more, their unconscious and true feelings seep out.

Most of us can sense when someone doesn't like us, even when she's serving us our favorite homemade dessert or asking us how our day went. The first step toward resolving this issue is to admit the truth to yourself. You don't like this or that about boys or, perhaps, you wish you'd had the girl you dreamed of.

Don't force yourself to be a father, too. Some single mothers feel the need to be both a perfect mother and a perfect father. They think they need to wrestle and play ball with their sons. But even if the boys enjoy that, they do not need their mothers to shoot baskets or play army with them. What sons need is to have those interests and inclinations respected. Striving unrealistically to be two parents is too much for anyone to handle. It is enough to be one good parent.

Consult with yourself. Ask yourself, "What would I tell another mother whose son was like mine?" Even when unable to provide it, mothers can often identify what is needed. Is your house boy-friendly? Do you and your four daughters decorate it as if it were one big girls' dorm, with little room for your son to feel belonging and identification as a male? Does he have good reason to feel jealous, given how much closer and more attentive you are to his sisters? And what—let's ponder the big question—is your not liking or enjoying him as much as the girls doing to your son?

Crossing Mother Nature is not only not very nice, it can wreak havoc. Raising a child against the natural tide of his temperament can make him feel bad about and alienated from who he is. Some boys will deal with this by trying to give you what you want, denying more of the traditionally masculine in themselves, developing inauthentic identities. Many more will find places where they are better liked and where they can feel more accepted than they do at home. A lucky few will find mentors and other second-mothers to fill the void. But some, having experienced your disapproval, may pull away, mistrusting the love they could find elsewhere, forever perceiving even loving girlfriends and wives as secretly disliking them, just as their mothers had. Going forth in this world as a man without having known the love and support of a mother is hard, especially for the son from a single-parent family.

A Kinder, Gentler Man

Ron was an interior decorator. He came to the profession late in life after having tried several "manlier" careers, including loan officer, retail manager, and service coordinator at an auto dealership. He was a strong man, a scratch golfer, and had a lifelong love for aesthetics. As a boy, he'd always noticed colors and textures. Even though he'd dressed as plainly as his friends, he noticed what people wore, who matched and who clashed. But it wasn't until his own father died that he had the nerve to give up the employment he hated to pursue the career he'd always felt born to.

How wonderful that Ron finally found his calling and that it resulted in his satisfaction and success. Many people are not so lucky and go to their graves still regretting dreams they have never pursued. How sad that Ron had to go through childhood hiding his interest and talent for fabric and decorating, and trying to please his father by being something he was not.

Many boys try with every fiber of their being to please their parents. They play baseball despite hating it. They try living up to their parents' expectations even when they don't share them. Sometimes parents lament, too, for their son, recognizing his giftedness for flower arrangement or crafts, for example. "He's in for such a hard life," one father worried.

In some ways, boys face more obstacles in following their dreams than do girls. Society, and most parents, now applaud the daughters who want to pursue Olympic and even professional sports. They encourage their girls to become pilots, doctors, or police officers, if that is their daughter's passion. For boys, however, the issue is clouded. It is a rare mother who doesn't worry when her little boy prefers dolls to trucks, wants to be a nurse instead of a doctor, or would rather dance than play team sports.

> Crossing Mother Nature is not only not very nice, it can wreak havoc. Raising a child against the natural tide of his temperament can make him feel bad about and alienated from who he is.

When you have a son who truly has a passion for drawing or high fashion, respect it. If you are concerned about the pressure he may face from society, then recognize how much more dearly he needs your love and support.

Oh, Boy

What's wrong with doing it the old-fashioned way? What's wrong with raising a boy with rough-and-tumble and a basement full of sports equipment? The short answer is nothing—but with lots of fine print.

Nothing, unless your son hates sports.

Nothing, unless your son likes life to be quiet and gentle.

Nothing, unless by rough-and-tumble you mean that he isn't to cry, be hurt, need consoling, or in any other way be emotional.

Nothing, unless the basement is the only place he is allowed, unless he is discouraged from going to the art museums and garden shows he secretly loves.

Nothing, unless you make it perfectly clear that you don't want a son who is anything but an All-American athlete.

Nothing, unless you are the kind of parent who won't allow painted bunnies in your young son's room because, you believe, it will make him a sissy.

But maybe we've lost sight of the original question. What's wrong with wanting our son to be a boy's boy? Again nothing, unless, of course, he isn't.

Gender De-Bending, Homosexuality, and Homophobia

Whatever the reasons, more mothers are raising boys who are confused about their gender identity, boys who worry about whether they are heterosexual, homosexual, or somewhere betwixt the two. Why wouldn't they worry? Despite the growing societal acceptance for homosexuality, homophobia is as much a problem as it ever was. It is no coincidence that teenage boys across the country are apt to call "gay" anything or anyone whom they wish to tease or they genuinely dislike.

What exactly is homophobia? It's the fear of being or becoming homosexual. Homophobia is the basis behind many boys' discomfort with feeling any kind of love toward men or other boys. It is a rare teenage boy who doesn't experience it to some degree. To some extent, homophobia is probably a psychological and developmental catalyst to keeping a child on the heterosexual straight and steady. But if overgrown or exaggerated—which it often is—it can obstruct a boy's capacity to be close to both men and women. At its most extreme it can lead to horrifying self-hatred.

What evokes such homophobia? Boys who've never known a father's healthy love

> In some ways, boys face more obstacles in following their dreams than do girls.

are apt to long for it. Though that yearning seems to go underground, it really only lies dormant, ready to be triggered by the slightest experience. When that boy, especially as an adolescent, finds himself attracted to a male friend or a teacher, for example, the longing that erupts can confuse him, for he hasn't had the foundation of a father's nurturing and nonsexual love. "Am I gay?" that boy may wonder, frightened by what he feels. He doesn't realize that what he wants is a father's love and admiration, and that nothing at all is homosexual about that. But this is just one dynamic, and hardly foolproof or true for every boy. For other boys, their attraction to boys or men may have other meanings, including jealousy over a favored sister,

The Couch Potatoes We Love

No one would have guessed that the advent of the television, the video recorder, and the computer would have such a huge impact on family life in this country. No one is quite sure why boys are more attracted to the screen than are girls. The truth is, however, that many boys spend a large proportion of their waking hours staring at a screen. They play Nintendo or PlayStation, they watch TV and movies, or they cruise the Internet, playing sophisticated games and exploring the world of the Web. What harm, you may wonder?

Well, for one thing, watching television or movies often involves little, if any, critical thinking. The human brain is quite passive while watching. Contrary to popular belief, children do not learn much language or social skills by watching. (We don't call it the "boob tube" for nothing!) The American Academy of Pediatrics has recommended *no* television—yes, you heard us correctly, none—during the first two years of a child's life.

Television viewing, especially before bedtime, appears to disturb sleep patterns in young children

envy for the girl's life, or, of course, a more purely overriding biology. These latter boys have not been made homosexual or bisexual, but are that way by nature.

How can a single mother help with all of this, especially when the culture may tell her son that warmth and

and may make falling asleep more difficult. Video games give young boys an unrealistic image of violence and warfare. After all, if the characters on the screen can be shot four times and still get up, why can't a real person? And all screen time involves physical inactivity. It is unarguably true that obesity in children is rising at an alarming rate, largely because children tend to sit still and snack on junk foods while staring at their favorite screen.

What can a mother do? Set reasonable limits on screen time. You may decide that two hours a day is all your son will get, and that two hours will include television, computers (unless being used for homework), and video games. After the time is up, he must find something else to do, something that involves his imagination and creativity, engaging with other people, and physical activity.

Many single mothers understandably, like many married parents, rely on the television as their "baby-sitter" at the end of a long day. Turning it off can mean extra work and effort for you. Difficult as it may be, all experts agree that it's worth the effort in terms of your child's health, intellectual growth, and social skills.

affection, physical closeness, and emotional intimacy with a mother may make him less of man? There is no simple prescription to follow. By being a good-enough mother in all of the ways our book describes and by helping him to have good relationships with good men (which we will discuss later), you will have done much to ensure that your boy develops a healthy gender identity and true self-esteem. A mother's healthy love does not create wimpy or homosexual boys. Affection and attachment do not mean a boy will be less of a man. They will sustain him whatever his eventual sexual preference.

A great deal of research in the field of human development, moreover, seems to tell us that young people are healthier and have better relationships when they are able to accept more androgynous aspects of themselves, meaning qualities more often associated with the other gender. Girls are better off when they can utilize their inherent strengths and confidence, and boys are better off when they have access to emotional and nurturing qualities.

Good mothering is not equal to feminizing; rather, it implies teaching a son to balance his strength, aggressiveness, and competitiveness with compassion, gentleness, and even sensitivity. It also helps if you are comfortable with your own gender. Life with a mother who is content in her own skin, who enjoys her femaleness but does not expect her son to share it, can help solidify a boy's growing sense of himself as a male.

Helping your son understand what he really wants can reassure him greatly. Listen to his concerns and doubts. Take him seriously. If he wishes, invite him to talk to a professional to help clarify what he feels and alleviate any undue and undeserved suffering. That also can help him to find resources, such as peer groups, to prevent shameful isolation and toxic self-rebuke. Even the most conservative of single mothers can appreciate the psychological risk that the homosexual boy faces. To hate oneself is the most destructive force a child can battle.

As with all other forms of hatred and bigotry, racial and sexual bigotry included, societal homophobia springs from fear of those who are different than we are. Even our most traditional institutions are not exempt: The Boy Scouts of America has been embroiled in controversy recently over admission of homosexual members and leaders. Our traditional ideals of masculinity, as warped and skewed as they may sometimes be, are familiar. The advent of AIDS and the Gay Pride movement have stirred up both confusion and strong feelings. Our boys are vulnerable to all of the emotional and political pressures so prevalent today.

Even the most loving mother cannot "fix" a boy's sexual confusion and doubts, but she can and should listen. Listen to your son's words, to his unspoken messages, and to his behavior. Don't be afraid to ask him how he's feeling and to offer your sup-

A great deal of research in the field of human development, moreover, seems to tell us that young people are healthier and have better relationships when they are able to accept more androgynous aspects of themselves, meaning qualities more often associated with the other gender. Girls are better off when they can utilize their inherent strengths and confidence, and boys are better off when they have access to emotional and nurturing qualities.

Barbies and Dump Trucks

What does it mean when a young boy asks for dolls instead of army men? The first answer you should give yourself is that it does not automatically mean any one thing. Some boys have a nurturing side that begs for expression. They want to feed and baby dolls no less than girls do. Over and over, we have seen in our clinical work that it is the boys—even the macho athletes—who most enjoy and use the dollhouse during play therapy. When such boys show wide-ranging and healthy interests in both boy and girl toys and activities and otherwise seem well-adjusted and happy, a parent should not be alarmed (and might even take pride and feel buoyed).

However, when a young boy seems to play more compulsively with girl toys, without much pleasure; frequently dresses like or pretends to be a girl; is socially isolated; appears unhappy; and, as sometimes happens, states a hatred for himself (or boys, or his body parts) or expresses a wish to become a girl, parents should take note. This child may be at some risk.

Such a child and his mother deserve sound therapy to help them understand his fantasies and frustrations. Although parents need to find a clinician whose perspective they trust, in general we recommend a therapist who is experienced working with issues of gender identity and one who is reasonable—meaning one who neither believes in "forcing" heterosexuality on a child nor one who does just the opposite, quickly confirming or celebrating a homosexual identity. Young children are still developing. What they need in therapy is the space to explore and question all their feelings and assumptions. A good therapy for a young child will likely assume that a heterosexual boy's identity is still possible and will provide the boy's parent with wise consultation on difficult questions, such as how much to push his *boy*ness and how much to discourage or indulge his *girl*ness.

In some cases gender confusion that results more from individual psychology and family dynamics will resolve itself, whereas that based more deeply in innate biology will not. But even in cases where a boy clearly seems headed for a bisexual or homosexual identity, sound therapy can help him to accept himself and establish a firm and cohesive self.

Most of all, good therapy that starts early not only has the best chance of helping a child resolve identity conflicts, but can help prevent his ever coming to hate himself for being a boy or for not being a girl. Therapy can also help that child have compassion for and insights into ways he will need to cope with his disappointing lot in life and the stigma he may experience from his community, his church, his family, and, sadly, even himself.

port and encouragement. Human beings, as a rule, are not good at unconditional love, but your boy needs something close to that. Help him discover his true self, and then do the best you can to love and embrace him just as he is.

You may have noticed that it is not easy to be a strong, healthy, and loving woman in this day and age. Neither is it easy to be a strong, healthy, and loving man. Despite the differences in your gender and the issues those differences create, your son needs your acceptance, your interest, and your love to face the difficult and complicated task of becoming a man.

CHAPTER 10

From Casanova to Prince Charming

Encouraging Healthy Attitudes Toward Women and Sex

Have you ever been to a mother-and-son Boy Scout breakfast? Look around the church hall. One boy in a uniform formal enough for the Café Budapest waits on his mother as if she were his queen. Another boy, who refused to wear his Scout shirt, pretty much throws a dish in his mother's direction. While many of the mother-son pairs enjoy each other's company, a few stand out. One son practically sits in his mother's lap, while another mother and son flirt shamelessly with each other. A few mothers and sons tease and banter more like brother and sister. There are parents and children who look like strangers, and many who look like the best of old pals. One boy politely asks his mother if he can get a Kleenex from her coat pocket. A second child takes it upon himself to rummage through his mother's pocketbook to reveal an embarrassing photo, despite her protests. Upon getting their merit badges, some boys accept kisses from their moms. Many more duck and pull away.

The assorted behavior you see is no wonder. Boys and their mothers come in all sizes and types. Their relationships are as varied and complex as any other intimate and long-standing relationships. These are people who share a history and memories, people who have both loved and hurt each other. However, many aspects of the mother-and-son relationship make it yet more special and worth exploring.

> That first relationship with his mother can help a son become capable of intimacy with other people. It can help lead him toward mature and responsible sexuality. It can help him to have a stable and satisfying marriage, or it can leave him more vulnerable for a lifetime of troubled relationships.

Unlike a marriage or partnership, for example, that is expected to last "till death do us part," a mother and son know that their relationship will one day culminate in his leaving home. Second, sons must depend on their mothers for both physical and emotional support for a good part of their early lives. Third, what a mother does or fails to do for her son will profoundly affect how well or poorly he makes his way in the world. And fourth, the mother–son relationship, an

experience in itself, becomes, or at least strongly contributes to, the template for how a son will relate to his
future girlfriends and wife.

That first relationship with his mother can help a son
become capable of intimacy with other people. It can
help lead him toward mature and responsible sexuality.
It can help him to have a stable and satisfying marriage,
or it can leave him more vulnerable for a lifetime of troubled relationships. With so much at stake, we must aim
our spotlight in that direction and must take time to understand the profound ways a mother influences her
son's view of women, relationships, sex, and himself.

Mothering Styles

Mothers can help their sons develop an authentic self, a
good conscience, and resilient esteem. Even as they employ those universal principles, however, single mothers,
like all mothers, have unique personalities and experiences that can lead them to relate to their sons in enduring and habitual ways. The single mother is the only
adult presence in the home, which intensifies the power
of her mothering ways. In most families these styles
pervade and affect almost every parenting decision and
moment. Let's consider these styles with a focus on how
they can influence a son's future life with women.

Baby-Keeper

For every mother who prays for the days of diaper-
changing and spoon-feeding to be over, there is a
mother who wants them to never end. The leading edge

of her son's development threatens her. *Growing up* are dirty words that she'd rather not think about. Doing her best to slow down the passage of time, she nurtures, celebrates, and rewards the qualities of her son that are more regressed and dependent. His growth, maturity, and increasing independence, she may believe, mean that she is no longer needed. And that thought is hard to bear.

To a coddling mother, her son's reaching the sink to wash his own hands is more sad than exciting. To her, each step forward is a punch in the belly that obliterates any joy and pride she may feel in his maturing. His graduation from elementary school is nothing but loss. That he did well and is moving on to the middle school honors program is lost on her.

Such infantalizing—the big word for treating a child as if he is much younger than his true age—affects a child in many ways, both obvious and subtle. The babied child can fall behind his peers. He will be less able to tolerate frustration, handle responsibility, and interact socially. He may come to resent the increasing demands of life that other children his age take in stride. Though a single mother may coddle her son because she loves him, she can unintentionally undermine his resilience. She may shelter her son to the point of smothering him, keeping him from experiences that would be good for him. She teaches him, so to speak, more about staying a baby than about growing up to be a healthy boy and, eventually, a healthy man.

Because they tend to be socially immature, baby-keepers' sons may spend their adolescence on the social margins. While their peers are getting to know who girls are, these boys may stand back, watching their friends joke and slow dance with the girls. As they get older, overly coddled boys may go in one of two directions. They can surrender to the cradle, never grow up, and never leave their mothers—which means never finding women of their own.

Or, they can do a 180-degree turn and break away from their mothers, finding girls who at first seem nothing at all like their mothers. They may initially be attracted to women who do not indulge them, who respect their autonomy and manhood. But a funny thing happens over time. These sons, never having grown up, may come to see their partners as too indulging this hour, not indulging enough the next, somehow never feeling loved with either. Babies fare better when they are infants in booties than when they are 32 years old and wearing three-piece suits.

Best Friend

Whereas the baby-keepers strive to stop their sons from growing up, some mothers are more devoted to keeping themselves from growing up. We do not refer here to vital parents who are active and engaged in life, but to mothers who reject the more traditional maternal roles. These women would rather be friends than mothers to their sons. Almost opposite of the baby-keepers, these mothers tend to enjoy their children more as the children grow older, as they acquire language and physical capability, making them more enjoyable companions.

This mother often dislikes disciplining her child. She'd rather go with her son and his friends to the movies than tell him he can't go because it's a school night. His pranks, even when they go too far, can make her laugh. In fact, she herself may get the prank going. She might not fret about report cards or that little incident with the police, feeling that her son's happiness, especially with her, matters most.

The best-friend mom and her son enjoy laughs together and take life as it comes. She may be the mother who sees single mothering as an exhilarating raft-ride down the rapids, something to be survived, not mastered; parenting advice is irrelevant to her. There is no doubt that such a mother can excel as a playmate and be a lot of fun. She may be the one who's out there playing catch or mountain biking, exposing her son to life, teaching him about its pleasures.

What does this imply for her son's future beliefs about women and his relationships with them? In the short run, this mother may enjoy the fact that her son is the guy that all the girls want. Rather than feeling jealous, this mother may live vicariously through her son and celebrate his having several girls whom he can dally with. She may teach him to see his difficulty with commitment as a virtue.

More important, growing up without ongoing expectations and limit-setting may retard his development into a competent and mature individual. Growing up in too loose of a home, though a gas, can ill-equip him for the responsibilities of life and relationships, for intimacy and investment in a long-term relationship. Their friendship also can obstruct some of the developmental changes that allow a boy to grow up and away from his mother, on toward other available women.

Obedient Wife

However feminist they may be, however twenty-first century, however uninterested in marrying a man, many single mothers play the dutiful wife to their sons. This kind of mother rushes home from work to have her son's favorite meal on the table when he comes home. She fills his requests quickly for fear of his wrath or disfavor. His wishes are her commands. What she needs or wants to do doesn't matter. If he says he might need sneakers in the morning, within hours she is at the mall buying them. She even deals swiftly with his demands for trivial items like candy or Pokemon cards, as if these desires were critical needs. She kids herself that because she gets him sometimes to say please, she is not really spoiling him. But any onlooker can see that her sense of priorities is out of kilter, for her son's priorities—his *me*-ness—are what set her agenda.

As you may decide, feeling deep love for a son does not guarantee that a mother will make wise parenting decisions. In fact, loving "too much" may lead a mother to focus only on the needs and feelings of the moment, rather than viewing parenting as the long-range proposition it truly is. Doing everything for a boy, buying him what he wants, and catering to his every whim may feel like good mothering at the moment, but what does it create in a boy's heart and mind? What kind of character does it mold?

This style does not bode well for anything in a son's development. As we stressed earlier, such indulgence weakens a boy's character and makes him more susceptible to an unhappy existence. He may have trouble handling the demands that teachers and other adults place on him. After all, he has grown accustomed to having people do everything for him, not the other way around. Boys who have been overindulged rarely develop respect for the needs and feelings of others, nor do they spontaneously become compassionate or generous. There is one person in such a boy's world, and that person is him. A more subtle risk in overindulgence is that doing too much for an otherwise capable young man may be the surest way to cripple his self-esteem. After all, if mom has to do everything for him, it must mean that he can't do anything for himself.

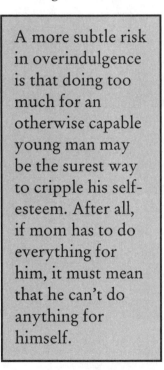

A more subtle risk in overindulgence is that doing too much for an otherwise capable young man may be the surest way to cripple his self-esteem. After all, if mom has to do everything for him, it must mean that he can't do anything for himself.

Obviously, this pattern can lay the foundation for big-time problems with women. Girls, and women, he may conclude, were created to serve men, particularly him. He may come to hold no expectations for himself and have huge expectations of his wife. A wife, he'll assume, should be as self-sacrificing, obedient, and enslaved to his desires as his mother was, while making no demands on him. Not exactly the formula for a happy marriage.

Queen Bee

The queen bee is antithetical to the obedient wife and very well may not be reading this book. Her son exists to meet her needs. He is there to tell her how pretty she looks, to tell her which shoes go better with her new skirt, and to massage the tension out of her neck. He may cook for her and do much of the housecleaning like some postmodern *Cinderfella*.

This queen bee is preoccupied with herself. Should her son talk of a sprained ankle, she remembers that she has a headache. After his piano recital, she talks all about her own musical exploits as a child. Even when she tries to ask how baseball tryouts went, she is prone not to listen to the answer and instead brings up the way her boss insulted her that afternoon.

Unable to appreciate or truly empathize with her son's perspective, she confuses her needs with his. "Do you want to go fix yourself a snack?" she asks when she is hungry. "Why don't you turn up the heat?" she suggests when she is cold. She has little interest in what interests her son. His accomplishments matter to her only as they highlight something about her. After all, if he is successful, if he is loving toward her, it must mean that she is a good mother. Their emotional communication is a one-way street, in which he is responsible for meeting her needs. In fact, sons of such self-absorbed and needy mothers learn to censor their own feelings and words. What is the point of asking for help or sharing successes when the only person who matters is mom?

The son of the queen bee is at great risk of losing his connection with himself. He may forsake his genuine interests and feelings in order to satisfy and amuse his mother. He will disguise his hurts and disappointments because he doesn't want to irritate his mother or shatter her image of him. When he takes his false self out into the world, this boy will find it hard to be close to girls (or women). He will tend to believe all women are as needy as his mother and fear that they, too, are using him for their own esteem and emotional benefit.

The concept of a mutual relationship, in which a man and a woman equally share with and care for one another, will be beyond him, for he'll never have experienced one. Because he has had to be attuned to and help regulate his mother's moods, this man will be exquisitely sensitive to his wife's moods and be apt to take her occasional distress and disappointment personally, believing they are somehow his fault. He also may carry suppressed rage over the way he was mothered—a rage that he couldn't show his mother—into his adult relationships with women, making marital harmony far less likely.

Star-Crossed Lover

It certainly sounds provocative and incestuous to refer to a mother as a star-crossed lover. And we have no wish to offend mothers. Yet neither do we want to overlook what is a fairly common dynamic between single mothers and their sons, especially when the son is an only child or the last one in the nest.

These mothers love their sons intensely, some might say too intensely. They feel passionately for their boys, and their relationship can at times look more like that of a girlfriend or a lover than a mother. They are physically close, and their relationship often involves entwining and merging.

Boundaries or their absence can frustrate these two. These are the mothers and sons who regularly get physical with each other, tickling and playing footsies. They regularly invade each other's privacy, whether in the bathroom or in the bedroom. Intrusiveness is the word of the day, and each often wants to know what the other is thinking.

These couples—who seem more like husband and wife than parent and child—can experience love and hate as an ever-swinging pendulum. Soulmates this minute, they may be the worst of enemies the next. As joined as they are, both are exquisitely vulnerable to feeling rejected and abandoned by the other. This mother sees girlfriends as competitors who are out to steal her son. Jealousy and envy abound; neither wants the other to share affection with anyone else. The mildest slight can lead to horrible fights. They can be mean, cruelly ridiculing, or say exactly what they know will devastate the other. At other times, they are seductive and adoring. Like tumultuous lovers or spouses in a troubled marriage, these two have wicked good and bad times.

How can this son possibly have good relationships with other women? All that he has experienced and learned tells him that women want to possess and control him (and, if he has some insight, that he now feels much the same way about them). His relationships with girls and women will tend to be stormy, full of sado-masochism and floor-stomping breakups and idyllic make-ups, until, of course, the next frustration arises. Right or wrong, he will view his wife as trying to emasculate him and take away his power. In the worst case this boy may become a man who, feeling threatened and helpless, is prone to mistreat his wife.

Having described these types, we must state a major qualification. These are broad images, unflattering portrayals of what a relationship can become if a mother is distressed, unaware, or just not paying attention. Most mother and son relationships are not so extreme, singular, and worrisome. A healthy mother and son relationship is flexible and varied. Most mothers occasionally play the part of baby-keeper, best friend, obedient wife, queen bee, and lover, just to name a few of the possibilities. And there is no one right way to mother a son, no one-size-fits-all mold for a healthy relationship. What matters is how responsively a mother meets her son's needs and what she teaches him about women.

It is always worth taking an occasional reading on how effective your mothering is, especially as mothering styles tend to be automatic and to go unquestioned for years (or until a crisis arises). If you routinely allow your son to put you down with name-calling or bullying behavior, he may well assume that his behavior is appropriate with every woman he encounters in his life. If you take delight in his conquest of girlfriends, he may decide that the thrill of the chase and the tally of victories is more important than mutual respect and lasting intimacy. If, however, you value and earn his respect—in addition to giving him the love and respect he needs—you will help him to become a good man who can have mature relationships with girls and the women they will become.

Healthy Sexuality

Sexuality involves much more than mere sex. Parents begin teaching their sons about healthy sexuality from the day they welcome the baby boys into this world. All of the good mothering detailed throughout this book will contribute to your son's healthy, safe sexual attitude. As with so many other aspects of his life, a child's knowledge of sexuality progresses through several stages as he grows and learns.

From Birth Through the Second Year

The well-mothered baby has been held with love and knows that he and his body are special and worth loving. Your responsive and reliable parenting has convinced him that the world is a trustworthy place, the foundation for good relationships. The good care you've given him has become part of him, so that he believes he deserves good care.

These early beliefs form the basis of self-preservation and self-care, increasing the likelihood that your son will not risk doing things that can cause him bodily harm (e.g., unsafe sex years down the road). The fun and good feeling he knows with you at bath or tickle times, for example, will promote a deep sense of comfort with bodily pleasure. And by hearing his body parts referred to matter-of-factly as what they are (e.g., *penis*), he will grow accustomed to regarding all of his body as okay, not as something secret or shameful.

Preschoolers

These children know and see more. They are curious, wondering about the women and men, boys and girls around them. They notice and wonder about the difference between boys and girls. At this age you will teach them more about their bodies, with a bit more information, but just as casually and openly, keeping in mind the child's developmental age. The old joke—about the child who replies, "Oh, I thought I was from Cleveland," when his mother answers his "Where did I come from" with a labored and anatomical explanation—is still relevant.

It is important to provide enough information but not so much as to overwhelm the child. Your acceptance and admiration for your son's character *and* his body will help him to develop a proud and comfortable identity as a boy.

Maintaining, too, the kind of boundaries discussed in chapter 4 will foster the child's naturally maturing wish for privacy. As Debra Haffner suggests, these are the years when boys should start knocking on bathroom and bedroom doors, as well as be taught that touching themselves is a private matter. ("It's okay to touch yourself in your bedroom; it's not okay at Grandma's dinner table.") Like all parents, mothers must strive to set appropriate limits in a compassionate and patient manner. If you are unsure what appropriate limits might be, consider asking your son's pediatrician or a professional who specializes in children and families. The ideal is to instill a positive sense of privacy, not to create shame, humiliation, or rejection.

School Children

Once again, all of the healthy mothering you've done (without even thinking about sex) will contribute to your son's healthy sexuality. He has learned to consider other people's perspectives and to control himself. He has a desire to be a good person who benefits the world. By working to foster his sense of competency and emotional self-understanding, you have nurtured his resilience and capacity to handle the stress of life, reducing the likelihood that as an adult he will be sexually compulsive or will see sex as an antidote to frustration, anger, or depression.

With their growing minds, these boys are ready to learn more about the biology of sex and how babies are really made. Again, consider carefully what your child is ready to hear. However, beware of not sufficiently informing your son because of your own discomfort, or because he never seems ready to listen. If he doesn't learn the truth from you, he will learn it, or a distorted version of it, from his friends on the street. Isn't it better that he learn what he can in the context of a loving home from a parent who can teach him the truth with care and sensitivity?

> A healthy mother and son relationship is flexible and varied. Most mothers occasionally play the part of baby-keeper, best friend, obedient wife, queen bee, and lover, just to name a few of the possibilities.

Though boys in this age range tend to play with other boys, you will start to see some attitudes toward girls and sexuality emerging. What kind of media do we expose our boys to? Mothers who think their boys seem overly interested in sex at this age may be right and should take their hunches seriously. Likewise, bad attitudes toward girls on the playground, for example, that go beyond the usual boy–girl rivalries should be noted and addressed. Sexual harassment is not something boys tend to grow out of, and it is a big problem. A 2001 study by the Harvard School of Public Health found that an alarming one in five teenage girls are either physically and/or sexually abused by their boyfriends. Little abusers tend to grow into big ones. Although we are the first to confess that distinguishing between innocent experimentation and more worrisome behavior is not always easy, looking the other way is never okay. This matter demands our best attention and efforts to notice, inquire, and do what, if anything, is necessary.

Grown in size and independence, your more social boys will also be out in the world more, out of your immediate supervision. Sad as it is, bad things do happen. Know the homes and families where your son plays or sleeps over. Is there ample supervision? Are older children present who might be a dangerous influence? Does drinking or drug use take place there? Do the children in that home get to watch whatever cable television shows or movies they wish? Today's parents must always err on the side of being too careful.

Preteens

These boys are getting ready for adolescence. Their bodies are changing and they may show interest in girls. They are intellectually able to understand more about puberty and the biology that is transforming their bodies.

Though some of this education will happen in school, a mother needs to make her two cents' worth known. These talks often are most effective when they focus more on your boy's ability to care for himself than on actual intercourse. Be sure you discuss with your son the possibility of pregnancy and the difficulty of sticking up for what he believes in a world that equates sexual exploits with manhood.

Open discussion about drug and alcohol use is critical here, too, for teens are much more likely to get into trouble sexually when high and out of control. Your discipline is needed more than ever, to sustain your son's moral behavior and his concern for others. It is much harder for a boy to sexually intimidate or harm a girl when he is empathic and appreciates how frightening and destructive such behavior is to her. Although you may not want to suppress your boy's growing interest in girls, you also don't want to fuel it prematurely. Slow him down. Don't rush to set up parties or accommodate dates to the mall, and don't push your sons to be more social than they are. Some mothers worry that their boys will be wallflowers even at this young age.

Middle Schoolers

The variation in children at this stage is remarkable. Visit the halls of any middle school and you will see tall young men with deep voices and facial hair walking beside shorter boys who still squeak when they talk. Some look like, behave, and feel as if they are still young children. Others look, act, and sense themselves as pubertal, unstoppably on the way to adulthood. Most feel uncomfortably stuck between the two. Some still play with toy cars, some kiss girls and go further, and some do both.

These children need good education and more good education. Messages about abstinence and self-protection are both needed. Your son needs your continued involvement, guidance, and supervision. Contrary to popular opinion, boys this age do not need less parenting. They just need their parenting in a different shape, one more respectful of their emerging selves. Left to their own devices, these children are apt to get into troubling situations and habits or come dangerously close. Know their friends and their acquaintances. Know the families. Don't give carte blanche to sleepovers (especially over vacations and during the summer), where your son tag-teams from home to home. Keep your son accountable here and there throughout the day. Set and keep curfews.

Unfortunately, these are the years when serious problems often begin, when mothers have been lulled into thinking that the risks come later, in high school, and have allowed too much freedom with too few limits and consequences. Hang onto every inch you can, for every inch you give quickly leads to more and more freedom, freedom that can be too much for any child to handle.

High Schoolers

Though prevention is the key, it is never too late. Stay in firm but respectful contact with your son when he is a high school student. The possibility that he is sexually involved is much greater now. Most parents worry that their adolescent sons will get into trouble at night, but in this day of working parents, the greatest risk is often during the day, when teens are out and about and parents are at work. It is impossible to control your son's behavior twenty-four hours a day, particularly when he begins driving or has a job. There is no substitute at this age for connection, for the trusting and respectful relationship you've built since his toddler days. Keep talking—about relationships, feelings, and his life in general. Keep talking, too, about his sexuality. Never surrender to what you think is inevitable.

Many teenagers do come to see the danger and destruction in their sexual promiscuity and learn to value a

The Internet

The World Wide Web is here to stay. Even if you are not connected, your son will likely use and explore the Internet at school, the library, and friends' homes. And as we know, cyberspace is full of graphic imagery that, even as it excites, can distress and preoccupy your son, and give him distorted and destructive messages about women, sexuality, and violence. The best you can do is to educate and socialize your son to use this resource wisely.

Teach and share. Get on the computer with your boy, the younger the better. As with most things it is much easier to prevent than "cure" Internet addiction. Teach him to browse wisely, to not give out personal information, and to stay out of chat rooms, newsgroups, etc. Show him how the computer can be used constructively. Help him learn to monitor himself and to come to you for help if he finds himself in "bad places" on the Web.

Monitor his use. Keep an eye on where your son is going on the Internet. Try not to allow all-day computing or late-night surfing. Don't use the computer as a babysitter. Allow him to go online only when you are around. Keep the computer in a common room where you or others can see what your son is up to. Of course, all of the teaching and effective parenting you have done will make it less likely that your son will get himself into trouble.com.

Get techno. Check the sites your child visits (click the History button on the Internet Explorer toolbar). Employ computer filters that block objectionable words and images. Encourage your child to use search engines that do the same, such as *www .google.com.* Consult sites, like *www.kidmon.com,* that show parents in detail what they can do and what software exists to help them stay one step ahead of their children. Catching up on technology yourself is not that hard and may be your best weapon to prevent your son from abusing his access to the Internet.

Get tough. Who can blame your teen for wanting to see all the Internet offers? Sexual curiosity is normal. While it's not his fault that so much is so easily available today, wise mothers remember that, however it begins, addiction to pornography is a real danger. If your son's use of the Internet is getting out of hand, get stricter about controlling his online access. If that doesn't work, you may need to disconnect (though, we admit, older boys will find their way on elsewhere).

Seek help. Internet addiction is as real as any other addiction. If your son cannot get off the computer, pleads or demands for even more time, ignores family and friends, appears restless when away from the computer, neglects school work, loses needed sleep to stay online, or loses interest in real people and activities, he may be headed toward addiction. If talking with him (and the above steps) doesn't help, consider finding professional help.

life of safer and less compulsive sex. We've seen wholly indiscriminate boys come to appreciate a more mature relationship with a girl who can be supportive and emotionally available. Rather than marvel that your son is going out with the cheerleading captain, observe how that relationship seems to be going. Get to know his girlfriends, watching out in case—it happens—she, not he, pushes for a sexual relationship.

And, we stress again, monitor his use of drugs and alcohol. Drunk boys and girls do more, do it more frequently, do more with more partners, and do more without protection. Studies show that teens with involved, caring parents get into less drug, alcohol, and sexual trouble. There is not a school in this country where drugs, alcohol, and sex are not readily available. Burying your head and saying, "not my boy!" does neither of you any good. Keep the lines of communication open, and be sure your son knows that you care, are listening, and are paying attention.

Teaching our sons healthy sexuality is a childhood-long enterprise that accumulates with every moment of good parenting and connection. We do not accomplish it with one big talk about the birds and the bees, not to mention AIDS and condoms (though such talks are needed, too). Nor is it mostly about penises and vaginas (though, of course, they have something to do with sexuality). We do it in baby steps, word by word and question by question, each one helping to create a boy, then a man, whose sexuality is lived out maturely, safely, and within the context of good, respectful, and loving relationships.

CHAPTER 11

School Boys

Promoting Educational and Career Success

Though little in life is certain, success in school is the best guarantor of a good life. Educational success tends to bring greater career income, security, and personal satisfaction. More highly educated people also enjoy better health and health care and are less likely to commit crimes and end up in jail. In short, education endows a child, and the man he'll become, with more personal freedom and opportunity.

Although it is a difficult fact to accept, statistics tell us that the children of single parents, whether mothers or fathers, do less well in school and drop out more often.[1] With so much at stake, her son's educational well-being must be one of a single mother's highest priorities. How can a mother motivate her son to try his best at school, to value education, and to succeed academically?

Blue Brains, Pink Brains

The findings of brain science and the new gender studies have been startling, especially as they relate to education. They have shown without question that on the average, boys and girls think and learn differently.[2]

Girls talk sooner and have more sophisticated language and vocabulary skills. They read better, listen better, and can do fine motor tasks, such as writing with a pencil, better. We know, also, that they are more adept both emotionally and socially.

Although it is a difficult fact to accept, statistics tell us that the children of single parents, whether mothers or fathers, do less well in school and drop out more often.

Boys are better at gross motor skills (e.g., throwing spitballs and juggling erasers) and are more curious. They tend to act out rather than verbalize what they feel. But they can read maps well and excel in activities that require visual-spatial manipulation.

Let's put this in plain terms. Girls can write neatly, can put their feelings into words, can peacefully work out problems with peers, can articulate ideas, and can sit at their desks quietly. Boys can't read their own chicken-scratch writing; they punch and kick out their feelings, punch and kick out their interpersonal conflicts, need to get outside and burn off excess energy, and fall out of their chairs a lot. When you compare these lists of traits, whom might you predict to have greater academic success, especially in the early years?

Even the boys know the right answer.

What can you do to protect your own son from falling by the academic wayside? First, assess how much of this applies to him. If you're not sure what your son's classroom behavior really looks like, volunteering in his classroom for an hour or two a week can give you some valuable clues. Share your thoughts and concerns with his teacher. Provide your son with support, not criticism, at home. Talk with him about the differences between boys and girls. Follow the strategies in this chapter and do whatever else you can to prevent his conscious or unknowing surrender to an identity as a bad student.

Encourage Doing One's Best

From as young an age as possible, encourage your son to do his best. Celebrate his baking you a cake, even if more chocolate mix ends up on the floor than in the pan. Encourage his self-initiated attempts to wash the car, bring you breakfast in bed, and tell you funny stories. Children who know how good it feels to try their best carry that desire to school. They are the ones who are happy to erase the board and do good work so that they can feel the pride and joy of not just their accomplishments, but their efforts, too.

Sadly, our society has almost systematically conditioned the wish to do one's best right out of many boys. Too many boys go out of their way not to do their best and, in order to defy authority and its demands, spite themselves. They will forgo their own learning and success so as not to please the adults around them. When these boys do their best, they feel like good little boys, a feeling that feels anything but good to them. Doing his best requires a boy to accept the fact that for all his macho posturing, he really does care.

Create a Learner

As soon as her adopted son, Matt, could walk, Kimberly, in her own words, "began training him for life." Whenever it was safe, Kimberly encouraged Matt to explore, marveling in his curiosity and adventures. She loved watching her little geologist, biologist, and physicist perform his experiments. And Matt could see her pleasure at his learning in the way her eyes lit up.

Sometimes Kimberly felt a little deceptive when, for example, she'd pack his favorite treats for them to share on the library lawn. "I want him to have good feelings about books and learning deep inside. I want him to think of me smiling and to taste those cookies every time he walks into a library for the rest of his life." But in her heart she knew she was doing the right thing. She could see it. Matt loved to learn.

—◦◦◦—

Kimberly made learning a priority in her family and discovered a formula for making a lifelong learner. To some this might sound like bribery, but what she did is not at all the same as giving a cookie or reward for every book read (though, admittedly, parents have tried all kinds of strategies with success). Kimberly applied the same principle that holds for the mother who lovingly reads with her son each night. Her warm and attentive presence, as much as any book, created her child's love of reading and books. Kimberly wasn't offering a treat for each page read—that would have undermined her son's inner motivation. She was simply, if profoundly, making his experience at the library a positive and memorable one.

Of course, even without a picnic, one of the best ways to prepare your son for school, to encourage language skills, and to enjoy time together is to read out loud to him. When your boy is a baby, you can prop him in your lap to look at board books. Point to objects and name them. Talk about colors and make animal noises. The sound of your voice, the physical warmth of being close, and the bright pictures can delight even the youngest child.

Make reading a story or two part of your nightly bedtime routine. As your son grows, introduce him to the classics of early childhood literature. Ask your librarian for other recommendations as your son matures. You can progress from reading short books at bedtime to reading chapters of longer books. Share your own childhood favorites, and discover the new, fine ones that are being published today. Many a mother can wistfully recall the day her son took a book out of her hands and said, "I can read this myself, Mom." In this way your son may become a man who will enjoy a lifelong love of books and ideas.

What *doesn't* work? Repeatedly ignoring your son's eager wish to involve you in his learning, his showing you the rings that a pebble makes in the sink or querying what a word means. When you don't respond, don't take an interest, or act bothered, he'll soon stop showing and asking you. He'll decide that learning isn't something worth caring about.

Also, too much rewarding can retard the maturing of a healthy inner motivation to learn. The educator and author Alfie Kohn has written convincingly on the dangers of rewarding children's learning and work too easily. Parents sometimes teach their children to work and learn *only* for external prizes, undermining development of an inner wish to learn for its own sake and pleasures. Children, especially at younger ages, love to earn prizes and admiration. But if this is always given or is forced on them, they may lose touch with their more inherent and natural incentives to learn and try.

Parents should strive for a balance. Observe. A child who hates to read may need more encouragement and external motivation to read more and better. However, once you see him reading on his own, laughing at what he reads, or staying up late to read one more page, recognize what is happening. It is now the reading itself that drives him from the inside.

Create a Worker

Remember Kimberly, the mother who used every minute of their daily life together to make her son a learner? Now, apply her philosophy to teaching your son to be a worker. What do we mean? Use every task at home as an opportunity to teach your child the value of working. Let him learn to put in that light bulb, empty the trash, and assemble that new computer desk. From an early age, invite him to work alongside you, learning the skills to do significant tasks that he is held accountable for. Is switching the laundry from the washer to the dryer too much to ask of your eight-year-old? He somehow doesn't mind wrestling with the laundry when he wants to find his new sweatshirt.

It is mind-boggling that baby-sitting teens ask upward of $10 an hour in some neighborhoods. Lucrative as it is for the night, where does it lead and what are these young people learning to expect for their future efforts? What a cruel awakening it will be when these spoiled children learn what the world is really like and how much is paid for what kind of work. Few bosses will pay a grown man $20 to play video games and eat snacks while his children sleep upstairs.

Expect some basic work as part of the privilege of living in your home. If you pay for extra work, go slow. Start with a dollar an hour. Just because a job really helps you out (and would have cost you $50 if a plumber had done it) is no excuse to pay your son $10 for 15 minutes of work.

Demonstrate that you believe his school work to be just as valuable—if not more so—than work he does for money. Create a good workspace for him in which to study and write. Guard against distractions. Don't tempt

A Penny Saved

Though it sounds less noble than fostering moral development, teaching our children the value of a dollar is a critical lesson. Children who don't appreciate that value are prone to reject hard work and to approach life with a spoiled and insatiable attitude.

Giving your children an allowance is one easy and time-tested way to begin teaching them about money and its management.

Here are some tips:

• *Start early:* Even toddlers can begin learning how to handle their money, with your guidance.

• *Give a reasonable amount:* Some parents give a dollar a week for each year of age (resist pleas to keep up with the neighbors), while others give their child what he needs to cover certain expenses. Under no circumstances does a child's getting excessive amounts of money do him any favor or teach him anything but plain old indulgence.

• *Establish and stick to guidelines:* Some parents require children to divvy their allowance between money to spend and money to go into the bank (and even money to go to charitable causes of the children's choosing).

him away from work with invitations to join you at the television or to run over to the mall because you want the company. Offer your help when asked for it. If he values his essay enough to ask for your opinion, read and com-

- *Pay it on time:* A reliable timetable is one aspect of an allowance that helps the child learn money management. It is also wise to consider whether you will allow borrowing against the allowance. If you do, be sure you kindly but firmly require prompt reimbursement. It is usually more effective to require that children save toward the things they want, rather than allowing them to buy on your credit.

- *Don't use it to punish or control behavior:* The purpose of an allowance is to give our children a chance to learn more about money, not to help us discipline them; they should do regular chores as part of the household, independent of the allowance.

- *Let them learn:* The way children learn from having an allowance is by making the same mistakes many adults do (e.g., spending their money quickly on junk and not having it for something better). Allow your children to use money for immediate gratification, as well as to save for bigger, more long-term items; try not to bail them out from the consequences of their spending decisions, for that will undo the lesson to be learned.

ment thoughtfully. A cursory, "yeah, great," may get you back to your favorite show, but what will it teach him?

Learning to work is perhaps the most necessary skill for succeeding in school and in life.

Create Futurists

No, we're not talking about space stations and laser swords. We're talking about boys who can study today for rewards that won't come until tomorrow. Many boys ask what the relevance of school is, why they should do today's stupid assignment. Many young people have a fast food mentality: If they can't have it now, they don't want to be bothered working and waiting for it. Opportunity and success that won't arrive for years is too abstract, too far-fetched a goal. They want a reward this very moment.

Not surprisingly, such boys have a great deal of trouble in school. They have no tolerance for the daily drudgery of lectures and worksheets that build up to quizzes and finals. And when they do put in some effort, the reward had better be big and fast. These are boys who hand in, excuse the expression, absolute crap and are indignant when they only get a C.

As with almost everything else in parenting, prevention is the best solution. How do you teach a child to tolerate work, perhaps even to enjoy it? By asking, without apology, that he work, and by gauging his rewards carefully. There's only one way your son can learn to delay gratification and that's by having to wait. Only by dealing with frustration will he learn how to tolerate it. Only by coping with failure does he learn how to master it.

In fact, contrary to popular belief in this era of warm-and-fuzzy self-esteem, failure is not fatal and often can be a highly valuable learning experience. Some mothers rush to school when their son gets a D, blaming the teacher, asking for another chance, or complaining that the assignment wasn't fair. It might be wiser to sit down with a boy who has failed or earned a disappointing grade to discuss what caused that to happen, how he feels about it, and what plans he has to improve his work in the future.

Create Respecters

Basil didn't give a [fill in the blank] about anyone. The terror of the seventh grade, he got detentions during his detentions—for wearing his hat, for chewing gum, for swearing at a teacher. He heard the most polite requests from teachers as harsh demands. "No one's going to boss my ass around," he'd even said to the principal. He was too busy breaking rules to study or learn.

———∾∾∾———

Basil grew up as the man of his house, more like its warlord. What he said was the law. His mother feared his tantrums when he was little, and now she feared his aggression, his size, and his verbal assaults. Having grown up with no respect for authority, he had none for his teachers or for the people who ran his school. His insecurity made complying with the constraints of school life too threatening. He eventually got thrown out of his school and then was thrown out of another, a private one for which his mother had borrowed a great deal of money. It was all for nothing. Basil did not respect himself, his mother, his teachers, or the value of learning.

For many young men, school is a frustrating, boring drill that leaves them feeling incompetent and resentful. Their primary goal becomes getting out, which they often do by misbehaving, cutting classes, coming to school drunk or high, or simply not showing up at all.

Mothers must begin early to teach their boys respect, not only for people but for the process of learning. Ironically, stressing academic success too strongly can backfire. The Josephson Institute of Ethics conducts a study every year on ethical beliefs and conduct among teenagers. Over the past few years that study has noted some disturbing trends. Seventy-five percent of teens admit to some form of cheating in order to improve their grades; 65 percent say they see nothing wrong with cheating on an important exam. The reason? They know good grades are important to future success. Apparently, *how* you get those good grades doesn't matter. These children believe that the end indeed justifies the means. And these are the young people who stay in school. Young men like Basil may never achieve even this disturbing degree of success.

> Mothers must begin early to teach their boys respect, not only for people but for the process of learning.

What can a single mother do? She can be involved on a daily basis with school. She can show an interest in homework and outside assignments without assuming personal responsibility for them. And she can demonstrate by her own words and actions that character and integrity mean as much to her, or more, as academic success.

Create Help-Takers

Joe had above-average intelligence. But he also had a bona fide learning disability that affected his writing. As the writing demands of the sixth grade grew, his work deteriorated. His classroom teacher and the special education teacher offered extra help, but Joe felt ashamed and frustrated by his inability to do the work others seemed to do so easily. He withdrew, snapping at his teachers when they pursued him. He ended the year with a mediocre report card and declared that he would never go back to school.

—◦◊◦—

To meet this crisis, Joe's mother consulted a therapist. She learned that Joe, like many boys, was especially prone to take his teacher's help as a signal that he was somehow defective and stupid. Though some boys' vulnerability stems from their having been subjected to early criticism or ridicule, or by having had mothers who excelled at everything, that wasn't true for Joe. He'd been raised by a kind and sensitive mother who spoke softly and wore kid gloves.

Armed with this insight, Joe's mother helped her son feel less ashamed and encouraged him to express the inadequacy he felt about his learning problem. Just being able to vent his frustration gave him much relief and awakened his old optimistic attitude. He also endorsed

Homework: Whose Work Is It?

Perhaps no one issue causes more conflict and consumes more family time than homework. Teachers believe in it and sometimes assign lots of it. Boys resent it and sometimes avoid it. Parents wind up taking responsibility for it. In some families, doing and checking homework can take hours per child per night, leaving little time for conversation, play, or other activities and leading to major power struggles between parent and child, family and school. Here are some suggestions to help you help your son manage his homework.

Be aware of your son's assignments. Many schools require students to keep daily planners or logs of assignments. Some require parents' signatures each day. Whatever the plan, do take time to ask your son what he needs to do and to encourage an orderly approach to getting it done. *What* and *how* questions are usually the best approach, rather than nagging or lectures: "What is your assignment?" "What things do you need to get it done?" "How do you plan to complete that project?" If your son routinely tells you he has no homework, a friendly call to the teacher may be in order.

Develop a homework routine. For most boys, sitting still in a classroom for six hours a day is hard enough. When school is out, they need an hour or two to run, to play, and to simply hang out with friends. Sit down with your son and make a plan together for getting homework done. "Homework time" may be after school, just before dinner, or right after dinner—it's the regularity that matters. Find out what works best for your son and encourages him to do his best, and then stick with it. This can present a challenge for working mothers. Invite your son's ideas in developing a plan, and then follow through.

Remember whose work it is. Unless we're mistaken, you probably have completed the fourth grade. Your son's homework is his responsibility and should be a matter he and his teacher resolve together. You can guide and encourage, but you should not do the work for him. If you do too much in the homework department, your son will gladly let you and will lose the opportunity to learn for himself. He'll almost certainly learn more from the F he receives for a missed assignment than from the B he receives when you do the assignment for him.

Be involved with the school. Join the parents' organization, go to parent-teacher conferences and open house nights, and make an effort to know your son's teachers and administrators. A personal knowledge of his school will help you know both what's going on—and what isn't.

his mother's offer to meet with his next year's teachers, to help them understand both his strengths and his weaknesses. During the school year, Joe's mother gave him special attention around big writing projects. By cooking his favorite meal, for instance, she gave him something to look forward to during a pained afternoon of writing.

> Learning to accept help is a valuable skill for any of us to have. Children who can ask for the help they need and use it when they get it are bound to thrive in school.

Admitting his learning problem also enabled Joe to take action. Now that he no longer had to waste energy denying it, Joe embraced his disability. He became proactive on his own behalf. He now searched the Internet to find out what other kids like him did to cope. He learned strategies to compensate and saw that writing might be something he had to work harder on, rather than an obstacle he could never overcome. Teachers no longer looked like the enemy; they became a resource he wanted and needed. Coming to terms with our limitations—something each of us must do—is always the surest road to mastering them.

Learning to accept help is a valuable skill for any of us to have. Children who can ask for the help they need and use it when they get it are bound to thrive in school. Boys have often absorbed the mistaken notion that being strong means never needing help, that real men don't have weaknesses. Gentle encouragement, empathy, and appreciation for the effort your son makes to learn and

Learning Problems

Although the good old days at school had some advantages, today's heightened awareness of how children learn and don't learn (and what sometimes complicates the process) is a godsend. If you suspect your son has a learning disability, or he appears to be doing poorly for no apparent reason, discuss it with your son's teachers.

Survey your son's behavior throughout his day. Maybe the reason he doesn't do well in reading at school relates to social problems with his peers. Perhaps he doesn't follow conversations well and often misunderstands what others say (in that case, a language disability). Or perhaps his utter disorganization in school completely resonates with the scattered and seemingly uncooperative child you battle at home (in this case, an organizational deficit).

If you are concerned, don't hesitate to ask your school to investigate this with formal psycho-educational testing. Do not let shyness or a wish that he'll grow out of it deter you. Many steps can be taken, at school and home, that can help a child overcome and succeed despite real learning issues. When it comes to learning disabilities, early intervention is always best.

(For more information about this significant topic, parents might begin with the classic *No Easy Answers: The Learning Disabled Child at Home and at School* (New York: Bantam, 1995).

grow will teach him that sometimes the strongest person is the one who can ask for help.

Create Self-Checkers

Many boys do not have the patience and stamina to rewrite drafts of their essays. They take their math tests as if they are in a 50-yard dash, even though they have 20 minutes to check it over. Their test grades are frequently knocked down because of careless errors on problems they knew how to do. Their reports come home covered with red pencil and the teacher's regretful comments that it was the sloppiness, the inattention to spelling and grammar, not the ideas, that accounted for the mediocre grade.

Closely related to the ability to accept help is the capacity and willingness to monitor one's own work. Writing this book, for example, required many drafts that we mutually edited and rewrote. The child who can check his own work will learn more, do better, and, more critically, he will know how to do his best on whatever task he pursues.

Fortunately, more teachers are addressing this skill within their classrooms. Even elementary school children are being asked to do their book reports in careful stages that must be checked before they can proceed. Help your child stay on track. Take an interest. Celebrate when children go the extra yard. If they decide midway that they need an extra resource, help them out; drive them to the library. (Yes, it's annoying to have to drop what you're doing, but it's well worth the effort.)

These are the little things that, more than rhetoric, reveal your true values to a child.

If your son persists in doing sloppy work, try not to sermonize or go on endlessly. Instead, allow yourself to commiserate, validate his own frustration, and help him understand how he can get a different result. "It must be so disappointing to get a B when you studied and knew everything." "You mean if you'd used the spelling checker, you'd have gotten an A? Bummer." Your son will start checking his work only when he decides it's worth the extra elbow grease.

Bad Boys

When we were children, parents usually took the teachers' side. It was always, "What did *you* do wrong?" Even when we complained of being mistreated, yelled at, or insulted, parents tended to ask, "What did you do?" As kids we hated it, sort of. Sure, we thought we wanted our parents to blame the school, but did we really? It felt good and safe to know that our parents valued and supported our second home, our school. They believed that learning to work and get along with different teachers was good for us and taught us about life. A bad or unfair grade was a reason to work harder, not a reason to call the principal or an attorney.

Horribly, today's schools are full of "bad boys," boys who are violent, hateful, or harassing, boys who cheat and steal and who would hurt anyone who gets in their way, especially weaker and more helpless children. Bullying has become such a problem on school playgrounds nationwide that entire curricula are devoted to peer mediation, conflict resolution, and prevention of aggression. More than ever, our schools and teachers need our loyalty and support, the old-fashioned kind. Rather than showing up at the school angry because your son never got his chance to be classroom weatherman, show up angry because he spoke rudely to his teacher. So he got a 93 when he deserved a 95 on a science quiz. What will he learn by watching you bully his teacher into another measly point or two, compared to your calm explanation that it doesn't matter and that you'd never bother his busy and trustworthy teacher with such a triviality? (Almost needless to say, this approach applies less aptly and well when your child has a teacher who proves not to be so trustworthy.)

> Bullying has become such a problem on school playgrounds nationwide that entire curricula are devoted to peer mediation, conflict resolution, and prevention of aggression.

It is never, absolutely never right to defend a son's bad behavior, to make excuses for him, or to let him off the hook from well-deserved consequences. If he is pushing his crotch into little girls at school, you need to make it clear that it isn't a joke. If your 4'5" son is defying his 6'6" principal, you'd better support the school's suspension. Be aware, however, that adding punishments at home to consequences at school may only increase your son's resentment and defiance. School issues are usually best dealt with at school, with support from parents. It is never a healthy thing for our children to hear us bad-mouthing teachers and school staff, even when we disagree with their actions. Learning to live with rules is part of life, as is learning to live with imperfect teachers. We owe it to our children to be their teachers' and schools' strongest allies, particularly in hard times.

Great Expectations for Tomorrow

We've met them both: mothers who expect their sons to go to Harvard when these boys can barely make it through remedial classes and mothers who expect nothing from their sons, despite the boys' talents and achievements.

How can you set the right expectations for your son? With careful thought and self-awareness. You have lived with your son. No one knows him better—his assets and liabilities—than you do. And, we hope, you have been involved in his educational life and understand something about his intellectual resources and motivation, as well as his interests. You can listen to his desires and help him assess his options.

Guide your son toward fulfilling his own dreams, not yours. Perhaps you wish you'd become a doctor and think he'd make a good one. But maybe he'd rather be a pilot or a salesman. Some mothers, nurturing and caring, want their sons to pursue altruistic professions. Their sons, however, want to go into business. Be assured that your goodness and all the compassion, moral

When Your Son and His Teacher Don't Click

What a painful and angering experience it is for a loving mother to think that the teacher doesn't seem to understand, appreciate, or like her son. What can she do to help bring her child and his teacher closer together?

Listen to your child. Go beyond his vague complaining. Ask him exactly what she doesn't like about him. And ask what he contributes to this mix. If he says "Nothing," he may not be giving his teacher a fair chance.

Listen to his teacher. Invite the teacher to share both likes and dislikes of your child. Try not to be defensive. The more open you are, the more his teacher can safely tell you.

Listen to yourself. What do you see in your child? Is the teacher on to something that you'd rather not admit? Or do you know what's behind his behavior: for example, that your son misses his beloved teacher of last year?

values, and concern for the world around him that you lived daily are in him and will guide him in whatever he does for a living. Character, when rooted in the heart, will spread through your son's endeavors, big or small, each and every one.

Be on guard, if your wish for him is too rigid or singular. If you have fantasies of his going to Yale Law School, you may be more in love with the idea of Yale

Try a little tenderness. Fending off or confronting the teacher is a caring mother's natural reaction. Your tit-for-tat rejection, however, will only push her further from your son. If it's true, let her know how you struggle with the same behaviors at home. Strive to be empathic, sympathetic, and constructive.

Keep a balanced view. When a mother knows her child is having difficulty at school, she is apt to focus on that, taking an inventory of how the teacher treated him on a daily basis. Give it a break. Instead, help your child see what he might do to get along with his teacher.

Seek help. If your best efforts don't help, speak to the school counselor or principal.

Fight, as your last resort. Working to get along is generally the best approach, but sometimes it isn't possible. In these unfortunate situations, children deserve to be with a teacher who'll give them a fair chance.

than with the reality of his being an attorney (something you might actually know nothing about). What is so special about Harvard, Stanford, or Duke? They are good schools, but so are lots of other colleges and universities. It is a sin that so many bright young high school seniors feel like second-class citizens because they didn't get into this or that school, a school that may have been a parent's dream much more than their own. What matters is the wish to learn and to succeed. Without that, it doesn't matter where your son goes to college.

And last, as mental health professionals, we have seen too many children who, after half-hearted and party-filled high school careers, go off to a 40K-a-year college to do more of the same. America, we think, has a hang-up with higher education and keeping up with Japan, much to our children's detriment. Many young men would be happier and more productive learning trades and crafts that pay well, are important to their community, and will bring them satisfaction. Any parent lucky enough to have money to put in a college fund might consider redirecting it to savings, to some day

Nurturing Giftedness

In nearly every community, the athletically talented child is recognized and given opportunities to excel. But boys who are gifted in other areas often go unnoticed and unnurtured, sometimes even feeling ashamed of their interests. Urge your school to offer your son the stimulation and challenge he craves. And help him to own and pursue his talents, be they musical, artistic, or intellectual. Because these gifts are frequently not adequately supported in our schools, you may also have to do some research to find people and programs that can support and fulfill your son's gifted needs.

help their son start a business or buy a home when he has a family of his own. College is a wonder for many boys; for others it is another four years of boredom, frustration, and indirection, an ill-advised and wasteful detour in their life's path.

Is learning important? Absolutely. But real learning can take many different forms as your son grows to manhood. He can learn from his friends, from his athletic experiences, from a good book, and from you, as well as from schools and colleges. Listening with your heart, paying attention, knowing just who your son is becoming, and gently guiding and encouraging both his academic and his personal growth will keep him on track for a lifetime of true success.

CHAPTER 12

Men 'Round
the House

Optimizing the Influence
of Ex-Husbands, Boyfriends,
and Other Male Role Models

No matter how loving, committed, and effective a single mother is, her son will still look for and to men in his life. The boy whose parents are divorced usually has a relationship with his father, for good or bad, that continues to be important to him. A boy can have relationships with the men his mother dates. Even the boy who never knew his father or whose mother doesn't date usually has an interest in men. How could he not? After all, he is male, too.

Whether boys need men in their lives is not our debate. We agree with the mainstream thinking that they do. Our focus is on finding ways to help your son enjoy the male influence he needs while staying true to the lifestyle and choices that you value. In this chapter, we look at the role of the men in your life and your son's: the lovely ex-husband, a divorced dead-beat dad, a new romantic interest, the soccer coach, the grandfather, or the neighbor downstairs. These men exist in the life of almost every boy. What can you do to help make their impact on your son a positive one?

Collaborating with Good Enough Ex-Husbands and Fathers Who Don't Live In

Some rare and fortunate women are divorced from impeccable husbands and fathers. Many more women, divorced or separated, once lived and still deal with men who, despite their marital problems, are pretty good or at least workable fathers, men who continue to love and support their sons. The number of women who've had sons with men they neither wed nor lived with is increasing also.

Coparenting—a challenge for happy couples who share a home—can be difficult with a man who lives in another apartment or house and for whom you may have complex and painful feelings. But it's a responsibility that must be faced. A divorced mother knows the potential fallout of divorce. She doesn't need any book to tell her that her son's psychological health heavily depends on how ably she navigates and negotiates post-divorce family life. What can she do to keep a divorce from disrupting the relationship between her son and his father?

Compartmentalize

By this awkward term, we mean separate your own feelings from your son's feelings about his father. This is undoubtedly easier said than done. How can you admire and appreciate the love your ex shows your son, when he so mistreated you? How can you calmly discuss the vacation he's planning to take with your son to Europe when you can't afford a weekend at a Budget Inn? How can you acknowledge and support his fathering when all he ever did was put down your mothering?

Sustaining your son's healthy relationship with his father may require setting aside your own pride and hurt. It isn't necessary or realistic to turn your other cheek or make believe that nothing happened during the time you spent with your ex. Compartmentalizing means creating space in your psyche and parenting life for both your experience and your son's. It means honoring the fact that while you may not love the father of your son or respect his choices, your son has a separate relationship with him, and that this relationship is a powerful and important aspect of your boy's life.

Put on More Objective Glasses

Although we all view the world subjectively, mothers can and often should attempt to see their sons' fathers as clearly and objectively as they can. The relationship between a man and a woman is a complex one, and anger and bitterness sometimes form just as strong a bond as did love. When you are blinded and consumed by your own feelings for your son's father, you may be unable to accurately assess what he is actually doing. Your own hurt and frustration can lead you to misread his actions and intentions.

> A divorced mother knows the potential fallout of divorce. She doesn't need any book to tell her that her son's psychological health heavily depends on how ably she navigates and negotiates post-divorce family life.

For instance, is your ex really giving your son spending money on the weekend just to undermine you, or is he genuinely trying to make your son happy? Perhaps he is even trying to teach your son financial management skills. Try to be candid with yourself. Do you genuinely believe it is coddling when your ex effectively works with your son on his history project, or are you upset that your son won't let you within a mile of his homework? Maybe your son talks openly to his father, not, as you want to think, because he's indulged, but because his father is better at listening than you are.

Of course, some of your suspicions and less generous assumptions may be true and may require that you intervene. Many of your concerns, however, will fall to the wayside when you can entertain other possibilities. A man who was a lousy husband may still be a caring father, even when his parenting style differs from yours. Confessing to yourself the personal hurts and anger you really feel can lift the fog, allowing you to see your ex-husband's fathering more objectively and to recognize when action on your part may be called for.

Be Flexible

A single mother, overwhelmed and fatigued by her responsibilities, can understandably resent it when her son's father does not do as he should—for example, when he brings their son home an hour late from a weekend visit. But again, take a look into your own heart. Are you truly being inconvenienced? Or do you feel resentful because he doesn't obediently honor your requests? Are you fearful that he is trying to steal your son's affection? Few things, and few people, are all good or evil. The same ex-husband who is always late may also be supportive of your desire to return to school or exceptionally generous with child support.

In the best of worlds, parenting partners complement each other. You may be more reliable or effective about one aspect of your son's life, but be less so with another, one where your ex shines. We know there are impossible fathers. We leave them for another discussion. The average, good-enough father typically has strengths and weaknesses that complement his ex-wife's, his son's good-enough mother.

Most single mothers can admit sometimes fearing that their sons will prefer to be with their fathers. Mothers worry that they might lose the boys who mean so much to them. The insecurity these mothers feel can lead them to see every action of their ex in the worst possible light and to create damaging and painful divided loyalties for their sons. A mother who demands that everything happen on her terms can miss seeing what her boy really wants or needs. Her inflexibility can strain her working relationship with her ex, show her son that she is rigid, and teach him to be the same. Collaboration takes cooperation and compromise, action that can be a lot to ask of a stressed-out single mother.

Give Credit Where It's Due

We know. Your ex may never have made you feel loved. He may be poor at acknowledging all that you do. Worse, he might be a critical you-know-what. All the same, you and your son will fare better when you are free to do what you think is right and best for your son. If you know that your ex loves the son you share, don't question or attack his devotion just because you are mad about something else, including what he says to you. That is a low and unfair blow. Should your ex be handling sex talks well, let him know you respect and appreciate the difficult task he's doing. Giving him credit takes nothing from you, nor does it weaken your status or position. In fact, supporting your son's relationship with a loving and effective father is likely to increase your boy's respect for and trust in you. Appreciating good fathering only increases the likelihood that it will continue.

Think and work optimistically, taking each day as a new beginning. Divorced spouses often hold grudges and bring them up over and over. This process is rarely the best use of your limited emotional energy. If you can't let past grievances go for your own sake, let them go for your son's well-being.

It also helps to recognize that your son and his father must work out their own relationship. Perhaps your ex-husband has a history of expecting too much from your son academically. It is almost always more effective to help your son find ways to talk about his feelings with his father than to step in and lecture or rebuke your ex yourself. It is highly unlikely that you will ever change your ex (if you could have, wouldn't you still be together?), but you can certainly let him know that you appreciate his efforts to be a good father.

Setting yourself up as the perfect mother by implication puts your ex in a one-down position. Should he admit a parenting misstep to you, let him know that you struggle, too, and that you know how bad it feels to mess up. Focus on finding solutions to the problem, not figuring out who to blame. Such generosity of spirit can only come back to reward you in the way he fathers the son you both love. Mothers who adopt this strategy find that it liberates them and that they feel pride in doing what is best for their son, rather than doing what is easiest or feels best at the moment.

Leave Loyalty to the Royal Family

Almost every married parent has known the agony of being in the doghouse and the ecstasy of being number one. The latter is a lot more fun. The former can be unbearable. Being runner-up is even tougher for a single mother.

A single mother has pretty much given up her life for her son, and most of her waking energy goes to caring and providing for him. Or so it seems. She does all the hard stuff, too. She's the disciplinarian. She's the one who hammers home the importance of studying and practicing trombone, habits she knows her son will one day thank her for instilling. She's the one who bothers to oversee the videos he watches, even giving up her favorite programs because, she judges, they don't suit her son's young eyes.

Meanwhile, her ex gets to be the good guy, the good cop to her bad cop. He serves pizza in front of the television and lets their son stay up school nights till midnight. He offers unlimited video rentals every Saturday. How can she compete, and why wouldn't she want to be her son's favorite? With all she does, is that too much to ask?

A mother's wish to be the favored parent is human, but it can create problems for the son she loves. Her son has a second parent whom he loves and who loves him, and that's the way it should remain after the divorce. It's a rare mother who doesn't intellectually agree with this. But honoring her son's love for his father in real life can threaten a single mother.

—◦◦◦—

Anthony, nine years old, sat on the couch in the therapist's office, twisting the hem of his sweatshirt between his fingers. "I sorta lied to my mom," he said uncomfortably. "I spent the weekend with my dad, and we had a great time. We worked on his motorcycle and then we watched a movie with his new girlfriend. She's really cool. But when I went home, I told my mom that I didn't have much fun."

Anthony sighed. "I'm all she's got, and I don't want to hurt her feelings. I don't want her to think I love my dad more than her. I love both my folks, but sometimes it just gets so complicated!"

—◦◦◦—

Boys go through developmental phases during which they idealize their fathers. This adoration says more about the child's psychological needs than about the father's qualities. Such periods are sometimes accompanied by a devaluing of mothers and are part of a boy's struggle with his dependence on his mother, and his natural desire to be more grown up and independent. Sons of divorce often treat the out-of-the-home father better than the full-time mother. But that is little consolation to a mother who feels shoved aside and taken for granted. However much a mother may understand it, being the chopped liver behind the filet mignon feels lousy. When she is in this painful position, why wouldn't she wonder what the point of it all is?

Nor is it fair to expect your son to share your perspective or your battles with your ex-husband. Social psychologists have shown that even more than wanting people we love to like those we like, we want them to hate those we hate. Sharing enemies is a powerful bond. But expecting or demanding such loyalty from a son can be terribly destructive. Mothers who try to turn sons against their fathers nearly always lose. "Winning" comes at a terrible cost for a boy. And should a mother succeed in persuading her son of a good father's "badness," she may do more damage than just depriving him of a good father. Because a boy often internalizes and identifies with his father, she may convince her son that he is bad, too, and that she never loved him either.

Children have the capacity to love many adults and to keep their roles straight. What children hate is having to choose between the adults they love. Wise parents never ask their children to choose.

Keep the Peace

Seventh-grade Kirin suffered splitting migraines that no medicine could touch. Although he had been a gifted student, he no longer cared about school. A fine athlete, he'd quit sports. He knew exactly why. His parents had been divorced two years earlier, but they still fought as fiercely as they did when married. They argued over everything, at every transition between the two homes. They didn't care if Kirin and his sister heard their cruel words and ugly accusations. Family therapy was recommended repeatedly, but his divorced parents couldn't put down their swords long enough to do any constructive work.

It took Kirin's suicide attempt to grab their attention. But sadly, even that truce didn't last. As soon as Kirin was released from the hospital, his parents' battling resumed.

—⟪⟫—

Anyone who has taken a history class or who owns a television should realize what civil war does to a country and its people. Kirin and his sister were virtually prisoners in the ongoing war between his parents. And *war* is not too strong a word here. Because of their own personalities and their own egocentricity, they were unwilling or unable to stop fighting. Their wish to protect

Kirin, even when they saw his pain, could not overcome their deep sense of injury and need to fight back against each other. Obviously, the physical and legal separation of divorce had done little to ease the twisted psychic tie that still bound them.

Subjecting a child to this kind of trauma, though common, is indefensible. Save your frustrations for later. Refuse to fight. No one can carry on an extended battle single-handedly. Let your ex have the last word, while

> Sharing enemies is a powerful bond. But expecting or demanding such loyalty from a son can be terribly destructive. Mothers who try to turn sons against their fathers nearly always lose.

you secretly congratulate yourself for being more grown up and a better parent for doing so. Prepare yourself for his using the provocative phrase that always gets you, and when you hear it, ignore it. Be the grown-up. Make sure that you aren't the instigator or the one to pour gasoline over a dying skirmish. Think of your child. Keep a picture of your son handy so you can look at it in heated moments; let it remind you of why you need to get a grip and let the argument go for now. Harsh as it may sound, think of your son all grown up, ruined from this fighting. If you can't stop yourself from waging war, get professional help.

Keep in mind that these strategies are meant for you, a single mother. We realize how frustrated you might feel by being asked to do more, especially if your son's father causes the problems. But who else can we appeal to? The fathers who need to hear this are probably not reading our book.

You likely have tried to change the men in your life for years, and to little avail. You may believe you don't need to change because your ex-husband contributes 90 percent to the problem. If so, you are doing yourself a disservice. Looking at your own 10 percent is always worthwhile and can bring surprising changes, not just to you but to him—and most especially, to your son. Of course, if you feel it is just too unfair, or you are determined to let *him* change first, this discussion will not help you.

Contending with Bad Fathers
If you choose, you can foster your son's relationship with his father. When fathers feel validated as worthwhile and valuable, many respond and improve. Sadly, though, some fathers are too toxic, neglectful, or abusive to be tolerated or waited out—fathers who betray custody settlements and who don't pay a dime of support. There are fathers who drink away their salaries. Other fathers beat and molest their sons, smoke dope with or buy booze for their sons and sons' friends. These situations are so extreme that a mother must protect her son, even if the boy protests.

Then there are the less dramatic horrors, such as fathers who deliberately undermine mothers' efforts to raise decent and caring sons. Some fathers go off to pursue their own business or social pleasure, leaving their young sons in the care of unknown or undependable people. Other fathers cancel weekend visits so they can carouse with pals or girlfriends, or they set bad examples, teaching their sons how to cheat and lie. Some fathers, starting new families with younger women, have dismissed their original children as second-class citizens, inconveniences they no longer need. Certain fathers, themselves unable to hold jobs, encourage their sons to screw up in school, condone their sons' defiance of teachers, and distract their sons from homework. There are fathers who simply vanish from their sons' lives.

This subject merits an entire book. Collaborating with a good, willing man and father can be sufficiently difficult. These bad fathers need more than just a little shaping. Do whatever you must to protect your son. Get support and help from family, friends, clergy, or professionals. If your son's health or safety is at risk, call the appropriate child protection authorities. Do something and do it today.

Boyfriends

Single mothers who date often worry about the effects of their choices on their sons. They don't want to harm their sons. Nor are they willing to go without romance and companionship. After all, just because a woman is a mother doesn't mean she must give up adult love. But what are the repercussions when some man plunks himself down in your son's life? The following steps can help to make your boyfriend more of an asset than a liability to your son.

Go Slow

The oldest advice is both the wisest and, often, the hardest to follow, especially if you are lonely and stressed. But the wrong male role model can do more damage to your son than no role model at all. In fact, statistics show that the risk of sexual molestation or child abuse rises when unrelated males live in a household with a woman and her children. A man who takes advantage of you, is physically or verbally abusive, or cannot treat you and your son with respect and kindness will not make your son healthier or your home happier. It pays to take your time, to be healthy yourself, and to look for mutual trust and respect.

Though initially comforting, rushing into a new romance can quickly bring its own strain and may lead to more pain and another failed relationship. For your son's sake, beware of rushing to find him a father figure. Anything worthwhile, including a boyfriend or a relationship, waits and lasts.

Balance Your Own and Your Son's Interests

Some single mothers are fortunate. The boyfriends they choose are good with and are liked by their sons. But some less lucky single mothers find themselves in a dilemma. Although we hope no mother picks or stays with a boyfriend who is bad for her son, we know that choosing a man solely as a good "father" can have its downside, too. Enduring an unsatisfying relationship for your son's sake deprives you of your needs, and lacking the support and love you need can stress your parenting. Also, you may come to resent your son for the misery and sacrifice you experience. Look for someone you like, who treats you well, and who is both a good-enough man and one who is motivated to be a positive influence on your son.

Don't Forget Your Son

Boyfriends can be preoccupying. Troubled or emotionally demanding relationships can consume a single mother's attention even when her boyfriend isn't around, leaving her less energy for her son. New and positive relationships likewise can preoccupy a mother. Although single mothers are only human and need to have space for their own relationships and time to assess their own honest reactions to these, they sometimes need to observe the effects on their sons, too.

Is your son's jealousy or resentment all in his head or is it justified? Are you always with your boyfriend or, when you're not, on the telephone talking with or about him? And if your boyfriend has little tolerance for your relationship with your son, it is probably a harbinger of troubling things to come.

When you begin a new relationship, it is usually helpful to create opportunities to listen to your son, both to his words and to his behavior. Spending one-on-one time with him on a regular basis can reassure him that he still has your love and attention and can help you know what to do to keep that connection strong. To children, attention and time are powerful measures of love and belonging. Being sure your son gets his share of your love and attention will prevent him from feeling undue resentment for the new man in your life.

Be Patient About Boyfriend–Son Connections
Your son does not need to meet or approve of everyone you date. Plan your dates to accommodate your son's needs and schedule and to allow for your social life without compromising your mothering. Let your son meet a boyfriend when you know that the relationship will be more than a night or two out on the town. Encourage their getting to know each other gradually, as your own relationship with this man grows. Although you may feel quick rapture, it is unfair to invite a child to become attached to a man who might well be out of the picture in a week or a month.

> The wrong male role model can do more damage to your son than no role model at all. In fact, statistics show that the risk of sexual molestation or child abuse rises when unrelated males live in a household with a woman and her children.

Consider that if a woman dates just one new man every six months, her son could lose more than a hundred father figures during his childhood. Respect your son's wishes as well. If he doesn't want to meet or connect with this man quite yet, don't force him to. It is usually much better to work toward respect and kindness than to insist on affection or love between your son and your new partner.

Be Discreet
You need not be deceitful or sneaky, for neither traits have a place in good relationships. But a single mother

who dates must be reasonably protective of her son's welfare, while managing the time that she needs with a boyfriend. Don't subject your son to frequent sleepovers with different men or in-your-face affection on the couch. This can be too stimulating, confusing, and destructive. Remember, too, that your own behavior is a powerful teacher. If you enjoy casual relationships, it is unwise and unfair to expect your son to avoid them.

Organize trysts out of your son's view, especially early in a relationship. Don't kid yourself that just because he doesn't see you in the act, he can't figure out what's going on. Make a boyfriend part of your home—that is, invite him to move in—only when you've gotten to know him well, believe there is promise in the relationship, have seen that he treats you and your son well, and know that your son is comfortable with him. And always, be aware of what your own choices teach your son.

Listen to Your Son
Give your son ample opportunity to share his feelings about your boyfriends and love life. Listen well and respect what he says. This doesn't mean using your son as your romantic consultant. Though good for movie plots, that is an inappropriate job for a son.

Listen closely if your son tells you that he doesn't like this man or thinks your boyfriend mistreats you. Do your best to understand where your son's distress comes from. Is it simple jealousy over a man in your life or a sense of disloyalty to his biological father? Or, in fact, does he see something that you are too close to or too blinded by love to see? Make your son's feelings and beliefs part of the equation, but make it clear that he does not necessarily have veto power.

Establish and Maintain Your Authority
Don't allow a new boyfriend to disturb the equilibrium you've established. Even as you nurture a social life, maintain the same limits, reliability, and availability that have served your son so well. Make it clear to boyfriends, too, that you are in charge of your home. If you don't allow your 12-year-old to watch R-rated movies, don't back down because a boyfriend insists on watching whatever he pleases, regardless of whether your son is there or not.

Single mothers sometimes believe that a man, any man, automatically knows more about discipline than she does and may give in too easily to a newcomer's opinions of her son's behavior. It should come as no surprise that most boys deeply resent the efforts of newcomers and strangers to control their behavior. In fact, when a new partner tries to step in and act like a dad too soon, even with the best of intentions, your son may respond with defiance, resentment, and more misbehavior.

You are your son's parent. Until the relationships between you and your boyfriend and between your boyfriend and your son are stable and healthy, it is probably best if you continue to set limits and follow through. Your watchfulness and instincts will tell you how trustworthy and capable a boyfriend is and when he has earned the privilege and right to exercise some parental authority.

If your boyfriend is a good man, instances will inevitably arise when he has opinions to offer that will benefit your son and maybe even improve your mothering. But in general, it's fair for you to expect your boyfriend to follow your rules and wishes concerning your son. After all, who knows your son better than you?

Be Careful

You've worked hard to get you and your son where you are. Be cautious about letting boyfriends change your family's direction. Guard your resources. Be wary of lending boyfriends money, for example, when you can barely get by as it is. Don't expect a boyfriend to change for you. If you find yourself having to care for a boyfriend as if he were another child, you might want to keep looking. Don't overlook suspicions or worries about this man, however much in love you feel. If you are afraid to ask questions of a boyfriend or he won't allow it, you are with the wrong man. If he mistreats you, you owe it to yourself and your son to get away from him.

Think Twice About Remarriage

You think the 50-plus percent divorce rate of first marriages is high? That's better than the more than 70 percent of second marriages that fail. Like it or not, the odds are stacked against you if you remarry. Most divorced men and women don't learn enough from their first marriage to succeed at their second. If you are contemplating remarriage, we have three pieces of advice: (1) go slow; (2) go slower, and (3) go slower yet.

Remember that you will not change your boyfriend. If he is far from what you want or need, if he is not good with your son, it will only get worse. For all of our psychological theories and optimism, history remains the best predictor of behavior. A man who meets you while cheating on his wife might just cheat on you. Beware of a man who showers you and your son with instant attention, while abandoning his three children from a previous marriage. People who easily leave children and wives are apt to repeat the pattern.

> Like it or not, the odds are stacked against you if you remarry. Most divorced men and women don't learn enough from their first marriage to succeed at their second.

Yes, people can change. Let a boyfriend prove himself over time before you commit your life and family. And don't neglect to look in the mirror. What have you done, what growth have you made to give you hope that this marriage will work? Painful and discouraging as it might be, the single mother who can be most honest with herself here will fare the best, as will her son.

Do stepfamilies and remarriages ever work out? Of course, they do. But most remarrying couples face obstacles in learning to deal peacefully with differing parenting styles, getting along with their various ex-partners, handling money, deciding where to live, and resolving the many issues that arise when children from different families must live with and accept new parents and each other. If you are considering remarriage, seek out a skilled therapist who deals with stepfamily issues, look into the many books and Internet resources (the Stepfamily Association of America Web site contains much information and a good resource list), and take your time.

Mentors and Role Models

Even boys who grow up with good fathers enjoy time with other men in their lives—grandfathers and uncles, coaches, teachers, the retired fireman down the street. It's natural and usually a good arrangement. So, why wouldn't sons whose fathers are divorced, unavailable, dead, or unknown do the same, perhaps even more?

Good father figures, so-called "role models," can do a lot for a boy. Every girl knows how important it is to have someone she can talk to, look up to, and identify with, someone who believes in her. And so do boys. In addition, sons of single mothers need men who have grown and succeeded to show them the way and to allow them to know in their gut that being male is a good thing.

Many boys find such role models on their own as they go through life. In such cases, all their mothers need do is respect and appreciate what those relationships mean and try to nourish them. Some boys, however, are not adept at finding such men. Boys who don't play sports or who are shy may have less opportunity to engage with healthy men in their lives. Although mothers cannot engineer friendships for their sons, they can certainly create opportunities for those friendships to happen.

If your son lacks the presence of healthy men in his life, consider finding time for him to join a community

Creating a Working Partnership

Whether you are dealing with an ex-partner or building a relationship with a new boyfriend, the following issues frequently become points of contention in raising children. Sit down with your partner, your ex, or, if necessary, a mediator, and give some thought to these questions. Having a well-thought-out plan will save you and your son a great deal of hassle.

- *Visitation.* Where does your son spend time? When? Having a consistent plan makes life easier for everyone.
- *Discipline.* Who is responsible for setting limits, for assigning chores, and for following through?
- *Vacations.* Can you or your ex take your child out of state without prior agreement?

or faith-related youth group, sports activities, or a chess or camping club. You can encourage your son to enjoy outings with his friends and their fathers. You can even sign him up for Big Brothers of America or another organized mentoring organization. Even the best mother can't quite know what it's like to be a growing boy or a grown man. This is, obviously, not your fault, but it may motivate you to create time and space for your son to explore relationships with other men. These relation-

- *Activities.* Who decides which activities a child will participate in? Who will transport and who will pay?
- *Religious training.* In what faith will your son be raised?
- *School.* Who has access to academic records? Who will supervise homework or grades?
- *Child care.* Who decides where and when a child receives child care? Who is allowed to drop off or pick up your son? Who selects baby sitters? When is it okay for your son to stay home alone?
- *Insurance.* Who will maintain medical insurance for your son? When he is old enough, how will you arrange for car insurance, and who will pay for it?

(For more information on coparenting, see Isolina Ricci, Ph.D.'s excellent and pragmatic book *Mom's House, Dad's House: Creating Two Homes for Your Children*, New York: Fireside, 1997.)

ships can not only benefit your son, they can provide you with ideas, energy, and support when you most need them.

A relationship with the wrong man—for you or for your son—has the potential to harm you both, and it is wise to be cautious. But a good relationship with a good man can do a lot for a growing boy, just as a loving and respectful relationship with the right partner can do a lot for a woman. To support such a relationship, or to help her son find one, is a healthy and worthy effort for a single mother. Such a healthy relationship can enhance not only a boy's journey toward manhood but a mother's own relationship with her son.

CHAPTER 13

MotherVision

Knowing Yourself and
Your Blind Spots

What we see is colored by what we think and feel. Psychologists rely on this principle when they hold up their Rorschach inkblots. Different people will look at the same blob of ink and see astonishingly different things: leaping lions and forlorn ballerinas. Pieces of a shredded tulip and a rotting castle. A monster, a baby, a bat. That people see virtually anything and everything in those vague and diffuse inkblots proves that the images must come from inside the person. Where else could they come from?

Now try it another way. Close your eyes. Do *not* think of a white bear. Most people find that try as they might, that white bear just insists on wandering into their mind. Our feelings and thoughts do indeed shape much of the way we see the world around us and reveal a great deal about the way we experience the world and ourselves. These different experiences and viewpoints, which are sometimes called perception, have a powerful influence on how we feel, what we believe, and how we choose to behave. In fact, it has been said that no two people have ever read exactly the same book, seen the same movie, or been in the same relationship. The reason? Each person's unique perception is shaped by his own feelings, thoughts, beliefs, and decisions. The difficulty arises when we assume, as we all do from time to time, that other people's perceptions are the same as our own.

When you feel joyous, you may see promise in the same untended garden that only last week, when you felt discouraged and weary, looked so irreversibly barren. It's more than just a matter of attitude. The pessimist actually *sees* a glass that is more empty than full; the optimist sees the same glass as being just the opposite; and each is certain that what she sees is truth, is reality.

Each human being has what might be called a separate reality, and this is true for all people, whether in or out of therapy, whether mothers or fathers, whether married or single. It is true, too, when the objects of our attention happen to be the objects of our affection—the sons we love.

Let's look at ways in which your *MotherVision*, your unique perception of your son and yourself, can make itself known.

Who Is Your Son?

Paint a word picture of your son. Take your time and use a fine brush.

Now stand back and look at the portrait you've created. Is that the boy you know each day? Or is your painting idealized, the boy you wish you had, or perhaps the boy or child you wish you had been. Or is it, more sadly, too bleak a portrait, too negative, missing your son's good qualities, perhaps qualities that just happen not to turn you on. Who is your son, really?

—⟨∽∾⟩—

Will was a good and hardworking student. He played varsity soccer and lacrosse and was a member of several school clubs, including the school newspaper and the debating society. He also served as junior class secretary. Though on paper he couldn't have been more involved, his teachers and coaches saw no spark in his eye, no passion for any of his interests.

Still, Will's mother believed her boy was everything a son should be. A shy woman, she hadn't participated in any extra activities at school, something she still regretted. To her pleasure, Will was spending his high school years just the way she'd wished she'd spent hers.

—⟨∽∾⟩—

Too enraptured with the son she needed to see, the active, happy student she wished she'd been, Will's mother didn't see the emptiness and depression that others saw. Nor did she see how his over-involvement was his way of pleasing her and bringing her to life.

When Will's mother discovered an empty vodka bottle in her car's trunk, she had to face what was truly happening. As a result, Will discovered the freedom to do less, while pursuing the activities that he really cared about with more zest and depth. By grieving the busy and accomplished childhood she'd never had, and by no longer relying on Will to satisfy her own longings, his mother found the energy to begin hobbies and college courses she'd believed it was too late for.

It can be a sobering experience to remove your MotherVision glasses and see your son clearly for the first time. But if you can find the courage, there may be no greater way to draw you closer together. Loving a son means loving the person he truly is, rather than loving an image that exists only in your own imagination. Real, flesh-and-blood boys have both strengths and weaknesses. They are like their mothers in some ways and very much unlike them in others. A clear-eyed mother will see who her son *is*, rather than see only what he does.

> Loving a son means loving the person he truly is, rather than loving an image that exists only in your own imagination.

Misreading Behavior

Jared had always been a quiet boy, one who seemed most comfortable when watching from the sidelines. He was liked by his peers, but was no social butterfly, though he did have a few long-standing and good friendships.

His mother wanted more for him. Tracy could see how lonely he was for more friends and how bored he was during evenings and on the weekends. She saw the phone ring off the hook for her daughter, but not for Jared. It broke her heart. So Tracy pushed him to join sports teams, Boy Scouts, and community youth programs. Though Jared disliked all of these activities and none made him more socially eager, his mother insisted that he stay with them. These, she was certain, would make Jared more happily involved with more people.

—◦◦◦—

It took an angry outburst from Jared for his mother to understand him and his behavior. "I like being alone," he screamed. "I like time to just hang by myself and to think about whatever I want to. Just because you need to be with someone every second, doesn't mean I do. And it doesn't make me a bad person either!"

Jared's words shocked his mother, but she was wise enough to learn from them. Never having learned to like her own company, she couldn't see that her son had. What she read as loneliness, something to be remedied, was instead a healthy capacity for being alone and a developmental achievement to be respected.

Is your adopted three-year-old rejecting you, or is that just the way you see his growing need to explore the world? Is your son's temper as explosive as it appears, or does your fear magnify what is a reasonable display of justifiable anger? You may benefit by looking and thinking twice before believing that you know for sure what a behavior means.

Of course, no mother, no matter how perceptive and loving, is a mind reader. A solid knowledge of both your son's development and his temperament will help you decipher his behavior. It also may set your mind at rest to check in occasionally with your son to be sure you understand *his* perception of his behavior.

Although sometimes boys just don't want to talk, especially about feelings, letting your son know that you notice his behavior (and asking with gentle curiosity what it means to him) can send him the message that you care and are paying attention. If he tells you that he's happy, it is often wisest to believe him, unless other evidence appears to the contrary.

All Behaviors Are Not Created Equal

Parents are prone to equate behaviors. Even when these look the same, however, similar behaviors are seldom equal. When your son curses at you (for not buying him the $150 sneakers), it is not the same as cursing at you (for calling him a dork), is not the same as cursing at the television newscaster (for reporting that his favorite team lost a game), is not the same as cursing to a friend (who dumped water on him), is not the same as cursing into thin air (after shutting the window on his own thumb). Though the expletive was the same in every instance, its meaning in each context varied substantially.

Your son might give you the cold shoulder when he's angry at you. But he might also be silent when he is tired, is preoccupied, or just feels quiet. Same behavior, different cause. If you make assumptions about your son's feelings based only on nonverbal behaviors such as facial expressions, phrases, or actions—his rolling eyes, for example—you will often be mistaken. You can use simple active listening to check out what is really going on for your son (e.g., "You look worried.").

Our Ears Are Only Human

Vision is not the only sense vulnerable to distortion. Hearing is just as precarious. Think how often we accuse, or at least assume, that someone sounds angry, critical, or impatient with us. Most of us do this with some regularity and with considerable inaccuracy, putting others into unnecessarily defensive positions. In some cases, the people we love most may avoid talking with us for fear of being misunderstood.

Try asking your son what he means, rather than jumping to damning conclusions. Many times, for example, you may think your son is trying to be rude or is mad when he isn't mad at all. In fact, when given the chance, he may express his surprise and even ask for your help in giving a better impression.

Your ears also may miss the messages that your son wishes you to hear and respond to. Perhaps he tells you of his sadness that he didn't make the major league at his Little League tryouts. "There's always next year. You're only ten," you reply. Or, "But you're a great athlete. What's wrong with those coaches?" Or "Quit bellyaching. It's life, get used to it." Or even, "Did you practice your piano?" How frequently we reply thoughtlessly, wholly missing our sons' heartfelt appeals. All he wanted and needed was an empathic ear, to know you understood his feelings. He needed to see his own sadness reflected in your eyes; he needed your quiet reflection of his thoughts and feelings. And maybe even your "You must be so disappointed. You wanted majors so badly," perhaps the most comforting words you could speak.

There is an old saying that what most people really need is a good listening to. It isn't easy hearing your child's sorrow and distress. Yet being heard and truly understood is arguably the most powerful of human experiences. Your son knows, even at a boy's young age, that

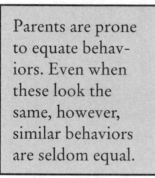

you can't get him into the majors, nor would he want you to. Nor does he want you cheering him up, for he doesn't feel cheery right now.

Parents are prone to equate behaviors. Even when these look the same, however, similar behaviors are seldom equal.

Truth is, many mothers have a large but perfectly understandable blind spot in their MotherVision. They love their sons and they want to fix their sons' difficult emotions. They want their boys to feel better. The only problem is, feelings aren't fixable by anyone other than the person who owns them.

Many a mother has sat by a son's bedside, hearing him weep for a missing father, watching him struggle to understand why he wasn't invited to his best friend's party, or, his shoulders shaking, telling how his first girlfriend dumped him for someone else. The overwhelming temptation is to offer verbal Band-Aids, to give advice or try to find the words that will make the hurt go away. But, as most mothers learn by experience, sometimes there simply aren't any.

The best response to your son's pain—as well as to his joy, frustration, or anxiety—is empathy. Ask yourself what he's feeling, then let him know you understand. Sometimes a hug or a hand on the shoulder is more effective than even the best words. There's plenty of time, too, for reminding him of his past achievements or all the good things that might happen tomorrow. All he wants now is to know that you, possibly the person he loves more than anyone in the world, get it, that you know why he hurts. There is no closer sharing between two people.

Devil-Making

Listening to Naomi talk, it was hard to believe that any seven-year-old could be so awful. And it wasn't just his misbehavior, somewhat routine for a young boy. She described his maliciousness: "There's nothing he loves more than irritating me." Naomi related as well how Justin had told her he hated her and how she'd replied that she regretted the day she'd adopted him. "It was just a huge mistake," she said. "A huge mistake."

———

Naomi didn't hate Justin any more than he hated her. They were stuck in a terrible and painful place. Sure, Justin could be a pain, a big pain. But the problem lay more with Naomi's perception of Justin's behavior. She interpreted his digging for worms as sadistic destruction of her garden, rather than natural curiosity. His attempts to make them lunch she saw as an excuse to mess up the kitchen that she'd cleaned all morning. His difficulty at school—later shown to be related to a learning disability—was, so she thought, intended to embarrass her with his teachers.

You could call Naomi paranoid. But she wasn't, not in that way. She saw Justin's behavior, fairly typical for an active boy his age, in an egocentric way. Locked into that perspective, she interpreted Justin's behavior as being somehow aimed at her. Once she came to see that everything he did wasn't about her and that he could have other motives, too, she began to see him and his behavior as less devious and sometimes even as well-intentioned.

Putting your son into neat categories, though simpler, makes for overly rigid and unresponsive mothering. Seeing your son as being bad and treating him that way can lead him to become the very bad boy you originally mistook him for. Even making an angel of your son, though better than creating devils, will impede your being able to see and raise him as the more complex person he is.

Seeing What We Want to See

It's as tragic as it is common: parents who didn't see the hints of a deep depression and wish to die that were strewn everywhere. Or who dismissed repeated failing progress notes and report cards from school as "a phase." Or who went along with their sons' assertions of just keeping the pipes and dope for a friend. Yes, those are extreme instances, but that's where this particular blind spot does the most damage.

Psychoanalysts call it denial. Cognitive scientists call it selective attention. Our grandfathers called it playing ostrich. Regardless of what we name it, refusing to see that our children or we ourselves are in trouble is dangerous. As understandable as our shame and reluctance to face the truth can be, there is never any good excuse for looking the other way. Help and a solution are almost always closer than imagined.

If you suspect that your son is in trouble—if his behavior has become unusually aggressive or withdrawn, if his grades are falling, if he adopts new friends you know little about, or he avoids activities he used to enjoy—do not hesitate to ask for help. Talk to a skilled therapist, a pastor, or a trusted friend. Yes, your son may object, but you may also save both of you much sorrow and struggle.

Weaving Virtue

Many of us not only see just what we want to see in others, we also manage to see only the aspects of ourselves that we choose. We are not cheap, we convince ourselves; we are frugal. We aren't afraid of our children and their displeasure; we just have good reasons to believe in a permissive household. We are not critical, even though everyone tells us we are; we have high standards. Like the alchemists who tried to make gold from lead, parents often try to turn their own shortcomings into virtues.

———◦◦◦◦———

Linda sometimes wondered whether Eli had been born worried. Having tried unsuccessfully to conceive for years with her ex-boyfriend and having adopted Eli on her own, her son was every-thing to her. Ever fearful of losing him, she hovered around him like a human bubble. Linda's vigilance succeeded only in making Eli an extraordinarily anxious kindergartner who feared being kid-napped, dying in his sleep, choking on grapes, being molested, contracting AIDS, and eating poison, just to name a few. A preco-cious reader, he used his skills to read labels in a search for food dyes and saturated fats, and he'd reduced his diet to bottled water and a few foods he could trust.

———◦◦◦◦———

Linda dearly loved Eli, and she did indeed fear los-ing him. But she didn't see herself as overly sheltering, smothering, or a worrier. She saw herself as a sensible parent who had an uncanny concern for safety. To her, wearing shoes in the house, in case there was a staple ly-ing about (which, she thought, could get into the blood-stream), was prudent. She believed that those who went barefoot were the foolish ones. As long as Linda viewed her own behavior as a virtue and not a problem, nothing would change.

But a vacation weekend with a friend and her chil-dren forced the issue. Eli could not eat, play, sleep, or do anything else like the "normal" children they traveled with. Breaking down with her friend, Linda admitted that *everything* scared her. "How," she asked her friend, "can you allow your children to go out in the world? So many dangers are out there." Her friend confirmed that it wasn't always easy, but that dealing with uncertainty was part of parenting.

Linda began to see that her behavior expressed her own anxiety and was not as admirable as she would have liked. She also realized that she had infected Eli with her own fear of the world around them. With this realization, she was able to see her son in a clearer light. She saw that he was much less fragile, and the world much less catastrophic, than she'd assumed. She also saw that her loving protection had ironically been "killing" and not preserving Eli, crippling his capacity to live life fully.

You can, if you choose, use your MotherVision to see yourself clearly. If you notice patterns in your son's behavior, it may be wise to ask yourself if you are contributing in any way to that behavior. If the answer is yes, recognize that change must begin with you. Learning to cope with your own fears, anger, or loneliness will give your son room to cope with his own.

Logical Versus *Psycho*logical

This distinction can be one of the subtlest and hardest to grasp.

═══∞∞∞═══

"'Cause I'm ugly!" Paul, a sixth-grader who only recently had been optimistic and well-adjusted, pointed to his mild acne. His mother had asked why he'd become so cranky and morose. "I'm stupid and I smell like shit," he added, meaning it.

"But you're a handsome boy," his mother countered, choosing for now to ignore the obscenity. "You always make honor roll and," she said, laughing, "the only time you smell is when you don't shower, just like everyone else."

"You don't get it, do you?" Paul screamed as he went out the back door, slamming it behind him.

———◦◦◦———

Paul's mother was right. Paul was good-looking, bright, and clean. She was wrong, though, in thinking she could rationally talk Paul into liking himself better. The onset of puberty—with its pimples, body odors, and expectations—was stressing him. What he needed at that moment was psychological understanding, not logical argument. If his mother had said, "You must feel awful" or given even a sympathetic shake of the head, if she had simply listened, she would have accomplished more. Paul would have felt understood and might then have been more open to hearing the factual reasons he shouldn't feel so bad.

If you suspect that your son is in trouble—if his behavior has become unusually aggressive or withdrawn, if his grades are falling, if he adopts new friends you know little about, or he avoids activities he used to enjoy—do not hesitate to ask for help.

Most people dislike hearing advice or logic when they're upset or hurt. When your son makes a statement that seems irrational to you, take a deep breath and pause before offering the three dozen reasons you think he's wrong. Listen and offer your empathy. And then, if the moment seems right, ask him, "Would you like to hear what I think?" He may say yes, in which case he'll be more willing to listen to your advice or comfort. And he may say no. If he does, smile and say, "I have faith that you can work this out. Let me know what happens." Then go for a walk, call a friend, or take a hot bath. Much like stand-up comedy, mothering a son is sometimes all about *timing*. If yours is off, your son will not hear your words, no matter how true or wise.

Perfect Parents

"You're a selfish little boy. You don't deserve to go to the circus." Five-year-old Bobby's crying and distress didn't slow his mother's tirade. "Me, me, me is all you can think about. Your mother is sick and all you can do is whine. A good boy would care about his mother, not the circus." Bobby and his flu-ridden mother spent the entire day battling.

———✺———

Bobby's single mother had planned this special outing months ago. Preoccupied for some weeks with a new baby girl, she was especially looking forward to this special day with her son. Now she felt that she'd neglected him again. Feeling too much disappointment and guilt of her own, she could not face Bobby's and condemned them both to an unnecessarily horrid day.

Like Bobby's mother, sometimes we feel so bad about ourselves that we can't bear it when our children complain about the same things that trouble us. Needing to be perfect parents and experiencing the utter shame we feel when we fall short can obstruct our ability to fully experience and learn from our parenting errors.

Mistakes, it has been said, are opportunities to learn. Rudolf Dreikurs, one of the pioneers of family therapy, spoke often of having the "courage to be imperfect"— as, indeed, we all are. If you make a mistake, fail in some way, or let your son down, perhaps the wisest and most loving thing you can do is to admit it and ask for his understanding. The hidden blessing in doing so is that you are teaching your son that it's okay to admit mistakes and ask for help, a lesson that may benefit you both as he grows up.

Blame-Throwers

Daily life is full of missteps. Some of us do not accept them as graciously or with as much humor as we might.

—◇◇◇—

Though her car was an automatic, Sandy was in overdrive. A meeting at work had run late, she'd picked up her teary four-year-old girl late from preschool, and now she was rushing her son to baseball practice. "I'm going to be the last one there," he complained. "I'm always the last one." Sandy drove even faster—until a policeman stopped her and gave her a speeding ticket.

"Look what you've done now," she screamed at her son. "I've got a hundred-dollar ticket and my insurance is going to go up. You've probably cost me five hundred dollars. Never mind your new baseball glove. We'll probably have the car taken away. Then you'll never get to another practice for the rest of your life!"

"I don't need a new glove," her son mumbled apologetically, feeling like the worst boy in the world.

"Good, 'cause you won't be getting one."

—⟨✿⟩—

It is painful even to imagine what Sandy's son was feeling and deciding about himself while listening to his frustrated mother. Sandy blamed her son for the speeding ticket and all the money it would cost her, money she didn't have. She preferred blaming him to admitting that she was stressed by a new job she'd volunteered for, that she'd gotten two other speeding tickets in the past four months (when her son wasn't in the car), and that it was she who drove the car above the speed limit. Besides unfairly chastising her son, Sandy's inability to accept responsibility for her own behavior kept her from facing ways in which her frantic lifestyle could be better managed.

Every mother has moments like this, moments when she is too frustrated, too stressed, or too anxious to be her best self. Many times you can hear the words you say to your son, and in your heart, you cringe yet are somehow unable to close your mouth. Such moments are a reminder that you must take care of yourself in order to take care of others and that maintaining your own emotional health and balance is a vital part of caring for your son. Investing time in your own welfare is not selfishness: It is wisdom.

Unique and universal in its existence, every mother's MotherVision can profoundly influence how she views her son. Since no mother has perfect MotherVision, all she can aim for is to see her son and her own mothering more clearly, so she can parent ever more effectively, genuinely, and from her heart.

CHAPTER 14

Mothering Solo

Taking Care of You

How does a woman become a single mother? Did it come about through tragedy, happenstance, or choice? Did she conceive thoughtfully or on impulse? In her teens, mid-50s, or somewhere in between? Was it an act of strength or weakness, rebellion or passivity? Was he her biological son or adopted? Did she welcome her son, or did she fear and regret her pregnancy? Each of these questions bears meaning, but in a more essential way, they are irrelevant to the reality she faces each day. For all the findings of fancy studies and pop psychology books, it comes down to this: She is a woman alone, raising a son and shaping a man's life. It is the central fact of her existence.

Taking for granted that mothering itself is a noble profession, consider for a moment other kinds of workers. Skilled electricians and carpenters, who have already experienced training and an apprenticeship, nearly always bring along a helper who stands around for those occasional instances when another arm is needed, to pull a wire along or support a joist to be hung. Executives want their secretaries, teachers have their tutors and classroom aides, and even garbage men work in pairs, helping each other with trash that is too bulky or heavy for one man to haul. Browse through the Sunday want-ads and you will find a nation of "second hands": baker's helper, dental assistant, prep cook. And these are just 40-hour-a-week jobs, unlike the "24/7" duty that single-mothering entails, especially in the early years.

Think of it. Single mothers set out to parent a child single-handedly not just for a month or a year, but possibly for a son's entire childhood. Many married parents find several hours in a single day with their own children to be too much. Want to see what relief looks like? Forget Rolaids: Observe harried married mothers when the baby-sitter finally comes, or overwhelmed fathers when their wives rescue them from a Saturday afternoon with the kids.

Going solo: When a leather-jacketed Lindbergh or Earhart does it in a plane, it is the stuff of heroic dreams. Even today, when a brave and solitary soul sails across the Pacific or peddles a bicycle through South America or trudges without oxygen up Mt. Everest, it captures our imagination. That these acts, however daunting and larger-than-life, may be full of ego, pride, and self-

centeredness (and may even waste life and limb) is ignored in this celebration of the human spirit. Meanwhile, millions of single mothers trek miles each day
with babies on their backs and groceries and diaper bags
in their arms, never getting enough sleep and yet still
cooking and cleaning and, often, working, even when
sick. Many single-mother families live in poverty or
have far less than they and their families need; many receive little sympathy and compassion. These dedicated
parents push themselves beyond human limits—not for a
week-long expedition but for months and years on
end—out of concern for their child's well-being, demon-
strating every day of their lives the real stuff of human
spirit and purpose. All too often, a single mother has to
clear an unrealistically high hurdle, be an Erin Brockovich, or mother a U.S. president to win our notice and
approval. Who are the real heroes? And whose values
are out of whack?

Doing It Alone

Although mothering by oneself undoubtedly involves
many hardships and limitations, these can be sur-
mounted and even turned to an advantage. In fact, many
single mothers are surprised to discover that parenting
solo can actually bring benefits and special joys. For this
to happen, though, requires first that we openly examine the potential hardships and pitfalls, for until a single
mother recognizes what is, she cannot truly take steps
to change or compensate for the better.

The Day-to-Day Drudgery

Some may judge as insulting and a waste of ink our bothering to highlight what must seem like a no-brainer. Single parents carry the daily work of two parents, which makes their job at best twice as hard. It's basic math. You survive on your lone income. You do all the driving, all the cooking, all the everything, not to mention the automobile repairs, snow shoveling, and home maintenance.

———✥✥✥———

"I've been the walking dead for ages," 38-year-old Teri said. "It's my own fault. No one made me. It's not Joey's fault there's only one of me to take care of him." With no time for an overdue haircut and dark shopping bags under her eyes, Teri's face mirrored her exhaustion. "I know. . . ." She paused, interrupted by a series of aching yawns, each of which she fought off. "I'm not even sure what I'm doing half the time. Have you ever driven on the highway and suddenly noticed you've gone miles without knowing it? That's how I'm mothering." She swallowed a yawn again and laughed. "On autopilot." Three-year-old Joey had fallen asleep on her chest and she didn't dare move for fear of waking him. She'd learned early on to take respite whenever or wherever it came.

———✥✥✥———

The single mother's need for sleep cannot be exaggerated. Nor can she afford to dismiss it jokingly as a "perk" of the job. Running on empty can pose great risk for both her and her son. Exhaustion is apt to compromise virtually every aspect of her mothering. She will be less patient, active, thoughtful, and resilient. She will be prone to act in ways designed just to survive the moment, rather than in ways that take charge and, with a broader perspective, master and put the moment to good use. Physical and extended exhaustion also takes its toll on a single mother's health and likely is one major reason that single mothers get sick more frequently than their married counterparts, stressing them more and fueling this unfortunate cycle.

As worrisome as fatigued performance is, however, dragging oneself from here to there and stretching the limits of one's energy invites even more profound hazards.

⸻

"I can't take it anymore. I can't." No reminders about Lorie's usually vibrant and strong mothering would help. She was beyond the comfort of words. "Michael couldn't have gotten a worse mother," she went on, sobbing and shaking. "I was the last one who should have had a child like him. He deserved a mother who had patience." For the moment, Lorie had lost sight of the everyday courage she showed in parenting the difficult child she'd had with her former husband, a man who, saying he "couldn't take it," bolted less than a year later. "Sometimes . . . sometimes I think about getting in my car, and just driving away." She buried her head. "And never," she choked on her words, "and never coming back." She pulled at her hair. "Never."

⸻

Lorie's words may sound desperate, but they are not necessarily a sign of danger or potential negligence. Lorie was as good a mother as a son could have. But

Taking Care of the Equipment: Your Physical Health

All mothers know times when they feel as if they can't stay awake another moment, walk one more step, or stand one bit more of misbehavior. Taking care of yourself involves paying as much attention to your own physical health as you do to your son's.

Try to:

Get adequate sleep. In your son's early years, this usually means sleeping whenever he does. If he takes a three-hour afternoon nap, give yourself permission to nap as well. Cleaning and cooking can wait. If you are unable to sleep soundly during the daytime, you can still curl up in a quiet corner with a cup of tea, some good music, and a book. Even a 10-minute power nap has been proven to do wonders for both our energy and our attitude.

Practice good sleep hygiene. Many mothers lie restlessly in bed, waiting for the next midnight crisis. But research tells us that lying in bed awake (as well as reading and watching television in bed) breeds sleeplessness. If you have difficulty falling

discouraged and depleted, she had less tolerance for Michael's high activity level and mischief. Sharing that frustration with an empathic and nonjudging ear was enough to begin replenishing her and restoring her perspective. Lorie was able to resume being the able mother Michael was accustomed to.

asleep or tend to lie awake and worry, get up. Sit on the sofa and read, do a quiet activity. Return to bed when you feel sleepy. And don't torture yourself by repeatedly checking the time. It only feels scarier to know that your son will be up and at 'em in three short hours.

Eat and drink well. Mothers often scrutinize their sons' food intake, while nibbling carelessly on whatever happens to be lying around the kitchen. You are the foundation on which your family depends. Eat healthful foods (remember those food groups?). Beware of drinking caffeine or alcohol late at night, as they affect your sleep cycle. Note marked changes in your appetite or sleep patterns, as they can be signals of depression.

Exercise. Research has demonstrated that moderate exercise, such as a walk after dinner, increases energy, is an effective antidepressant, and can enhance sleep. You needn't buy Spandex and a gym membership (though there's nothing wrong with that). You can do something you enjoy. Try yoga, tai chi, or dance. Or simply put your son on the back of your bicycle and explore the neighborhood.

Many single mothers live endless days of feeling themselves sucked dry by their sons' demands, needs, and wants. Much of good-enough mothering requires that a mother not be wiped out and saturated. Much of what mothers do is to hold their children. By hold, we do not simply mean the physical picking up of a child. This holding involves a deeper sense, on the child's part, of being heard and soothed, protected from not just the outside world but from his own inner anxieties and impulses.

> Many single mothers are surprised to discover that parenting solo can actually bring benefits and special joys. For this to happen, though, requires first that we openly examine the potential hardships and pitfalls, for until a single mother recognizes what is, she cannot truly take steps to change or compensate for the better.

When a mother quiets her whining baby, she does so by somehow absorbing his undifferentiated distress. And a child can tell whether mother is just mouthing the words or meaning it, and whether she really does feel his sadness or upset. But even the world's largest bath sponge can soak up only so much water; eventually, not one more drop will fit. Not until that sponge is at least partially squeezed out does it have the room to take in more. Mothers are the same way. No single mother can give and give and give of herself without growing resentful and ineffective. In other words, taking care of you is neither selfish nor a luxury; it is a wise and caring part of your mothering.

Many mothers, especially those with young children, report that feeling isolated is one of their greatest struggles. For single mothers, the problem can be even more serious. Each of us needs to be heard; being listened to cannot be overvalued in helping a single mother avoid saturation. Find someone—a friend, a family member, other single mothers, or even a therapist—who can comfortably hear your complaints, and who will not make you feel bad for feeling what you feel. All parents sometimes feel helpless and hopeless; many find themselves wishing they could do it all again, perhaps without children—and then feeling horribly guilty for having harbored such thoughts. Suppressing those feelings does little good and is likely to stress you further. When negative thoughts are brought into the light of day, they often lose their power, leaving us feeling lighter and somehow ready to take life on again.

But for all that kind listening can offer, single mothers need more. Single mothers need feeding, loving, holding, and consoling no less than the young sons who hold onto their apron strings. How you find this comfort is another question. Many single mothers seek out family, friends, and companions, but others are lonely and have little or no outside support. None of us ever seems to have enough time for simple fun, but whatever you can find will help. Begin to build yourself a network of friends and helpers; be sure you watch that one show you enjoy; and buy yourself that truffle and save it for after Junior's bedtime. Single mothers need treats, too—regularly. Consider this suggestion: Every time you find yourself thinking of something that will please or surprise your son, do something for yourself instead (or perhaps, as well). It is healthy and will help support and strengthen your mothering.

Making Decisions

Single mothers rarely feel more alone than when an important decision needs to be made—and it's up to them to make it. What's a good bedtime? Should you push the

Ways to Replenish Yourself

You wouldn't expect a car to run forever without fuel. You, too, may occasionally find yourself running on empty. Here are a few ways to energize and replenish yourself along the path of mothering. Let your imagination and creativity suggest others.

Connect with others. A listening ear is vital. If you don't already have good friends to support you, make a determined effort to find some. Look for groups like Mothers of Preschoolers or Parents Without Partners. Find a parenting class and sit in. Churches often provide a wonderful sense of community and support. Most important, make time to chat, to get together, and to commune with people who care. A simple phone call at the end of a weary day can make all the difference.

Do things you truly enjoy. Even ten minutes spent reading poetry, playing the piano, or digging in the garden can carry you through the day with grace and patience. Remember, your son will learn

school for reading help? Should you intervene in your son's conflict with the Phillips' boy or should you stay out of it? Will letting him stop Tae Kwan Do make him a quitter or will it rescue him from an activity that he doesn't enjoy? Should you let him have the car keys on Friday night? And how late should he stay out?

a great deal about self-respect by watching you. Seeing your joy in life is a good thing for a child.

Create moments of beauty. Find ways to surround yourself with things that give you pleasure. Paint your walls teal blue. Buy flowers and put them in pretty jars. Frame favorite photos and spread them around your rooms. These touches need not involve a great deal of money, but they can make home, wherever it is, a place you and your son love and enjoy being together.

Learn to ask for help. It is astonishing how many capable, competent women believe that they are somehow expected to know everything. Those who are truly strong know when to ask for help from others. Rugged individualism isn't all it's cracked up to be, especially when you're the single mother of an active boy. You may be pleased and surprised to discover just how many people are willing to help out with skills and information, if you only ask.

Parents continually make choices on their children's behalf, even when they are not aware of it. The dinner menu, when and how much of an allowance to give, how much to push the homework, how much to spend on his holiday gifts—all are decisions. And all decisions have consequences.

This demand stresses the single mother by its relent-lessness. No sooner does she figure out one dilemma than she's tripped by another. We all know the feeling of being too tired and too "thunk'd out" to decide what to make for supper or even what to watch on television. Pathetic, no. It's something we all feel. And yet single mothers must be on 24-hour duty to handle every kind of problem, whether it's his bed-time procrastination or his social shyness, his educa-tional needs or his tummy ache. And as any of us can attest, it's not the choosing that most beleaguers us. It is the responsibility.

> Parents continu-ally make choices on their children's behalf, even when they are not aware of it. . . . And all decisions have consequences. This demand stresses the single mother by its relentlessness.

———❧———

"You'd think I'd have gotten used to it by now," said Luisa, a single mother by choice of two school-aged boys. "But I haven't. I look at my sister and brother-in-law. You wouldn't believe what they go through just to decide what kind of birthday cake to get their kids. I'm not saying that's good. But when I make a big decision, like what school Eric should go to, I am so afraid of making a mistake. At least Julie and Tim can share the blame if things don't work out for my nieces. But I'm it. The buck stops here."

———❧———

Successful companies have dozens of vice presidents and committees of committees for good reason. Despite the caution about too many cooks, others can help us to think things through. They can offer alternatives we hadn't considered. They can poke holes in what we believe to be our impeccable logic. They can hear the neurotic and unconscious motives behind our supposedly rational plans and can help us put what feels like an urgent situation into a more balanced and deliberate context.

The burden Luisa felt is one most of us share. Why, there are people who don't want to order Chinese for the whole table out of fear of ordering the wrong dishes. When our child's well-being is at stake, the consequence of what we choose carries awesome implications—or seems to.

—◊◊◊—

"And I worry," Luisa continued, "that I'm not even seeing what I should. Eric complains that he's bored and yet he isn't doing all that well, and when his teachers have cranked up his work, he says it's too hard. But his best friend is going to a private school that has a writing program, and Eric's a gifted writer. I don't know. Sometimes I worry that I'm making decisions based on what I want and not what's best for him." Luisa sighed. "It's times like these I almost wish I'd married Gus."

—◊◊◊—

Having your knees buckle or convictions soften under such duress is to be expected. Picking out the wrong size shower curtain is one thing; choosing the wrong school placement is another. As Luisa said, sharing the blame is a natural, comforting, and most human device. "I knew you didn't like the kitchen," a husband will say, preferring to be his wife's protector than admit that he was shaking in his boots at the prospect of buying their first home. But finding someone to share the blame should not be a single mother's goal. She can pursue more constructive avenues.

Talk to others. You can best decide who those others should be—not just others who will agree or love you anyway, but others you can trust to be honest and who aren't afraid to call it as they see it. However discouraging they can seem on a daily basis, nay-sayers and devil's advocates can make you think, leading you to better and stronger decisions. And if you are really stuck, bounce your ideas off anyone, even an anyone with no expertise or experience in the subject, for that can help to clarify your own thoughts.

> Learn to use consultation. Think of yourself as a CEO or president. Who are the people in the know who can help you in this situation? Seek out people who can inform, guide, and challenge you.

Learn to use consultation. Think of yourself as a CEO or president. Who are the people in the know who can help you in this situation? Seek out people who can inform, guide, and challenge you. If, for instance, you are contemplating an educational decision, talk with teachers and other professionals, as well as with parents who have children at both schools. If you are unsure about your pediatrician's advice, seek other doctors' opinions. Even books, articles, and the World Wide Web, while they cannot actually make the best decision for you, may lead you to resources that give you useful information or that lead you to find helpful advice and to ask more incisive questions. Besides granting immunity against helplessness, actively analyzing your choices is the surest antidote to lukewarm, resigned, and poor decisions.

And when you have gathered the facts and opinions, trust your own wisdom and knowledge of your child, and do the best you can. In the end, it is all you can do, and it is enough.

It's Lonely at the Top

In our therapeutic work with single mothers we've seen that what they wish most, however, is not consultation or practical opinions. What they want is to be heard and to have their experience validated.

—⁓—

Anita, a divorced mother of a daughter and son, had not spoken for forty minutes of her therapy session. "You made me waste my one hour a week," she accused. She was genuinely annoyed. Only several weeks later did she reveal the hurt behind her frustration. "I don't want you offering your advice. Just because I bring things up in here doesn't mean I'm asking you to figure anything out. I can get real help and advice anywhere. What I need from you is something harder to find."

—⁓—

Anita's protest was as deserved as it was heartfelt. More than advice and well-intended suggestions, most of us want empathy and compassion. That is why Anita bristled at well-intentioned suggestions for dealing with her son's fresh mouth and an auto mechanic who had cheated her.

———✦———

"When we spend time talking about the kids and what to do," she elaborated, "it's as if I lose you. I know it sounds petty and self-centered. It's all about me. But I spend every waking moment taking care of them, and this is the only place that I get all for myself, where what I feel matters most."

———✦———

What Anita wanted was empathy and understanding for what she endured. One of the toughest parts of being a single mother is that there is no one else to confirm what she experiences. Married spouses often ask one another if they are being unreasonable, if what they see is really there. "Am I being unfair in feeling so angry? Was Kevin as rude to me as I think he was?" Single mothers lack this luxury.

Anita wanted, too, someone who could share her pride and joy in her children and her parenting. Anyone can celebrate a child's winning first prize at the science fair. But how often do these big events happen? Single mothers need others to notice the important, small changes they make in their parenting and the promising ways that their children respond. "Mark held his temper today when I asked him to repeat what he said." "Rye stayed at soccer practice for twenty minutes even though I ran an errand." "Chip slept in his own bed for two hours last night!" Such seemingly tiny triumphs make up a whole childhood and keep us afloat and motivated during harder times.

And finally, Anita needed a place—which means a person—where she could fall apart, be out of control, let it hang out. Even when good mothers are under the harshest of stress, they struggle to protect their children from seeing it. Single mothers need times, lots of them, where they can shout their darkest thoughts and most hopeless fears without hearing back "We told you so" or "It's your bed, baby, you made it"—harsh critiques that too many single mothers have already bullwhipped themselves with. Again, finding friends, family, support groups, or therapists with whom they can share their feelings should be high on the to-do list.

Such places inevitably also become havens where single mothers can share their deepest dreams and wishes, dreams kept secret lest they be ridiculed or trampled.

—◈—

"Last night I dreamed it was thirty years ago," Anita said, stammering through obvious embarrassment. "But me and the kids were the same age we are now. The children had a father who looked like Robert Young and I was the perfect wife and mother." Anita looked away in shame.

—◈—

Single mothers often harbor enormous regret that they haven't made their children and homes as wondrous as they'd once hoped. Some mothers question whether their choice—to be or remain single—was in itself the ultimate injury to their child. Even those who are single mothers by abandonment or by being widowed can feel responsible. Confessing this, and revealing the ideal homes they've sometimes, maybe always, dreamed of, can be a huge step toward grieving what wasn't, making room for more realistic and optimistic mothering and for seeing the very real benefits in creating a good-enough home.

> Just as flight attendants instruct mothers to put the oxygen masks on their own faces before doing the same for their children, we encourage single mothers to do something that is wholly against their instincts: Take good care of themselves first.

A mother who is drowning can do little to save her child. Just as flight attendants instruct mothers to put the oxygen masks on their own faces before doing the same for their children, we encourage single mothers to do something that is wholly against their instincts: Take good care of themselves first. We hold no illusions that having read this, you will put yourself at the front of the line. We know it will be your son's hunger that you feed before your own and his scrape that you bandage while your own cut bleeds. That is a mother's way. We just hope that you will work at making your own well-being a higher priority—if not for your sake, for your son's.

CHAPTER 15

Letting Go

Celebrating and Coping
with the Inevitable

It had to happen. You always knew it, from the day you
first played with his little toes. When he fell asleep on
your breast, you knew it. You knew it his first day of
school and the day he got his acceptance to college.
Through the birthday parties and the soccer practices,
the lazy naps and the sleepless nights; you knew it when
he played safely at your feet, just as you knew it when he
stayed out till dawn and didn't call.

Much of the time you looked the other way, preferring not to see what lay ahead. When he outgrew his
pants, you busied yourself by shopping for new ones,
distracting yourself from the twinge you felt seeing him

grow yet another inch. You rejoiced each last day of school to have him around the house more, but the autumn came so soon, as did the turning of the seasons, the report cards, and the eventual promotions to the next grade.

How does a childhood pass so fast? Where do the days go? A childhood encompasses 6,570 days, four presidencies, 1.8 decades, and nearly one million minutes—and during every one of them you never stopped loving that boy, never stopped trying your best to raise him well. However we parse it out, the precious years have gone. He's ready to leave.

But are you ready for him to go?

Getting Ready

Divorced after just a year of marriage, Natalie had decided to go it alone. She'd had a few brief relationships but, in the end, had judged herself to be too free a spirit to remarry. So she'd raised her only child, a son, by herself. And now she was saying good-bye to him. He was off to the university.

Like her fellow mothers, Natalie dreaded Patrick's growing up. Natalie, however, was a resourceful and thoughtful woman. She hadn't turned away, blind to what was happening. He won't be here forever, she'd told herself, painful as it was to know. Recognizing that his leaving would be hard, she began to prepare beforehand for its eventuality. Long before.

During Patrick's toddlerhood, Natalie was quite isolated. Devastated by her divorce, she'd felt unworthy of friends and spent most of her time at home with Patrick. Those were lonely, difficult times.

But her love of Patrick moved her to do what might otherwise have been out of her reach. She forced herself to meet other mothers so that Patrick would have playmates and so that she could learn from them better ways of parenting. That she also found friendship was an unexpected bonus.

As Patrick grew, so did Natalie. In fact, she'd made a deliberate effort to grow and learn. When Patrick quit piano, for example, she took it up, realizing that her musical interests, unlike her son's, were genuine. Watching him play soccer and baseball rekindled her own passion for sports. So, taking care of herself, too, she took to walking, often circling the enormous fields while her son played. And reading to him led her to discover and appreciate the many books she'd neglected during her own troubled adolescence and young womanhood.

When Patrick went off to junior high, he grew busy with friends and activities. Natalie could feel the loss, though she still saw him every morning, at night, and on the weekends. She could feel his separateness more and knew that he needed space. He shared a bit less of his inner world with her. Fortunately for Patrick, his mother understood and appreciated this. It saddened her, but felt right and made her believe that she had raised him well, for her son was where he should be in his development.

Again something in Patrick's growth sparked Natalie's own. They would have heated arguments about politics, social issues, and the relationship of children to adults. He felt children were subjugated and enslaved; she countered that they were cared for and protected. Though they seldom agreed, they enjoyed their discussions, and they often had guests for dinner and conversation.

Patrick's young idealism touched his mother's. She became more involved in the community. She lobbied successfully to stop the use of pesticides near school grounds and campaigned for a congressional candidate. She thought about a new career, too. For several years she'd worked as a paralegal in a small law office, and now she found she wanted something more.

The week that Patrick went off to high school, his mother enrolled in an art school to take night courses in photography, something she'd always fantasized about. Over the next four years, while Patrick was doing pre-calculus and honors English, she learned about lighting, perspective, and composition. She also learned that she was good at it.

By the time Patrick packed his bags, Natalie had made a life for herself, a life that had real meaning and that would help fill the space that her son had once wholly occupied. She didn't know if she'd ever make a true career change to be a photographer. But that didn't matter. She realized that life is a process that continues until the last breath. She also knew that having her own life was good for her son, too.

—⦿⦿⦿—

It's Not the End

We're not just saying this to make you feel better: It's really not the end. In fact, most grown kids come home and stay there long after their parents wish they would move out on their own. The average child now lives at home beyond age thirty. Hard to believe—and, if you don't find the idea particularly appealing, one more reason to encourage confidence, life skills, and independence in your son.

For good or bad, young adulthood has become a late phase of adolescence. It is likely that your sons will not marry or settle permanently on a career for quite some time. They will be checking in with you, asking what they should do, wondering who they should be, and, perhaps, asking to borrow money.

Stay in Touch

For those of you whose sons are going off to live at college, joining the military, backpacking through Africa, or simply striking out on their own, take heart. You will hear from them. Through the miracle of cell phones, phone cards, e-mail, and other such technology, you will have far more contact with them than any previous generation has enjoyed.

In case, though, you have one of those many sons who drifts off, out of sight, don't hesitate to take the initiative to keep your connection alive. Of course, we don't mean intrusive and unreasonable contact. But neither should you stay too far away. Some respectful mothers so fear getting in their children's way that they let themselves fade into the distance. Remember those boys we told you about, the ones who don't know what they feel and can't ask for the help and hugs they need? However well you've raised your boy, he might be one of these.

> It's really not the end. In fact, most grown kids come home and stay there long after their parents wish they would move out on their own.

Call him periodically. Write to him—a real, hand-written letter that can be held and carried around can convey a love and presence that an electronic memo cannot. Listen to the little things: what he did last night, what he had for lunch today. Conversations with college students and other newly independent young men can easily drift into one-way queries about your expectations: how school is going, how the grades are, and so on, same-every-week calls that go nowhere. These interrogations may alienate your son instead of keeping him connected. If you really want to know how your son is doing, ask less and listen more.

> Conversations with college students and other newly independent young men can easily drift into one-way queries about your expectations: how school is going, how the grades are, and so on, same-every-week calls that go nowhere. These interrogations may alienate your son instead of keeping him connected. If you really want to know how your son is doing, ask less and listen more.

Tell him about your life, too. Some mothers sound as if they are zombies, living now only for that 15-minute call every week. This, we can imagine, can make some young men feel like guilt-ridden abandoners, a feeling they would understandably wish to avoid. Be direct. Tell him about the new neighbor, what the dog is doing, about the book you read.

And be truthful. White lies have no place in a good relationship. If the cat is sick, let him know. If Grandma is having a breast removed, tell him. Many parents think they are doing their grown children a favor by sparing them news that will upset them and distract them from their work or studies. Your son deserves to know about illness, tragedy, and the like, so that he can grieve them and so he can make the choice whether he wants to send cards, call, visit, or attend a funeral. In other words, he needs to be treated like the adult he is so quickly becoming.

And even if your son cannot respond in words or isn't the type to call or write back on his own, he'll deeply appreciate your gentle reminders of the love and interest you have in him, wherever his life's journey takes him.

Be Available

Though he is off on his own, sort of, your son still needs your presence. When he comes home to visit, try to be there. Have food in the fridge and his favorite cookies on the counter. Invite his friends to come home with him. You may want him all to yourself, but don't you still want to see who he hangs out with? Get to know his girlfriends, and be respectful enough to do so in a way that sits well with your son. Invite him on vacations, even if you know he won't go. Invite him to dinner or to a concert he might like. Don't stop inviting him because you expect him to decline. Let him tell you that he can't make it. Holding the door open today without insisting he enter—and without making him feel guilty for having interests of his own—will help keep that door open for the years to come.

Be a Good Consultant

The young adult years can be difficult ones. Questions about identity, career, and romance pervade every aspect of his existence. Even as he drinks frappé cups of beer and plays Ultimate Frisbee, he is plagued by uncertainty. Will he pass physics? Will he get into law school? Will he ever find a job he likes and is good at? Will he ever amount to anything?

Although it can be unnerving to watch, these are the proper years for utter confusion. Beware of forcing premature closure, pushing your son to settle down before he's ready. Choosing a career or marriage can provide immediate relief and make a young man think he is on his way, but hasty decisions may get him nowhere fast, creating problems and hurting and possibly cutting him off from opportunities that just yesterday were open to him.

> Many parents think they are doing their grown children a favor by sparing them news that will upset them and distract them from their work or studies. Your son deserves to know about illness, tragedy, and the like, so that he can grieve them and so he can make the choice whether he wants to send cards, call, visit, or attend a funeral.

Of course, some boys know early in life just which path they want to pursue. They have always wanted to be a veterinarian, a professional baseball player, or a concert violinist, and they have the energy and focus to make their dreams come true. For most young men, however, life is not so clear. Help your son bear his distress and uncertainty. Let him know that this is the right time to look around, to not know exactly what he wants to do. Let him know it is okay to try this major, then that. It is okay to teach English in Japan or learn cabinet-making, even though he may find that he wants to do something else as his lifetime's work.

Learn to listen for such self-doubt when you speak on the phone or sit together over a cup of coffee. Listen with open ears and heart. "You are young," let your calm and steady presence say, "and you have plenty of time to figure it out."

A wise mother who keeps her faith in her son will be the safe harbor to which he can return time and again when his voyage grows stormy or dark. Your confidence in your son can give him confidence in himself, enabling him to leave safety and set out on his own again.

Hard Feelings

Some sons leave home and their mothers with a "good riddance" on both ends. But often that is just an act, however persuasive. Few mothers and sons, if any, truly like being so at odds. What a heartache it must be to be estranged from the one person you love most and who raised you by herself. If you and your son parted with hard feelings, don't give up. Be patient.

When you have a chance to see or talk to him, try to not be defensive. If he accuses you of this and that, try to hear the underlying hurt he conveys. Your natural reflex may be to defend yourself and to point out his shortcomings and errors, but you can build a better bridge to communication when you hear what he tells you, even if you believe that half of it is exaggerated or distorted. Don't stubbornly reject, don't withhold love, don't hang up on him, don't refuse to answer letters, and don't stand on principle. Ask yourself what you'd prefer: to be right or to have your son back?

> Although it can be unnerving to watch, these are the proper years for utter confusion. Beware of forcing premature closure, pushing your son to settle down before he's ready.

We're watching a home movie of a grandfather's 60th birthday party. Look at all the mothers and sons in this extended family:

―◦◦◦―

A little boy sits on his mother's lap, picking French fries off her plate. She unconsciously caresses his hair while talking with her sister. Grandfather walks off to the bathroom and his grown son jumps into his seat to get his mother's advice about the trouble his own son, her grandson, has sleeping. Two school-aged boys tickle their mothers' noses with feather-blowing party favors. Another cousin, a sophomore in college, leans on his mother as if she were an easy chair. She doesn't seem to mind. The oldest grandson argues the death penalty with his mother, a law professor. A daughter sits off in the corner, blissfully breastfeeding her new baby, the latest grandson. The birthday boy returns and his own 82-year-old mother grabs his arm, then pulls him toward her so that she can fix his tie, a flimsy excuse to give him another hug. Everyone applauds and hoots, as if watching newlyweds kiss.

———⟨∿∿⟩———

It really never ends. Generations and passing decades can't tarnish the shine. Our sons go off, but they come back again, and again, and again, always the apples in their mothers' eyes.

You've done all you can. Now you must let him go and trust that he'll take good care of himself. You must accept the likelihood that he will make mistakes, will suffer pain and disappointment, and will eventually know loss as well as joy. And you must allow him to let you go, too, to create enough space for him to make his own way, to find out just who he is. When he does, he will likely find that a good part of him resembles the mother who was always there, the mother who is now and will always be within him. You have raised a boy to be a man.

NOTES

Chapter 1

1. We can only fantasize about which of his own emotional issues motivated Einstein's preoccupation with the passage of time. Curious readers—especially mothers who hang onto the past and can feel every minute fleeing—might enjoy and find comfort in Alan Lichtman's short and insightful novel *Einstein's Dreams* (New York: Warner Books, 1994).

2. The questions and results are adapted from a survey conducted by Bruskin Research for Women.com, reported on its Web page on Monday, May 21, 2001.

Chapter 2

1. Reported by the University of Chicago Hospitals, 2001.

2. Sung by Leadbelly in 1944.

3. Daniel Kindlon and Michael Thompson, *Raising Cain* (New York: Ballantine, 2000).

4. *Oxford English Dictionary.*

5. It is thought that the seemingly higher curiosity associated with boys may also involve cultural influences. Boys are more likely encouraged to boldly act on their curiosity, to take risks

associated with a wish to explore that may be less welcome, if not subtly discouraged, in girls.

6. Susan Gilbert, *A Field Guide to Boys and Girls* (New York: HarperCollins, 2000).

7. Deborah Tannen, *You Just Don't Understand: Women and Men in Conversation* (New York: Ballantine, 1990).

8. First one seeing a VW Beetle calls out, "Punch-buggy [Beetle color]" while punching the arm of the person next to him.

9. Kindlon and Thompson, *Raising Cain.*

10. Gilbert, p. 73.

11. William Pollack, *Real Boys* (New York: Random House, 2000).

Chapter 3

1. As told in Lionni's lovely children's book *Frederick* (New York: Knopf, 1990).

2. In Maria Montessori's *The Absorbent Mind* (New York: Henry Holt, 1995).

Chapter 4

1. Of course, this is true for families where a mother spends sufficient time with her child. This is not meant for mothers who already give their sons too little nurturing and attention.

Chapter 5

1. In Stanley Greenspan's *The Challenging Child* (Cambridge, MA: Perseus Books, 1995). Parents who find their sons especially sensitive, self-absorbed, defiant, inattentive, or aggressive might consult this book for insights and useful strategies.

Chapter 6

1. Jane Nelsen, Ed.D., and Cheryl Erwin, M.A., *Parents Who Love Too Much* (Roseville, CA: Prima Publishing, 2000).

Chapter 7

1. Brad J. Bushman and Roy F. Baumeister. "Threatened Egotism, Narcissism, Self-Esteem, and Direct and Misplaced Aggression: Does Self-Love or Self-Hate Lead to Violence?" *Journal of Personality and Social Psychology* 75, no. 1, 1998.

Chapter 8

1. Edward Hallowell, *Connect* (New York: Pocket Books, 2001).

Chapter 9

1. Kindlon and Thompson, *Raising Cain.*

Chapter 10

1. Some of this discussion has been stimulated by and adapted from Debra Haffner's *From Diapers to Dating: A Parent's Guide to Raising Sexually Healthy Children* (New York: Newmarket, 2000), an excellent reference for any parent.

Chapter 11

1. In Sara McLanahan and Gary Sandefur, *Growing Up with a Single Parent* (Cambridge: Harvard University Press, 1994).
2. Readers are strongly urged to read Michael Gurian's *Boys and Girls Learn Differently* (San Francisco: Jossey-Bass, 2001), an important book that much more elaborately details this subject.

INDEX

A

Adolescents
  chores for, 163
  drugs, sex, and, 170–171,
    215, 220
  ethics and academics, 232
  at family meals, 177–178
  homophobia in, 190–195, 198
  impossible demands from,
    44–45
  reckless behavior in,
    167–169, 172
  sexuality in, 217, 220
Adoptions, single-mother, ix
  difficulty attaching, 46
  stories about, 3–5, 52–55, 66–67
Aggression
  in boys, 21–23
  bullying, 239–240
  dealing with, 33
  discipline for excessive,
    184, 185

Allowance, 228–229
Amends, making, 141–143
Anxiety, mother's, 50–51
Apologies
  from mother, 286
  from son, 141–143
Art, supporting love of, 176
Askable mothers, 170–171
Attachment
  building secure, 37–41
  dependency and, 57–59
  difficulty in creating,
    45–50
  separating too early, 51–55
  strengthening healthy bond,
    55–56
  urge to grow and, 42–43
Attitudes toward single mothers,
    8–12
Authors, xi
Autism, 86
Availability, 55–56, 313

B

Baby boys
  attachment to, 37–38
  boundaries and, 62–64
  crying, 30, 45–47
  cues from, 40, 72
  healthy sexuality and, 211–212
  postpartum depression and,
    49–50
  private time for, 41
  temperaments of, 87
Baby-keepers, 201–203
Beauty, creating moments of, 299
Bedtime
  reading to your son, 33,
    225–226
  routine, 70–71
  television before, 192–193
Behavior and temperament, 93
Belonging, sense of, 173–178
Best friend mothering style,
  203–205
Big Brothers of America, 268
Biology as destiny, 87–88
Boundaries
  body, 75–76
  early childhood and, 62–66
  family bed, 68–70
  healthy separation, 66–68
  importance of, 61–62
  intense motherly love and, 209
  listening versus probing, 73–75
  mother's emotions and, 77–78
  parenting role and, 78–81
  privacy issues, 80–81
  solitude, 71–73
Boy Scouts of America, 195
Boyfriends
  advice on, 259–261
  boyfriend-son connections, 262
  careful attitude toward, 265

  discreet relationships, 262–263
  parenting role and, 264–265
  remarriage and, 265–267
  son's feelings about, 263–264
Boyishness
  embracing, 183–188
  variability of, 183
Boys' development
  aggression, 21–23, 33
  competitive spirit, 27–28
  curiosity, 18–20, 40
  description of "average boy,"
    14–16
  emotional life, 28–34
  energy, 16–18
  impulse control, 23–25
  noise, 20–21
  temperament and, 92–93
  tips for mothers on, 32–33,
    39–41
  verbal skills, 25–27, 33
  what boys are made of,
    13–14, 29
Brain development, 39–41
Bribes, 119
Brockovich, Erin, 291
Buckley, William F., Jr., 26
Bullying, 239–240

C

Careers and callings, 188–189
Chores
  appropriate, 79
  family work, 162–163
  skills for, 152–155
  work ethic and, 160–167,
    226–229
College, 241–245
College students, conversations
  with, 311–313

Communication. *See also*
Listening
baby's cues, 40, 72
boys' verbal skills, 25–27, 33
conveying empathy, 96–97
parent's expectations and,
131–132
probing versus listening, 73–75
sons as confidantes, 77–78
talking about sex and drugs,
170–171, 215, 217, 220
Competency, 150–152
Competitive spirit, 27–28
Concern for the world, 115–118
Connections, making, 173–178
Conscience, social, 117
Consultant, being a good, 314–315
Consultation and decision-
making, 302–303
Coparenting
bad fathers and, 258–259
challenge of, 248–249
compartmentalizing and, 249
father as favored parent,
253–256
fighting with ex, 256–258
flexibility for, 251–252
giving credit to ex, 252–253
objectivity and, 249–251
questions to settle in, 268–269
Couch potatoes, 192–193
Courage, teaching real,
167–169, 172
Criticism, 99–100, 158–159
Curiosity
boys', 18–20, 40
mother's genuine, 97

D

Decision-making, 297–303
Delayed gratification, 230–231

Dependency
boy's struggle with, 57–59
cutting the cord, 66–67
Depression in boys
denying, 273, 280
divorce and, 256
protection against, 173
Depression in mothers
anxiety and, 50–51, 78
postpartum, 49
Development, boys'
aggression, 21–23, 33
competitive spirit, 27–28
curiosity, 18–20
description of "average boy,"
14–16
emotional life, 28–34
energy, 16–18
impulse control, 23–25
noise, 20–21
temperament and, 92–93
tips for mothers on, 32–33,
39–41
verbal skills, 25–27, 33
what boys are made of,
13–14, 29
Disciplinary environment,
139–140
Discipline
apologies from son and,
141–143
babies and, 41
boyishness and, 185
children's need for, 108–109
choices and, 132, 134
coparenting and, 268
custom-made, 110–111
defined, 106–107
doling out justice, 123–124
encouragement and, 137–138
guilt over, 120–121, 145

Discipline, *continued*
  hypocrisy and, 121–123, 171
  limit-setting, 112–113
  morality and, 105–106
  mother's rights and, 113–114
  natural and logical conse-
    quences, 127–131
  no's of, 133
  privileges, 138–139
  proper, 109–110
  punishment versus, 125–126
  routines and, 134–135
  as serious business, 140–141
  signs of improper, 107–108
  strictness versus permissive-
    ness, 111–112
  teaching skills, 131–132
  temperament and mis-
    behavior, 93
  time outs, 135–137
  when nothing works, 143–145
  why children misbehave,
    126–127
Divorce rate, ix
Divorced parenting. *See*
  Coparenting
Dreikurs, Rudolf, 286
Drudgery, 292–297
Drugs, talking about, 170–171,
  215, 220

E

Educational success
  bad behavior at school,
    239–241
  boys versus girls, 222–223
  creating a futurist, 230–231
  creating a help-taker, 233,
    236, 238
  creating a learner, 224–226
  creating a respecter, 231–233
  creating a self-checker,
    238–239
  creating a worker, 226–229
  encouraging one's best,
    223–224
  expectations for, 241–245
  giftedness, 244
  homework, 234–235
  importance of, 173, 221–222
  learning problems, 233,
    236, 237
  teachers, 242–243
Emotional life, a boy's, 28–34
Emotional miseducation, 54, 180
Emotional needs, mother's, 41
Empathy for single mothers,
  303–304
Empathy for sons
  clashing temperaments and,
    94–95
  conveying, 56, 96–97
  listening with empathic ear,
    277–279
Encouragement, 137–138
Energy, high, 16–18
Environmental conscience,
  116–118
Erikson, Erik, 38
Erwin, Cheryl, 118, 144
Exercise for mothers, 295
Ex-husband
  abusive or neglectful,
    258–259
  compartmentalizing relation-
    ship with, 249
  coparenting with, 248–249,
    268–269
  as favored parent, 253–256
  fighting with, 256–258
  flexibility in dealing with,
    251–252

giving credit to, 252–253
objective view of, 249–251
Expectations, communicating,
131–132

F

Family bed, 68–70
Family meals, 177–178
Family meetings, 174–175
Family work, 162–163
Fathering, single, xi, 11
Fathers
bad, 258–259
compartmentalizing relationship with, 249
coparenting with, 248–249,
268–269
as favored parents, 253–256
fighting with, 256–258
flexibility in dealing with,
251–252
giving credit to, 252–253
objective view of, 249–251
Feelings
emotional life of a boy, 28–34
identifying, 32
validating, 48–49
Ferber, Richard, 71
Forgiveness, 114
Freud, Sigmund, 167
Friends, 175, 274–275
Frustration
acknowledging, 91–92
blame-throwing moments,
286–287

G

Gangs, 173
Gender identity
careers and callings, 188–189
embracing boyness, 183–188

genetics, 182
homophobia and, 190–195, 198
misconceptions about, 179–182
television and boys, 192–193
therapy for confusion over,
196–197
variability of boyishness, 183
Giftedness, 244
God, 176
Goluston, Mark, 177
Good character. See Discipline;
Values
Greenspan, Stanley, 101
Guilt, mother's
clashing temperaments and,
95, 98
discipline and, 120–121, 145
over parenting mistakes, 8,
285–286
Gurian, Michael, 31, 172

H

Haffner, Debra, 213
Hallowell, Edward, 173, 174
Healy, Jane M., 41
Help-takers, 233, 236, 238
High schoolers. See Teenagers
Homework, 234–235
Homophobia, 190–195
Hypocrisy, 121–123, 171

I

Impulse control, 23–25
Independence
boy's struggle with, 57–59
cutting the cord, 66–67
grown children at home,
310–311
hard feelings and, 315–317
mother's growth and, 308–310
passing of childhood, 307–308

Independence, *continued*
as purpose of parenting, 3–5
staying in touch with adult
son, 311–313
in young adult years, 314–315
Infant mortality rates, 11
Infants. *See* Baby boys
Insurance, 269
Integrity, 106
Interests, understanding son's, 56
Internal locus of control, 106
Internet use, 218–219

K
Kindlon, Daniel, 30, 54, 59, 172
Kohn, Alfie, 226

L
Language skills, 25–27, 33
Lazy kids
couch potatoes, 192–193
fostering work ethic, 160–167,
226–229
reforming, 164–166
Learning problems
accepting help for, 233, 236, 238
early intervention for, 237
Letting go
boy's struggle with, 57–59
cutting the cord, 66–67
grown children at home,
310–311
hard feelings and, 315–317
mother's growth and, 308–310
as part of parenting, 3–5
passing of childhood, 307–308
staying in touch and, 311–313
in young adult years, 314–315
Limit-setting
functions of, 112–113
importance of, 103–105

loving too much versus, 67,
118–120
as part of discipline, 107
single mom's guilt and,
120–121
Listening
active, 277
conveying empathy by, 56, 96,
277–279
identifying feelings by, 32
importance of, 49
probing versus, 73–75
to son's feelings about your
boyfriend, 263–264
to teachers, 242
Logical consequences, 128–131
Loudness, 20–21
Loving sons "too much"
consequences of, 67, 118–120
obedient wife mothering style,
205–207

M
Meals, family, 177–178
Meetings, family, 174–175
Men around the house
boyfriends, 259–267
ex-husbands, 248–259
role models, 267–270
Mentors, 267–269
Miller, Alice, 78
Mistakes, parenting, 8, 285–286
Money management, 228–229
Montessori, Maria, 40
Morality
discipline and, 105–106
hypocrisy and, 121–123, 171
Mothering solo
as challenging job, 289–291
day-to-day drudgery, 292–297
decision-making, 297–303

replenishing yourself, 298–299
sleep hygiene, 294–295
Mothering styles
baby-keepers, 201–203
best friend, 203–205
healthy and varied, 210–211
obedient wife, 205–207
queen bee, 207–208
star-crossed lover, 208–210
Mothers of Preschoolers, 298
MotherVision
blame-throwing moments,
286–287
clear picture of son, 273–274
defined, 271–272, 288
denial and, 280–281
listening with empathic ear,
277–279
logical argument vs. psychological understanding,
283–285
misreading behavior, 274–277,
279–280
parenting mistakes, 8, 285–286
seeing yourself clearly, 281–283

N
Narcissistic disorders, 155–156
Natural consequences, 127–128
Nature, appreciation of, 176
Nature versus nurture, 86–88
Nelsen, Jane, 118, 144
Nolte, Dorothy Law, 150

O
Obedient wife mothering style,
205–207

P
Parenting. *See also* Coparenting;
Discipline

as challenging job, 289–291
day-to-day drudgery of,
292–297
decision-making in, 297–303
discipline and, 125–145
mistakes in, 8, 285–286
modern knowledge of, 5–6
opinions on solo parenting,
8–12
as perplexing challenge, 7
Parents Without Partners, 298
Pasteur, Louis, 20
Perfect parents, 7, 285–286
Perfectionism, 156–160
Physical affection, 76
Play, 33, 40
Pollack, William, 31, 172
Pornography, 219
Preschoolers
chores for, 162
healthy sexuality in, 212–213
Privacy issues. *See also*
Boundaries
bedrooms and bathrooms,
80–81
listening versus probing, 73–75
Punishment, 125–126, 127

Q
Queen bee mothering style,
207–208

R
Reading to your son, 33, 225–226
Reality testing, 64
Recklessness, 167–169, 172
Remarriage, 265–267
Resilience, fostering
competency, 150–152
connections to others, 173–178
courage, 167–172

Resilience, fostering, *continued*
 perils of perfectionism, 155–160
 self-love, 148–150
 skills, 152–155
 work ethic, 160–167, 226–229
Respect
 educational success and,
  231–233
 for mother, 113–114
 mutual, 97
Ricci, Dr. Isolina, 269
Rights, mothers', 113–114
Risk-taking behavior
 daredevil sports, 167–169, 172
 drugs and sex, 170–171,
  215, 220
Role models, 267–269
Role playing, 132

S

School performance
 bad behavior at school, 239–241
 boys versus girls, 222–223
 creating a futurist, 230–231
 creating a help-taker, 233,
  236, 238
 creating a learner, 224–226
 creating a respecter, 231–233
 creating a self-checker, 238–239
 creating a worker, 226–229
 encouraging one's best, 223–224
 expectations for, 241–245
 giftedness, 244
 homework, 234–235
 importance of, 173, 221–222
 learning problems, 233, 236, 237
 teachers and, 242–243
Schoolchildren
 chores for, 162–163
 sexuality and, 213–215

Second marriages, 265–267
Self-care, single mother's
 blame-throwing moments and,
  286–287
 empathy and compassion,
  303–306
 importance of, 306
 replenishing yourself, 298–299
 sleep hygiene, 294–295
Self-checkers, 238–239
Self-esteem
 competency and, 150–152
 overindulgence and, 67, 206
Self-love, healthy, 148–150
Self-protectiveness. *See also*
  Resilience, fostering
 daredevil behavior and,
  167–169, 172
 drugs and sex, 170–171,
  215, 220
Sex, talking about, 170–171, 215,
  217, 220
Sexual identity
 careers and callings, 188–189
 embracing boyness, 183–188
 genetics, 182
 homophobia, 190–195, 198
 misconceptions about, 179–182
 television and boys, 192–193
 therapy for confusion over,
  196–197
 variability of boyishness, 183
Sexuality, healthy. *See also*
  Mothering styles
 birth through second year,
  211–212
 in high schoolers, 217, 220
 Internet use and, 218–219
 in middle schoolers, 216–217
 in preschoolers, 212–213

in preteens, 215–216
in schoolchildren, 213–215
Shore, Rima, 41
Single-mother adoptions, ix
  difficulty attaching, 46
  stories about, 3–5, 52–55, 66–67
Single mothers
  attitudes toward, 8–12
  decision-making by, 297–303
  depression in, 49–50, 78
  drudgery and, 292–297
  guilt felt by, 120–121, 145
  renewal for, 298–299
  sleep hygiene for, 294–295
Single mothers and sons, theory
  on, 5–8
Sleep hygiene, mother's,
  292–295
Sleep issues for son
  bedtime routine, 70–71
  family bed, 68–70
  television before bedtime,
  192–193
Social conscience, growing a, 117
Solitude, 71–73
Spirituality, 176
Sports, daredevil, 167–169, 172
Star-crossed lover mothering
  style, 208–210
Strengths, building on son's,
  99–100
Strictness, 111–112. *See also*
  Discipline
Styles of mothering
  baby-keepers, 201–203
  best friend, 203–205
  healthy and varied, 210–211
  obedient wife, 205–207
  queen bee, 207–208
  star-crossed lover, 208–210

T
Tannen, Deborah, 26
Tantrums, 118–120, 127, 231
Teachers
  disliked, 242–243
  learning problems and, 233,
  236, 237
  respect for, 231, 240, 241
Teaching
  housework/chores, 152–155
  social skills, 131–132
  work ethic, 160–167,
  226–229
Teenagers
  chores for, 163
  drugs, sex, and, 170–171,
  215, 220
  ethics and academics, 232
  at family meals, 177–178
  homophobia in, 190–195, 198
  impossible demands from,
  44–45
  reckless behavior in,
  167–169, 172
  sexuality in, 217, 220
Television, 192–193
Temperaments, clashing
  behavior and, 93
  building on strengths, 99–100
  compatibility of mother and
  son, 83–86
  development and, 92–93
  empathy and, 94–95
  examples of, 88–91
  frustration over, 91–92
  mother's temperament, 94
  nature versus nurture, 86–88
  self-blame over, 95, 98
  solutions for, 98–99,
  100–101

Thompson, Michael, 30, 54,
    59, 172
Twain, Mark, 23

U
Unmarried mothers
    attitudes toward, 8–12
    day-to-day drudgery and,
        292–297
    decision-making by, 297–303
    depression in, 49–50, 78
    empathy for, 303–306
    guilt felt by, 120–121, 145
    realities of, ix, xi
    renewal for, 298–299
    sleep hygiene for, 294–295

V
Values
    concern for the world, 115–118
    discipline and morality,
        105–106

hypocrisy and morality,
    121–123, 171
importance of discipline and,
    103–105
of smart people, 114–115
work ethic, 160–167, 226–229
Verbal skills, 25–27, 33
Video games, 192–193
Visitation, 268

W
Wayne, John, 59
Women, son's attitude toward
    encouraging healthy sexuality,
        211–220
    mothering styles and,
        201–211
    mother-son relationship as
        template, 199–201
Work ethic
    creating a worker, 226–229
    fostering, 160–167